D0915620

GUIDE TO STATISTICAL MATERIALS PRODUCED BY GOVERNMENTS AND ASSOCIATIONS IN THE UNITED STATES

GOVERNMENT DOCUMENTS BIBLIOGRAPHIES

Series Editor   Steven D. Zink

The other titles in this series are:

An Annotated Guide to Current National Bibliographies
by Barbara L. Bell

Checklist of Government Directories, Lists and Rosters
by Richard I. Korman

Bibliography of Official Statistical Yearbooks and Bulletins
by Gloria Westfall

Guide to Presidential Advisory Commissions, 1973–1984
by Steven D. Zink

GOVERNMENT DOCUMENTS
BIBLIOGRAPHIES

Guide to Statistical Materials Produced by Governments and Associations in the United States

Juri Stratford
and
Jean Slemmons Stratford

CHADWYCK-HEALEY INC
ALEXANDRIA, VA

© 1987 Juri Stratford and Jean Slemmons Stratford
All rights reserved. No part of this work
may be reproduced, stored in a retrieval system,
or transmitted in any form or by any means,
electronic, mechanical, photocopying or otherwise
without the prior permission of the
copyright owner.

First published 1987 by:
Chadwyck-Healey Inc.
1101 King Street
Alexandria, VA 22314

Distributed outside the USA by:
Chadwyck-Healey Ltd
Cambridge Place
Cambridge CB2 1NR
England

Reprinted 1988

ISBN: 0 85964 127 9

Library of Congress Cataloging-in-Publication Data

Stratford, Juri, 1955–
  Guide to statistical materials produced by governments
  and associations in the United States.

  (Government documents bibliographies)
  Includes index.
  1. United States—Statistics—Periodicals—Bibliography.
  2. United States—Government publications—
  Periodicals—Bibliography. I. Stratford, Jean Slemmons,
  1955–   . II. Title. III. Series.
  Z7554.U5S8 1987 [HA203]   016.3173   86–32722

British Library Cataloguing in Publication Data

Stratford, Juri
  Guide to statistical materials produced
  by governments and associations in the
  United States.—(Government documents
  bibliographies)
  1. United States—Statistical services
  —Bibliography
  I. Title   II. Stratford, Jean Slemmons
  III. Series
  016.3173   Z1215

Printed by Unwin Brothers Ltd.
Old Woking, Surrey.

CONTENTS

INTRODUCTION

The *Guide to Statistical Materials Produced by Governments and Associations in the United States* is an annotated bibliography providing subject access to the statistical contents of over seven hundred publications. It is intended to serve as a bibliographic guide and acquisitions tool.

The scope of the *Guide* is defined by the following criteria. In order to be considered for inclusion, a work must:

(1) be produced by, or at the expense of, a federal or state agency, or a U.S. based association;

(2) be a recurring title of regular frequency (generally biennial or more frequent);

(3) be either primarily statistical, or include recurring statistical features of consistent content;

(4) provide a geographic, industrial or thematic orientation to the data;

(5) provide data primarily in tabular or chart form;

(6) provide data for the United States, its regions or states (a work may also provide world and/or foreign data but publications dealing exclusively with other regions of the world have been excluded).

These criteria are discussed more fully below, as are exceptions which have been made in order to allow for the inclusion of appropriate titles.

Publications included have been produced by governments and associations in the United States. At the federal level, this includes publications produced by, or at the expense of, a federal agency or the Congress. State publications have been defined as those produced by, or at the expense of, state agencies or state-funded educational and/or research institutions. In addition, publications of the District of Columbia have been included with state publications. For the purposes of the *Guide*, association publications have been defined as those produced by non-profit membership organizations in the United States, generally those representing a specific industry, profession or sector of the economy. Publications of private research institutions which are affiliated with associations have also been included; e.g., the publications of the U.S. Travel Data Center of the Travel Industries Association.

The *Guide* emphasizes publications having a regular frequency. However, appropriate statistical compilations meeting other criteria have been included regardless of frequency.

7

The various censuses conducted by the U.S. Bureau of the Census are not included in the *Guide*. Only the social and economic compilations of the Census Bureau, such as the *Statistical Abstract of the U.S.* and its supplements, are included here.

In general, annual reports dealing with the finances and operations of the issuing source have been excluded. Budget documents have also been excluded from the scope of the *Guide*. Several exceptions have been made for publications considered to be of broad interest such as *U.S. Budget in Brief* and the Tax Foundation's *Facts and Figures on Government Finance*.

Publications included in the *Guide* were examined first hand. A few publications which could not be consulted directly were included and annotated on the basis of bibliographic records in combination with detailed abstracts or reviews.

For federal and association publications, no specific guidelines for subject content were developed beyond the criteria outlined above. Some industries or sectors of the economy are not represented because appropriate publications were not identified for inclusion. Other industries (e.g., finance) may be represented by several publications, indicating only that federal and/or association publishing activity is prolific in that area.

At the state level, it was necessary to establish subject guidelines in order to provide access to a useful body of data with some consistency of coverage from state to state. Therefore, the following types of state publications have been included in the *Guide*:

(1) State statistical abstracts (or in the absence of a statistical abstract, population data);

(2) Vital statistics (generally including data on birth, death, marriage and divorce);

(3) Employment or annual planning reports (generally including data on employment, unemployment and personal income);

(4) Economic conditions (including economic indicators and/or analyses of specific industries);

(5) Agriculture industry (generally including data on crop, livestock, dairy and poultry production).

Due to their importance as sources of statistical data, state statistical abstracts have been included regardless of issuing source. In addition, privately published economic studies for the states have also been included where no equivalent state government publication was identified.

Finally, some consideration was given to cost and availability. All titles included in the *Guide* were evaluated on the basis of cost in relation to the usefulness and/or uniqueness of the coverage provided. Only those titles available to the public for free, for sale, or through depository library programs are included in the *Guide*. Titles priced in excess of $100.00 were not included. In several instances, potentially appropriate publications were omitted when availability was not confirmed by the issuing source.

HOW TO USE THE GUIDE

Entries in the *Guide* follow the basic format outlined below:

Entry Number
Issuing Source.
Title.

Approximate number of pages.	Frequency.	Date.
ISSN:	LCCN:	
SUDOCS:	ITEM NO:	
Availability:		
Annotation.		

Each entry has a five character, alphanumeric "Entry Number". The number consists of a one letter prefix followed by four digits. The prefixes, A, F, or S, indicate the category of publication, either association, federal or state.

The "Issuing Source" is generally the publisher or intellectual authority for the title. The cataloguing records on the national networks were consulted in an attempt to provide standard (that is, A.A.C.R. or A.A.C.R. II) forms for issuing sources. However, conflicts frequently arose between cataloguing copy and the issuing source as indicated on the item itself and changes have been made to accommodate those conflicts and reflect the current forms of entries (to the best of our ability to determine them). Any change in issuing source over the publishing history of the title is noted in the body of the annotation by the phrase "issuing source varies".

The "Title", again, reflects the standard form for the work except where conflicts arose between the item and cataloguing copy. In addition, there seemed to be little standardization in cataloguing records for titles which include the year of coverage or issue. The presence of a date in the title is indicated by one of several notations: (year) for calendar year, (fy) for fiscal year, (py) for program year. Any change in title over its publishing history is noted in the body of the annotation by the phrase "title varies".

9

The average length of the work is indicated by the "Approximate number of pages". This notation should be taken only as a general guideline as some titles vary substantially in length from edition to edition.

The "Frequency" of issue is also noted. For titles which have experienced changes in frequency, only the current frequency is given.

The "Date" given is generally the date of first issue. In cases where the date of first issue was not readily available in cataloguing copy or standard bibliographic sources, this date can reflect the best approximation of the issuing source, examination of major library holdings as reflected in union lists of serials, or the date of first available data.

The "ISSN" (International Standard Serial Number) and the "LCCN" (Library of Congress Card Number) are noted where available.

For publications of the Federal government, the "SUDOCS" and "ITEM NO" are noted where available. The "SUDOCS" number is the number assigned to a title or series in the Superintendent of Documents classification scheme. The "ITEM NO" is the number assigned to a title or series for selection through the Federal Depository Library Program.

The "Availability" note indicates the current price and source for the title. Addresses for sources are given in the appendices. Though every attempt has been made to provide accurate price information, prices given reflect conditions in late 1985 and should be used with caution.

The body of the "Annotation" is organized as follows. The general scope of the work is described. The time span of coverage, including the presence of trends or projections, is outlined. Breakdown of data by geographic area or subject is indicated where appropriate. The inclusion of comparative data (such as data for other areas or industries) is noted. The approximate number of tables and/or charts is given. Changes in title or issuing source are noted. The type and range of data sources used in the compilation of the title is indicated, and the edition upon which the annotation is based is noted.

The industry groups employed in the annotations are based upon Standard Industrial Classification groups and are outlined in the "Glossary of Terms". The "Glossary of Terms" also provides brief explanations of several terms employed in the annotations. A key to abbreviations used in the *Guide* is provided in the appendices.

PUBLICATIONS OF ASSOCIATIONS

A0010
Administrative Management Society.
Annual Guide to Management Compensation.
Approximately 45 pages.   Annual.   1973-
ISSN: 0278-1506   LCCN: 81-643450
Availability: $60.00 to members, $100.00 to non-members from the issuing source.

Provides data on salaries and benefits paid for approximately twenty middle management positions for the United States. Most data cover a one year period. Includes data by city and region. Provides select comparisons to Canadian data. Contains approximately 15 tables.
Data from survey of approximately 3,200 companies with 55,000 middle management employees.
Description based on 1984 imprint covering 1984 data.

A0020
Administrative Management Society.
AMS Annual Office Salaries Directory.
Approximately 40 pages.   Annual.   1947-
                LCCN: SN83-11874
Availability: Free to members, $90.00 to non-members from the issuing source.

Provides data on weekly salaries paid for approximately twenty job categories of clerical and word processing positions for the United States. Most data cover a one year period. Includes data by type of business and location. Provides select comparisons to Canadian data. Contains approximately 27 tables.
Data from survey of approximately 5,200 companies with 350,000 office employees.
Description based on 1984 imprint covering 1984 data.

A0030
Aerospace Industries Association of America.
Aerospace Facts and Figures (years).
Approximately 170 pages.   Annual.   1953-
                LCCN: 46-25007
Availability: $10.95 from Aviation Week & Space Technology.

Provides data on the civil and military aerospace industry for the United States including production, research and development, imports and exports, employment and financial and operating data. Most data cover a one year period; select trends are included.

Provides select comparisons to foreign data. Contains approximately 12 tables. Title varies.

Data from federal and private sources.

Description based on 1984 imprint covering 1983 data.

Also publishes updated data as "Aerospace Economic Indicators" in *Aerospace* (quarterly).

A0040
Air Transport Association of America.
Air Transport (year).
Approximately 20 pages.　　　Annual.　　　　1937-
ISSN: 0190-552X　　　　　LCCN: 70-613485
Availability: Free from the issuing source.

Provides data on the air carrier industry for the United States including volume of air traffic, number of passengers and freight volume, safety, financial and operating data, employment and the air carrier fleet. Most data cover a two year period; select trends and projections are included. Includes data by air carrier and select data by airport. Contains approximately 20 tables. Title varies.

Data from federal and private sources.

Description based on 1984 imprint covering 1982-1983 data.

A0050
Aluminium Association.
Aluminium Statistical Review for (year).
Approximately 70 pages.　　　Annual.　　　　1962-
ISSN: 0065-6666　　　　　LCCN: 72-131
Availability: $7.50 to members, $20.00 to non-members from the issuing source.

Provides data on aluminium industry for the United States including ingot and mill production, shipments, supply, and imports and exports. Most data cover a one year period; select trends are included. Includes data by product type and company. Provides select comparisons to foreign countries. Contains approximately 30 tables/charts. Title varies.

Data from federal and private sources.

Description based on 1984 imprint covering 1983 data.

Also publishes historic data in *Aluminium Statistical Review Historical Supplement* (quinquennial) which provides coverage for a twenty year period and updated data in *Aluminium Situation* (monthly).

A0060
American Association of Engineering Societies. Engineering Manpower Commission.
Engineers Salaries: Special Industry Report, (year).
Approximately 250 pages.　　　Annual.　　　　1958-
ISSN: 0071-0415　　　　　LCCN: 79-8565
Availability: $100.00 from the issuing source.

Provides data on salaries paid for engineers for the United States. Most data cover a one year period; select trends are included. Includes data by industry/sector, years of experience, supervisory level, educational degree and region. Contains approximately 10 summary tables/charts and 4 lengthy tables. Issuing source varies.

Data from survey of approximately 1,000 establishments and 135,000 engineers.

Description based on 1983 imprint covering 1983 data.

Also publishes the following annual salary surveys: *Engineers' Salaries: Professional Income of Engineers*, and *Salaries of Engineers in Education.*

A0070

American Association of Fund-Raising Counsel.
Giving U.S.A.: A Compilation of Facts and Trends on American Philanthropy for the Year (year).
Approximately 105 pages.   Annual.   1956-
ISSN: 0436-0257   LCCN: 59-1874
Availability: $25.00 from the issuing source.

Provides data on philanthropy for the United States including contributions by type of contributor and source. Also provides data on areas of opportunity for philanthropy. Most data cover a one year period; select trends are included. Contains approximately 60 tables/charts. Title varies.

Data from survey, federal and private sources.

Description based on 1984 imprint covering 1983 data.

A0080

American Association of University Professors.
Academe: Bulletin of the American Association of University Professors.
Approximately 65 pages.   Bimonthly.   1915-
ISSN: 0190-2946   LCCN: 79-642918
Availability: Free to members, $30.00 per year to non-members from the issuing source.

Bimonthly journal of the American Association of University Professors includes recurring statistical feature, "Annual Report on the Economic Status of the Profession, (years)", as its July/August issue. Provides data on university faculties for the United States including employment, salaries and benefits. Most data cover a two year fiscal or school period; select trends are included. Includes data by rank and affiliation. Contains approximately 15 tables. Title varies.

Data from survey of approximately 2,200 institutions and federal sources.

Description based on 1984 imprint covering FY1982-FY1983 data.

A0090

American Bankers Association.
ABA Banking Journal.
Approximately 120 pages.   Monthly.   1908-
ISSN: 0194-5947   LCCN: SN83-2366
Availability: $15.00 per year to members, $20.00 per year to non-members from the issuing source.

Monthly journal includes recurring reports providing statistical data on the banking industry for the United States including commercial lending, bank marketing, retail banking, community banking, correspondent banking, assets and liabilities of commercial banks, international banking and select data for the real estate industry. Most data cover a two year period; select trends are included. Statistical content varies from issue to issue. Title varies.

Data from federal and private sources.

Description based on 1984 imprint covering 1983-1984 data.

A0100
American Bankers Association.
(year) Retail Bank Credit Report.
Approximately 90 pages.   Annual.   1960-
ISSN: 0276-9093   LCCN: 81-641421
Availability: $35.00 to members, $52.50 to non-members from the issuing source.

Provides data on the retail banking industry for the United States with emphasis on credit and lending activity including employment, installment loans, bank cards, overdraft line-of-credit, credit life insurance and other types of lending. Most data cover a one year period; select short term trends are included. Includes data by bank asset size and census division. Contains approximately 122 tables.

Data from survey of approximately 600 member banks and private sources.

Description based on 1984 imprint covering 1983 data.

A0110
American Bureau of Metal Statistics.
Non-Ferrous Metal Data (year).
Approximately 150 pages.   Annual.   1920-
ISSN: 0360-9533   LCCN: 75-649952
Availability: $45.00 + P/H from the issuing source.

Provides data on the world minerals industries including production, consumption, imports and exports for nonferrous metals including copper, lead, zinc, aluminium, silver, gold, and uranium. Most data cover a one year period; select trends are included. Includes data by commodity/sector and country. Contains approximately 185 tables. Title varies.

Data from federal and private sources.

Description based on 1984 imprint covering 1983 data.

A0120
American Cancer Society.
Cancer Facts and Figures (year).
Approximately 30 pages.   Annual.   1951-
ISSN: 0069-0147   LCCN: SN84-10362
Availability: Free from the issuing source.

Provides data on cancer for the United States including incidence, deaths, and research grants awarded by the association. Most data are one year projections; select trends are included. Includes data by type and site of cancer, and state. Provides select comparisons to foreign data. Contains approximately 15 tables/charts.

Data from federal, international and private sources.

Description based on 1985 imprint covering 1985 data.

A0130

American Chamber of Commerce Researchers Association.
Inter-City Cost of Living Index.
Approximately 25 pages.   Quarterly.   1967-
ISSN: 0740-7130   LCCN: SC83-2115
Availability: $65.00 per year from the issuing source.

Provides data on comparative cost of living for approximately 225 United States cities (U.S. average equals 100). Most data cover a one quarter period with the most current figures available. Includes data by item (for approximately sixty items), city and S.M.S.A. Contains approximately 4 tables. Title varies.
Data from original research by participating chambers of commerce.
Description based on 1984 imprint covering 1984 data.

A0140

American Chemical Society.
Chemical and Engineering News.
Approximately 60 pages.   Weekly.   1923-
ISSN: 0009-2347   LCCN: A41-2413
Availability: Free to members, $35.00 per year to non-members from the issuing source.

Weekly journal includes significant recurring statistical features. Provides data on the chemical industry for the United States; annual features include "Facts and Figures for Chemical R&D", "Salary Survey", "World Chemical Outlook" and "Facts and Figures for the Chemical Industry". Most data cover a one year period; select trends and projections are included. Provides select comparisons to foreign data. Contains approximately 30 tables. Title varies.
Data from federal and private sources.
Description based on 1984 imprint covering 1983 data.

A0150

American Council of Life Insurance.
Life Insurance Fact Book (year).
Approximately 130 pages.   Annual.   1946-
ISSN: 0075-9406   LCCN: 47-27134
Availability: Free from the issuing source.

Provides data on the life insurance industry in the United States including sales, ownership, annuity benefit payments, income, and earnings and assets of life insurance companies. Also provides data on life expectancy and causes of death. Most data cover a two year period; select trends are included. Includes data by type of insurance, state and region. Provides select comparisons to Canadian data. Contains approximately 90 tables. Issuing source varies.
Data from survey, federal and private sources.
Description based on 1983 imprint covering 1981-1982 data.
Also publishes *Life Insurance Buying* (annual) which provides socioeconomic data on persons insured by life insurance policies purchased in (year).

A0160
American Council of Life Insurance.
Pension Facts (year).
Approximately 55 pages.   Biennial.   1974-
                               LCCN: 75-39762
Availability: Free from the issuing source.

Provides data on major private and government administered pension plans for the
United States including plans with life insurance companies, IRA and Keogh plans,
Railroad Retirement System, Social Security System, and other federal, state and local
plans. Data includes numbers of persons covered, assets, reserves and benefits paid. Most
data cover a two year period; select long term trends are included. Includes data by type
of plan. Contains approximately 20 tables. Title and issuing source vary.
Data from federal and private sources.
Description based on 1984 imprint covering 1982-1983 data.

A0170
American Council on Education.
(year) Fact Book for Academic Administrators.
Approximately 200 pages.   Biennial.   1959-
ISSN: 0198-8425   LCCN: 80-648845
Availability: $39.95 from Macmillan Publishing Co.

Presents a broad range of social and economic data for the United States of relevance
to the field of higher education. Provides data on population, birth, death, employment,
unemployment, personal income, Gross National Product or other measures of production, and data on education including enrollment, institutions, faculty, staff, students
and degrees earned. Most data cover a twenty-three year period; select projections and
long term trends are included. Contains approximately 200 tables. Title varies.
Data from federal sources.
Description based on 1984 imprint covering 1950-1982 data.

A0180
American Financial Services Association.
(year) Finance Facts Yearbook.
Approximately 80 pages.   Annual.   1961-
ISSN: 0430-4705   LCCN: 61-14409
Availability: $8.50 to schools, libraries and members, $10.00 to non-members from the
issuing source.

Provides data of relevance to the consumer finance industry for the United States
including population, education, employment, personal income and expenditures, consumer finance, consumer credit, and financial and operating data for consumer finance
companies. Most data cover a one year period; select trends and projections are included.
Contains approximately 60 tables/charts. Title and issuing source vary.
Data from survey of approximately 550 consumers, federal and private sources.
Description based on 1984 imprint covering 1983 data.

A0190
American Frozen Food Institute.
Frozen Food Pack Statistics, (year).
Approximately 65 pages.   Annual.   1969-
ISSN: 0469-7405   LCCN: SN81-4602
Availability: $50.00 from the issuing source.

Provides data on the frozen food industry for the United States including production
figures for fruits and berries, concentrates, potato products, vegetables and seafood and
poultry. Most data cover a five year period; select long term trends are included. Includes
data by commodity/sector. Contains approximately 68 tables.
Data from federal and private sources.
Description based on 1984 imprint covering 1979-1983 data.

A0200
American Gas Association.
Gas Facts (year): A Statistical Record of the Gas Utility Industry.
Approximately 220 pages.   Annual.   1945-
                             LCCN: 72-622849
Availability: $30.00 from the issuing source.

Provides data on natural gas industry for the United States including supply, reserves,
distribution, consumption, sales, revenues and prices. Most data cover a one year period.
Provides select comparisons to foreign data and other forms of energy. Contains
approximately 175 tables/charts. Condensed as **Gas Data Book**. Title varies.
Data from federal and private sources.
Description based on 1984 imprint covering 1983 data.
Also publishes updated data in **Monthly Gas Utility Statistical Report** and **Quarterly
Report of Gas Industry Operations.**

A0210
American Hospital Association.
Hospital Statistics, (year).
Approximately 240 pages.   Annual.   1946-
ISSN: 0090-6662   LCCN: 72-626765
Availability: $39.50 to members, $49.50 to non-members from American Hospital
Publishing.

Provides data on the health care services industry for the United States with emphasis
on hospital services and operations including capacity, utilization, employment, facilities
and financial and operating data. Most data cover a one year period; select long term
trends are included. Includes data by hospital site, city, state and census division.
Contains approximately 25 lengthy tables. Title and issuing source vary.
Data from survey of approximately 6,500 hospitals and private sources.
Description based on 1984 imprint covering 1983 data.
Also publishes updated data as "Hospital Indicators" (approximately fifteen statistical
charts) in **Hospitals** (semimonthly).

A0220
American Humane Association.
Highlights of Official Child Neglect and Abuse Reporting, (year).
Approximately 20 pages.   Annual.   1978-
                                 LCCN: 84-186062
Availability: $5.00 from the issuing source.

Provides data on cases of child abuse and neglect for the United States including characteristics of cases and child protective services. Most data cover a one year period. Includes data by state. Contains approximately 16 tables. Title varies.
Data from federal and state sources.
Description based on 1984 imprint covering 1982 data.

A0230
American Iron and Steel Institute.
Annual Statistical Report- American Iron and Steel Institute, (year).
Approximately 115 pages.   Annual.   1879-
                                  LCCN: 14-3046
Availability: $15.00 from the issuing source.

Provides data on the iron and steel industry for the United States including employment, production, receipts, shipments, imports and exports. Most data cover a one year period; select trends are included. Includes data by product and production method. Provides select comparisons to foreign data. Contains approximately 75 tables. Title varies.
Data from federal and private sources.
Description based on 1984 imprint covering 1983 data.
Also publishes more general *Steel and America: An Annual Report.*

A0240
American Iron Ore Association.
Iron Ore (year).
Approximately 110 pages.   Annual.   1957-
ISSN: 0075-0883   LCCN: 59-42154
Availability: Free from the issuing source.

Provides data on the iron ore industry for the United States including production, inventories, receipts, consumption, shipments, imports and exports. Most data cover a ten year period. Includes data by region. Provides select comparisons to Canadian data. Contains approximately 66 tables.
Data from federal and private sources.
Description based on 1984 imprint covering 1974-1983 data.
Also publishes updated data in *Iron Ore and Iron Ore Agglomerates,* and *Shipments of U.S. and Canadian Iron Ore From Loading Docks Destined to the Great Lakes* (monthlies).

A0250
American Meat Institute.
Meatfacts (year).
Approximately 40 pages.   Annual.   1971-
Availability: $5.00 to members, $10.00 to non-members from the issuing source.

Provides data on the livestock sector of the agriculture industry for the United States including livestock inventories, slaughter, meat production, wholesale, retail and producer meat prices, farm marketing receipts, meat consumption, imports, exports, and financial and operating data for the meat packing industry. Most data cover a one year period; select trends are included. Includes data by state. Contains approximately 40 tables.
Data from federal and private sources.
Description based on 1984 imprint covering 1983 data.

A0260
American Medical Association.
Physician Characteristics and Distribution in the U.S. (year).
Approximately 300 pages.　　　Annual.　　　1943-
ISSN: 0731-0315　　　LCCN: 82-644625
Availability: $17.00 + P/H from the issuing source.

Provides data on health care services industry for the United States including physician manpower and licensing, data on women and foreign graduate physicians, hospital facilities, population and income served. Most data cover a one year period; select trends are included. Includes data by S.M.S.A., county, state, and region. Contains approximately 36 tables. Title varies.
Data from private and state sources.
Description based on 1982 imprint covering 1981 data.

A0270
American Medical Association.
Socioeconomic Characteristics of Medical Practice, (year).
Approximately 150 pages.　　　Annual.　　　1972-
ISSN: 0742-2709　　　LCCN: 84-640340
Availability: $12.00 + P/H from the issuing source.

Provides data on medical practice for the United States including hours spent in practice, volume of patient visits, surgery, hospital utilization, fees and expenses. Most data cover a one year period. Contains approximately 40 tables. Title varies.
Data from private sources.
Description based on 1984 imprint covering 1983 data.

A0280
American Newspaper Publishers Association.
(year) Facts About Newspapers.
Approximately 25 pages.　　　Annual.　　　1976-
Availability: Free from the issuing source.

Provides data on the newspaper publishing industry for the United States including number of papers, circulation, price, advertising volume, revenues, employment, newsprint consumption and prices. Most data cover a thirty-eight year period. Provides select comparisons to Canadian data. Contains approximately 17 tables.
Data from federal and private sources.
Description based on 1984 imprint covering 1946-1983 data.

A0290
American Petroleum Institute.
Basic Petroleum Data Book.
Approximately 225 pages.   Three/year.   1975-
ISSN: 0033-3654   LCCN: 47-36541
Availability: $40.00 per year from the issuing source.

Provides data on the gas and oil industries for the United States including production, demand, consumption, reserves, exploration, drilling, refining, imports, exports and financial data including employment, personal income and prices. Most data cover a ten year period; select projections and long term trends are included. Provides select comparisons to foreign data including OPEC. Contains approximately 150 tables. Title varies.
Data from federal and private sources.
Description based on 1984 imprint covering 1973-1984 data.
Also publishes updated data for the United States in *Weekly Statistical Bulletin* and *Monthly Statistical Report.*

A0300
American Public Transit Association.
Transit Fact Book, (years).
Approximately 80 pages.   Annual.   1943-
ISSN: 0149-3132   LCCN: 45-31939
Availability: Single copies free from the issuing source.

Provides data on urban mass transit for the United States including financial and operating data such as revenues, expenses, employment, usage, transit fleets, and energy consumption. Most data cover a three year period. Includes data by mode of transit and state. Provides select comparisons to other modes of transportation and Canadian data. Contains approximately 35 tables/charts.
Data from federal, foreign and private sources.
Description based on 1985 imprint covering 1981-1983 data.

A0310
American Textile Manufacturers' Institute.
Textile Hi-lights.
Approximately 35 pages.   Quarterly.   1957-
ISSN: 0040-4950   LCCN: 75-616538
Availability: $50.00 per year from the issuing source.

Provides data of relevance to the textile industry for the United States including Consumer Price Index, Producer Price Index, fiber consumption, production, loom hours, shipments of various textile products, imports, exports, inventories, and financial and operating data including employment in the textile manufacturing industry. Most data cover a six year period. Includes data by fiber type. Provides select comparisons to other industries and foreign data. Contains approximately 35 tables. Title and issuing source vary.
Data from federal sources.
Description based on 1985 imprint covering 1979-1984 data.
Includes monthly supplements which provide updated data.

A0320
American Waterways Operators.
Inland Waterborne Commerce Statistics, (years).
Approximately 60 pages.   Annual.   1975-
ISSN: 0157-518X   LCCN: 77-642119
Availability: Free from the issuing source.

Provides data on the barge and towing sector of the transportation industry for the United States including number of towing vessels and barges, barge traffic and commodities transported. Most data cover a two year period; select trends are included. Includes data by commodity and United States waterway (exclusive of the Great Lakes). Provides select comparisons to other modes of transportation. Contains approximately 85 tables. Data from federal sources.
Description based on 1984 imprint covering 1981-1982 data.

A0330
Association of American Railroads.
Railroad Facts (year).
Approximately 70 pages.   Annual.   1923-
ISSN: 0742-1850   LCCN: 84-640303
Availability: Free from the issuing source.

Provides data on the railroad transportation industry for the United States including financial and operating data, traffic, train miles, employment, fuel costs and consumption. Most data cover a one year period; select trends are included. Provides select comparisons to other modes of transportation. Contains approximately 55 tables. Title varies.
Data from federal and private sources.
Description based on 1984 imprint covering 1983 data.

A0340
Association of Information Systems Professionals.
(year) Annual Salary Survey Results.
Approximately 100 pages.   Annual.   1975-
Availability: $25.00 to members, $40.00 to non-members from the issuing source.

Provides data on salaries paid for approximately forty-five positions in the information industry for the United States including word processing positions. Most data cover a one year period. Includes data by metropolitan area and region. Provides select comparisons to Canadian data. Contains approximately 110 tables. Issuing source varies.
Data from survey of approximately 23,000 employees in 2,500 companies.
Description based on 1984 imprint covering 1984 data.

A0350
Association of Research Libraries.
ARL Statistics (years).
Approximately 75 pages.   Annual.   1963-
ISSN: 0147-2135   LCCN: 77-647280
Availability: $8.00 to members, $10.00 to non-members from the issuing source.

Provides data on research libraries for the United States including total and new volumes,

microforms by type, current serials, interlibrary loan, operating expenses by function including salaries and FTE staff. Most data cover a one fiscal year period. Includes data by size and institution. Contains approximately 20 tables. Title varies.
Data from survey of 115 member libraries.
Description based on 1984 imprint covering FY1983 data.

A0360
Atomic Industrial Forum.
Nuclear Power Facts and Figures.
Approximately 15 pages.   Annual.   1975-
Availability: Free from Publications Office.

Provides data on the nuclear power industry including number of reactors, reactor construction, employment, energy production, consumption and capacity, financial and operating data and data on uranium reserves, production and consumption. Most data cover a twenty-six year period; select projections are included. Includes data by state and region. Provides select comparisons to foreign data and data for other forms of energy. Contains approximately 28 tables.
Data from federal, foreign, international and private sources.
Description based on 1984 imprint covering 1957-1982 data.

A0370
Bank Administration Institute.
U.S. Bank Performance Profile, (year).
Approximately 125 pages.   Annual.   1973-
Availability: $7.50 to members, $15.00 to non-members from the issuing source.

Provides data on the commercial banking industry for the United States including income, expenses, growth, employment, yield, interest rates, capital productivity, assets and liabilities. Most data cover a one year period. Includes data by asset size and state. Contains approximately 110 tables. Title and issuing source vary.
Data from reports filed by approximately 14,000 federally insured banks.
Description based on 1984 imprint covering 1983 data.

A0380
Battery Council International.
(year) Battery Council International Statistics Annual.
Approximately 45 pages.   Annual.   1940-
Availability: $5.00 from the issuing source.

Provides data on the automotive battery manufacturing industry for the United States including production, shipments, imports and exports, and world lead production, consumption, stocks and prices. Also provides data on automobile production, registration, usage, imports and exports. Most data cover a two year period; select trends from the 1940s are included. Includes data by state. Provides select comparisons to foreign data. Contains approximately 40 tables. Title varies.
Data from federal, foreign and private sources.
Description based on 1984 imprint covering 1982-1983 data.

A0390
Book Industry Study Group.
Book Industry Trends, (year).
Approximately 130 pages.   Annual.   1977-
ISSN: 0160-970X   LCCN: 78-642241
Availability: Free to members [$75.00 for library membership], $150.00 to non-members
from the issuing source.

Provides data on the book publishing industry for the United States including sales,
manufacturing and library acquisitions. Most data cover a ten year period with actual
figures for six years and four year projections. Includes data by type of market and book.
Contains approximately 6 lengthy tables.
Data from private sources.
Description based on 1983 imprint covering 1978-1987 data.

A0400
Chamber of Commerce of the U.S.
Economic Outlook.
Approximately 20 pages.   Ten/year.   1971-
Availability: $60.00 per year from Forecast Section.

Periodic report contains recurring statistical tables. Provides data on business and
economic conditions for the United States including forecasted change in approximately
fifty-three economic indicators such as Gross National Product or other measures
of production, employment, unemployment, personal income and expenditures, and
financial and operating data for the private sector and the federal government. Most
data cover a four year period with actual figures for two years and two year projections.
Contains approximately 2 recurring tables.
Data from original research, federal and private sources.
Description based on 1985 imprint covering 1983-1986 data.

A0410
Chamber of Commerce of the U.S.
Employee Benefits.
Approximately 35 pages.   Annual.   1947-
ISSN: 0194-3499   LCCN: 84-642678
Availability: $7.00 from Survey Research Center, Economic Policy Division.

Provides data on employee benefits for the United States including distribution of
benefits, types of benefits, benefits as percent of payroll, pension and insurance payments
as payroll deductions. Also provides data on personal income. Most data cover a one
year period; select trends are included. Includes data by type of benefit and industry/
sector. Contains approximately 25 tables/charts.
Data from survey of approximately 1,000 employers.
Description based on 1984 imprint covering 1983 data.

A0420
Clothing Manufacturers Association of the U.S.A.
Special Statistical Report on Profit, Production, and Sales Trends in the Men's and Boys' Clothing Industry.
Approximately 15 pages.   Annual.   1982-
ISSN: 0740-7424   LCCN: SC83-8116
Availability: $20.00 from the issuing source.

Provides data on the men's and boys' clothing industry for the United States including production, shipments, sales, profitability, imports and exports, employment and survey data on consumer purchases of men's clothing. Most data cover a five year period; select trends and projections are included. Includes data by fabric type and wholesale price range of garment. Contains approximately 20 tables. Title varies.
Data from survey of 30,000 consumer households, federal and private sources.
Description based on 1984 imprint covering 1979-1983 data.

A0430
College Placement Council.
CPC Salary Survey.
Approximately 125 pages in twenty-eight issues.   Six/year.   1962-
ISSN: 0196-1004   LCCN: SC79-4046
Availability: Price per volume varies from the issuing source.

Provides data on starting salaries paid and jobs offered to college graduates for the United States including number of job offers, average, ninetieth and fiftieth percentile salaries offered. One report (issued three times per year) provides national data. Five reports (each issued five times per year) provide data for five United States regions. Most data cover a one school year period. Includes data by field of study and type of employer. Contains approximately 1 detailed table per report. Title varies.
Data from private sources.
Description based on 1984 imprint covering 1983-1984 school year data.
Also publishes *Recruiting (year)* (annual) which summarizes college recruitment activities.

A0440
The Conference Board.
Business Executives' Expectations.
Approximately 2 pages.   Quarterly.   1977-
                                 LCCN: SN83-10646
Availability: Price on request from the issuing source.

Provides data on projected business and economic conditions for the United States by chief executive officers of American firms including a Composite Measure of Business Confidence. Most data cover a one year period with actual figures for six months and six month projections; select trends are included. Includes data by industry/sector. Contains approximately 5 tables/charts.
Data from survey and private sources.
Description based on 1984 imprint covering 1984 data.

A0450
The Conference Board.
Consumer Attitudes and Buying Plans.
Approximately 2 pages.   Monthly.   1968-
ISSN: 0547-7204   LCCN: SC79-4258
Availability: Price on request from the issuing source.

Provides data on projected business and economic conditions for the United States by consumers including Consumer Confidence Index and Buying Plans Index (projections for durables purchases and travel). Most data are six month projections. Contains approximately 3 tables/charts. Issuing source varies.
Data from survey and private sources.
Description based on 1984 imprint covering 1984-1985 data.

A0460
The Conference Board.
Economic Policy Issues.
Approximately 15 pages.   Quarterly.   1981-
                              LCCN: 81-643431
Availability: Price on request from the issuing source.

Quarterly series on economic policy for the United States includes several recurring statistical features. First issue of each year provides data on U.S. monetary policy; second issue of each year provides data on the federal budget; third issue of each year provides data on world economic conditions. Most data cover a two year period; select trends and projections are included. Contains approximately 5 tables/charts. Incorporates the Conference Board's former annual publication *The Federal Budget: Its Impact on the Economy.*
Data from federal and private sources.
Description based on 1983 imprint covering 1981-1982 data.

A0470
The Conference Board.
Economic Road Maps.
Approximately 4 pages.   Monthly.   1936-
                              LCCN: SN82-20303
Availability: Price on request from the issuing source.

Monthly series of brief reports on business and economic conditions for the United States including several recurring (generally annual) titles. Provides data on inflation, income, taxes, and corporate profits. Most data cover a ten year period; select long term trends are included. Provides select comparisons to foreign data. Contains approximately 12 tables/charts. Title and issuing source vary.
Data from federal and private sources.
Description based on 1983 and 1984 imprints covering 1975-1984 data.

A0480
The Conference Board.
Financial Indicators and Corporate Financing Plans: A Semiannual Survey.
Approximately 5 pages.   Semiannual.   1976-
                               LCCN: SN83-10770
Availability: Price on request from the issuing source.

Provides data on business and economic conditions for the United States including corporate financial executives' general economic expectations, and past and planned sources of corporate financing. Most data cover a one year period. Contains approximately 1 table/chart. Issuing source varies.
Data from survey of thirty-seven executives.
Description based on 1984 imprint covering 1984 data.

A0490
The Conference Board.
International Economic Scoreboard.
Approximately 4 pages.   Monthly.   1979-
ISSN: 0270-045X   LCCN: 80-429
Availability: Price on request from the issuing source.

Provides data on world business and economic conditions including comparative indexes of economic performance, growth rates and leading business cycle indicators for the United States, Canada, United Kingdom, West Germany, France, Italy, Japan and Australia. Most data cover a one quarter period with the most current figures available; select trends are included. Includes data by country and by region for Europe. Contains approximately 5 tables/charts. Issuing source varies.
Data from private sources.
Description based on 1984 imprint covering 1984 data.

A0500
The Conference Board.
Manufacturing Investment Statistics: Capital Appropriations and Capital Investment and Supply Conditions.
Approximately 10 pages.   Quarterly.   1972-
ISSN: 0195-8313   LCCN: 79-644427
Availability: Price on request from the issuing source.

Provides data on the manufacturing industries for the United States including capital appropriations, expenditures and assessment of investment capital levels and external funds supply. Most data cover a one year period; select short term trends. Includes data by industry/sector. Contains approximately 10 tables/charts. Title and issuing source vary.
Data from survey and private sources.
Description based on 1984 imprint covering 1984 data.

A0510
The Conference Board.
Report: Annual Survey of Corporate Contribution, (year) Edition.
Approximately 45 pages.   Annual.   1970-
ISSN: 0416-0986   LCCN: 76-24946
Availability: Price on request from the issuing source.

Provides data on philanthropy for the United States including tax deductible contributions by corporations to charitable organizations and public interest groups. Most data
cover a one year period. Includes data by corporate level of contribution, size, assets and
industry/sector. Provides select comparisons to foreign data. Contains approximately 30
tables/charts. Title and issuing source vary.
Data from survey of approximately 550 U.S. companies and private sources.
Description based on 1984 imprint covering 1982 data.

A0520
The Conference Board.
Report: Top Executive Compensation (year) Edition.
Approximately 65 pages.   Biennial.   1942-
                                         LCCN: 73-151220
Availability: Price on request from the issuing source.

Provides data on base salaries and total compensation of the highest paid executives in
various industries for the United States. Most data cover a one year period. Includes
data by industry/sector for construction, energy, finance, and manufacturing. Contains
approximately 120 tables/charts. Issuing source varies.
Data from survey of approximately 1,000 executives and private sources.
Description based on 1982 imprint covering 1981 data.

A0530
The Conference Board.
Research Bulletin.
Approximately 15 pages.   Irregular.   1975-
                                         LCCN: SN82-21176
Availability: Price on request from the issuing source.

Irregular series of reports includes several annual statistical reports. Annuals include
U.S. Regional Economies: An Updated View of (years) which provides data on the
status of the eight U.S. regional economies; *Labor Outlook* which provides data on
employment and personal income as forecast by union and corporate leaders; *International Outlook* which provides data on world business and economic conditions as
forecast by corporate analysts and O.E.C.D.; *Economic Outlook* which provides data on
business and economic conditions for the United States including Gross National
Product or other measures of production, Consumer Price Index, Producer Price Index
and Corporate Profits. Most reports cover a two year period. Statistical content varies.
Title and issuing source vary.
Data from original research, federal and private sources.
Description based on 1984 imprint covering 1982-1983 data.

A0540
The Conference Board.
Statistical Bulletin.
Approximately 15 pages.   Monthly.   1968-
ISSN: 0010-5554   LCCN: 73-644166
Availability: Price on request from the issuing source.

Provides data on economic and business conditions for the United States including leading economic indicators, diffusion indexes, business executives' expectations, capital appropriations in manufacturing industries, federal receipts and outlays, employment, consumer confidence and spending. Most data cover a two year period; select projections are included. Provides select comparisons to foreign data. Contains approximately 10 tables/charts. Title and issuing source vary.
Data from federal and private sources.
Description based on 1983 imprint covering 1982-1983 data.

A0550
The Conference Board.
Utility Investment Statistics: Utility Appropriations.
Approximately 5 pages.   Quarterly.   1958-
ISSN: 0360-523X   LCCN: 75-648802
Availability: Price on request from the issuing source.

Provides data on the investor owned electric and gas utilities including capital appropriations and expenditures. Most data cover a two year period. Contains approximately 4 tables/charts. Title and issuing source vary.
Data from survey of ninety-five percent of electric companies and sixty percent of gas companies.
Description based on 1984 imprint covering 1983-1984 data.

A0560
The Conference Board.
Worldbusiness Perspectives.
Approximately 5 pages.   Bimonthly.   1970-
ISSN: 0084-1455   LCCN: SF77-252
Availability: Price on request from the issuing source.

Bimonthly periodical on world business and economic conditions with recurring statistical reports. Semiannual report provides data on foreign capital expenditures by U.S. companies; annual report provides data on U.S. foreign trade. Most data cover a one year period; select trends are included. Contains approximately 4 tables/charts. Issuing source varies.
Data from survey, federal and private sources.
Description based on 1984 imprint covering 1983 data.

A0570
Copper Development Association
Annual Data, (year).
Approximately 20 pages.   Annual.   1963-
ISSN: 0589-6835
Availability: Free from the issuing source.

Provides data on the copper industry for the United States including production, consumption, imports and exports, and stocks for copper, brass and bronze. Most data cover a twenty-one year period. Includes data for copper produced from primary and secondary sources. Contains approximately 4 detailed tables. Title varies.
Data from federal and private sources.
Description based on 1984 imprint covering 1963-1983 data.

A0580
Council of the Great City Schools.
Statistical Profile of the Great City Schools, (years).
Approximately 55 pages.   Biennial.   1983
Availability: Free to members, $10.00 to non-members from the issuing source.

Provides data on education in twenty-two large city school districts for the United States including population, geographic area, enrollment, facilities, employment, municipal bond debt ratings, revenues and expenses. Most data cover a thirteen year period. Includes data by city. Contains approximately 40 tables/charts.
Data from district and federal sources.
Description based on 1983 imprint covering 1970-1982 data.

A0590
Council for Financial Aid to Education.
Corporate Support of Higher Education.
Approximately 20 pages.   Annual.   1954-
ISSN: 0270-4501   LCCN: 80-644000
Availability: $5.00 from the issuing source.

Provides data on philanthropy for the United States including corporate income and contributions to education, purpose of support, contributions by corporate foundations, gifts of company products, research grants and matching gifts. Most data cover a one year period; select short term trends are included. Contains approximately 24 tables. Title varies.
Data from survey of approximately 800 corporations and federal sources.
Description based on 1984 imprint covering 1982 data.

A0600
Council for Financial Aid to Education.
(years) Voluntary Support of Education.
Approximately 70 pages.   Annual.   1954-
ISSN: 0363-3683   LCCN: 81-641373
Availability: $14.00 from the issuing source.

Provides data on philanthropy for the United States including voluntary support of educational institutions from various sources. Most data cover a two school year period; select trends are included. Includes data by type of institution, source and purpose of gift. Contains approximately 20 tables. Title varies.
Data from survey of approximately 1,500 schools and federal sources.
Description based on 1984 imprint covering 1982 and 1983 school year data.

A0610
Credit Union National Association.
Credit Union Report, (year).
Approximately 7 pages.   Annual.   1954-
                          LCCN: SN82-21126
Availability: $5.00 from the issuing source.

Provides data on the credit union industry for the United States including number and
membership of credit unions, deposits, loans, reserves, assets, services offered, dividends
paid, and financial and operating data including employment and performance. Most
data cover a one year period; select trends are included. Includes data by asset size and
state. Provides select comparisons to other financial institutions. Contains approximately
12 tables. Title varies.
Data from survey of approximately 16,000 credit unions.
Description based on 1984 imprint covering 1984 data.

A0620
Distilled Spirits Council of the U.S.
Annual Statistical Review, (years), Distilled Spirits Industry.
Approximately 60 pages.   Annual.   1939-
ISSN: 0066-4367   LCCN: SN82-2979
Availability: Free from the issuing source.

Provides data on the distilled spirits industry for the United States including Consumer
Price Index, distillation, stocks, withdrawals, bottling, sales, shipments, imports, exports,
apparent consumption, revenues, prices, consumer expenditures, and state and local
controls. Most data cover a one year period; select trends are included. Includes data by
class of distilled spirit and state. Provides select comparisons to foreign import and export
data. Contains approximately 55 tables. Title and issuing source vary.
Data from federal, foreign, private and state sources.
Description based on 1984 imprint covering 1983 data.

A0630
Distilled Spirits Council of the U.S.
(years) Public Revenues From Alcoholic Beverages.
Approximately 90 pages.   Annual.   1935-
ISSN: 0148-0863   LCCN: 77-642153
Availability: Free from the issuing source.

Provides data on federal, state and local revenues from the sale, taxation and regulation
of alcoholic beverages for the United States. Most data cover a one year period; select
trends are included. Includes data by beverage type and state. Contains approximately
85 tables. Title and issuing source vary.
Data from federal, local and state sources.
Description based on 1984 imprint covering 1983 data.

A0640
Edison Electric Institute.
Statistical Yearbook of the Electric Utility Industry, (year).
Approximately 95 pages.   Annual.   1928-
ISSN: 0361-3607   LCCN: 82-641051
Availability: $27.50 (20% discount to members) from the issuing source.

Provides data on the electric utility industry for the United States including generating capacity, supply of electricity, fuel consumption and costs, customer sales, average bill by consuming sector, revenues, expenditures, and assets and liabilities of electric utility companies. Most data cover a one year period; select trends are included. Includes data by state and census division. Contains approximately 100 tables.
Data from federal and private sources.
Description based on 1982 imprint covering 1981 data.
Also publishes updated data as "Statistical Review" in *Electric Perspectives* (quarterly), and two annual surveys of electric power industry capacity and requirements: (year) *Annual Electric Power Survey*, and *(year) Electric Power Annual Report.*

A0650
Electronic Industries Association.
Consumer Electronics Annual Review, (year): Industry Facts and Figures.
Approximately 60 pages.   Annual.   1980-
Availability: Free (send 6" by 9" SASE with $0.73 postage) from the issuing source.

Provides data on the consumer electronics industry for the United States including production, factory sales, sales to dealers, imports and exports. Most data cover a five year period; select trends are included. Includes data by product type and region. Contains approximately 43 tables/charts.
Data from federal and private sources.
Description based on 1985 imprint covering 1980-1904 data.

A0660
Electronic Industries Association.
Electronic Market Data Book, (year).
Approximately 150 pages.   Annual.   1956-
ISSN: 0070-9867   LCCN: 72-627504
Availability: $55.00 from the issuing source.

Provides data on the electronics industry for the United States including employment, production, sales, research, development, imports, exports, and financial and operating data. Most data cover a ten year period; select long term trends are included. Includes data by product for consumer electronics, communications equipment and industrial electronics. Provides select comparisons to foreign data. Contains approximately 150 tables/charts. Title varies.
Data from federal and private sources.
Description based on 1984 imprint covering 1974-1983 data.
Also publishes updated data as "Monthly EIA Statistics" in *Electronics Market Trends* (monthly).

A0670
Fibre Box Association.
(year) Fibre Box Industry Annual Report.
Approximately 15 pages.   Annual.   1941-
ISSN: 0190-6151   LCCN: SC78-1709
Availability: $10.00 from the issuing source.

Provides data on the fibre box industry for the United States including value and volume of corrugated and solid fibre container shipments, production, consumption, inventory, Corrugated Price Index, Producer Price Index, employment and personal income. Most data cover a three year period; select trends are included. Includes data by geographic area. Contains approximately 23 tables.
Data from federal and private sources.
Description based on 1984 imprint covering 1981-1983 data.

A0680
Food Marketing Institute.
(year) Annual Financial Review- Food Marketing Institute.
Approximately 20 pages.   Annual.   1975-
ISSN: 0192-374X   LCCN: 79-644937
Availability: $7.50 to members, $15.00 to non-members from the issuing source.

Provides data on supermarket industry for the United States including income, sales, and financial and operating data for firms with sales in excess of $2 million. Most data cover a three year period; select trends are included. Contains approximately 125 tables/charts.
Data from survey of approximately 130 companies with 11,000 stores and 10K reports filed with the Security and Exchange Commission.
Description based on 1983 imprint covering 1980-1982 data.

A0690
Food Marketing Institute.
Trends: Consumer Attitudes and the Supermarket, Update (year).
Approximately 40 pages.   Annual.   1974-
ISSN: 0278-6346   LCCN: 81-645577
Availability: $10.00 to members, $20.00 to non-members from the issuing source.

Provides data on consumer practices and attitudes of relevance to the supermarket industry for the United States including shopping patterns and general economic concerns. Also, provides data on business and economic conditions for the United States including unemployment, personal income and prices. Most data cover a five year period. Includes data by age, budget size and region. Contains approximately 45 tables.
Title varies.
Data from survey of approximately 1,000 shoppers and private sources.
Description based on 1981 imprint covering 1978-1982 data.

A0700
General Aviation Manufacturers Association.
General Aviation Statistical Databook (year).
Approximately 30 pages.   Annual.   1980-
                                 LCCN: SC83-1662
Availability: Free from the issuing source.

Provides data on the general aviation industry for the United States including aircraft shipments, fleet and flight activity, aviation personnel, airports and aeronautical facilities. Most data cover a five year period; select trends and ten year projections are included. Includes data by region and state. Contains approximately 24 tables.
Data from federal and private sources.
Description based on 1985 imprint covering 1980-1984 data.

A0710
Gold Institute.
Modern Gold Coinage, (year).
Approximately 30 pages.   Annual.   1976-
ISSN: 0149-4279   LCCN: 77-643382
Availability: $10.00 from the issuing source.

Provides data on world gold coinage including number of coins issued, coin and issue values, gold content and value, and physical characteristics of coins. Most data cover a one year period. Includes data by country for approximately seventy countries. Contains approximately 70 tables.
Data from federal, foreign and private sources.
Description based on 1984 imprint covering 1983 data.

A0720
Gold Institute.
World Mine Production of Gold, (years).
Approximately 10 pages.   Annual.   1979-
Availability: Free from the issuing source.

Provides data on the world gold mining industry including production figures. Most data cover a five year period with actual figures for one year and four year projections. Includes data by county for fifty-seven gold producing countries. Contains approximately 3 tables.
Data from private sources.
Description based on 1985 imprint covering 1983-1987 data.

A0730
Health Insurance Association of America.
(years) Source Book of Health Insurance Data.
Approximately 100 pages.   Annual.   1959-
ISSN: 0073-148X   LCCN: 60-187
Availability: Free from the issuing source.

Provides data on the health insurance industry for the United States including the extent of private insurance coverage, benefit payments, premium income, government health

care programs, medical costs and health services manpower. Most data cover a two year period; select trends are included. Includes data by type of insurance company, state and region. Contains approximately 65 tables. Issuing source varies.
Data from federal and private sources.
Description based on 1983 imprint covering 1981-1982 data.

A0740
Independent Petroleum Association of America.
Oil Producing in Your State, (year) Edition.
Approximately 130 pages.   Annual.   1939-
                                  LCCN: 41-10748
Availability: Free from the issuing source.

Provides data on the oil and gas industries for the United States including production, reserves, value, exploration and development. Most data cover a one year period; select trends are included. Includes data by state for thirty-three oil producing states. Contains approximately 115 tables. Title varies.
Data from federal, private and state sources.
Description based on 1982 imprint covering 1981 data.
Also publishes updated data as "Facts and Forecasts" in *Petroleum Independent* (bimonthly) and a pocket sized annual *U.S. Petroleum Statistics, (year), Revised.*

A0750
Independent Sector.
Dimensions of the Independent Sector.
Approximately 80 pages.   Annual.   1984-
                                  LCCN: 85-23520
Availability: $35.00 from the issuing source.

Provides data on philanthropy and voluntary action ("the independent sector") for the United States including percent of national income, personal income and employment in the independent sector, contributions, characteristics of supporting sources and profiles of organizations in the independent sector. Most data cover a seven year period. Includes data by industry/sector. Provides select comparisons to other sectors of the economy. Contains approximately 50 tables.
Data from federal and private sources.
Description based on 1984 imprint covering 1974-1980 data.

A0760
Institute of Real Estate Management.
Expense Analysis: Condominiums, Cooperatives and Planned Unit Developments (year).
Approximately 150 pages.   Annual.   1954-
ISSN: 0191-2208   LCCN: 79-642606
Availability: $30.00 from the issuing source.

Provides data on the real estate industry for the United States including expenses for condominiums, cooperatives, and planned unit developments. Expenses covered include administrative, operating and repair costs, and fixed expenses. Most data cover a one year period; select trends are included. Includes data by building type, size, age and

price, region and metropolitan area. Contains approximately 38 tables. Title varies.
Data from survey of 900 developments and private sources.
Description based on 1983 imprint covering 1982 data.

A0770
Institute of Real Estate Management.
Income/Expense Analysis: Apartments (year).
Approximately 220 pages.   Annual.   1954-
ISSN: 0194-1941   LCCN: 79-643863
Availability: $49.00 from the issuing source.

Provides data on the real estate industry for the United States including apartment
building income and expenses, operating ratios, turnover, vacancies and utility costs.
Most data cover a one year period; select trends are included. Includes data by building
size and type, region and metropolitan. Contains approximately 46 tables. Title varies.
Data from survey of 5,000 apartment projects and private sources.
Description based on 1983 imprint covering 1982 data.

A0780
Institute of Real Estate Management.
Income/Expense Analysis: Office Buildings, Downtown and Suburban (year).
Approximately 120 pages.   Annual.   1976-
                             LCCN: SC83-8040
Availability: $35.00 from the issuing source.

Provides data on the real estate industry for the United States including downtown and
suburban office building income and expenses, vacancies, and heating costs. Most data
cover a one year period; select trends are included. Includes data by building type, size,
age, and rental range, metropolitan area and region. Provides select comparisons to
Canadian data. Contains approximately 39 tables. Title varies.
Data from survey of 700 buildings and private sources.
Description based on 1983 imprint covering 1982 data.

A0790
Institute of Scrap Iron and Steel.
Facts.
Approximately 15 pages.   Annual.   1939-
ISSN: 0163-3899   LCCN: 78-646697
Availability: $5.00 from the issuing source.

Provides data on the ferrous scrap metal industry for the United States including
production, consumption, price, shipment, and import and export. Most data cover a
one year period; select trends are included. Includes data by furnace type and scrap
grade. Contains approximately 6 tables/charts. Title varies.
Data from federal and private sources.
Description based on 1983 imprint covering 1982 data.

A0800
Insurance Information Institute.
Insurance Facts, (years) Edition.
Approximately 120 pages.   Annual.
ISSN: 0074-0713   LCCN: 73-2557
Availability: Free from the issuing source.

Provides data on the liability and property insurance industry including number and value of policies written, losses, financial and operating data. Most data cover a one year period; select trends are included. Includes data by type of policy and cause of loss. Contains approximately 70 tables. Title varies.
Data from federal, private and state sources.
Description based on 1983 imprint covering 1982 data.

A0810
International City Management Association.
Municipal Yearbook (year).
Approximately 420 pages.   Annual.   1914-
ISSN: 0077-2186   LCCN: 34-27121
Availability: $46.00 from the issuing source.

Provides data on urban areas for the United States including population, educational attainment, municipal revenues, expenditures, debt and employment data for police, fire and refuse collection and disposal departments. Also includes salary information for municipal and county officials. Most data cover a one year period. Contains approximately 120 tables. Title varies.
Data from federal, municipal, private and state sources.
Description based on 1984 imprint covering 1983 data.

A0820
Investment Company Institute.
(year) Mutual Fund Fact Book.
Approximately 100 pages.   Annual.   1966-
ISSN: 0077-2550   LCCN: 80-647954
Availability: Free from the issuing source.

Provides data on the investment company or mutual fund industry for the United States including growth, sales, redemptions, dividends, dividend reinvestment, assets, equity, capital gains, composition of mutual fund portfolios, and data on money market funds. Also includes a survey of investor needs. Most data cover a one year period. Includes data by region and state. Contains approximately 60 tables. Issuing source varies.
Data from survey of 1,500 heads of households and private sources.
Description based on 1984 imprint covering 1983 data.
Also publishes updated data in *Trends in Mutual Fund Activity* (monthly).

A0830
Menswear Retailers of America.
Annual Business Survey.
Approximately 60 pages.   Annual.   1927-
Availability: $20.00 from the issuing source.

Provides data on menswear retailers for the United States including sales, profit, inventory, assets, liabilities, and financial and operating ratios. Most data cover a five year period; select trends are included. Includes data by sales volume, merchandise class and region. Contains approximately 35 tables.
Data from survey of approximately 185 retailers.
Description based on 1984 imprint covering 1979-1983 data.

A0840
Morris, Robert Associates.
Journal of Commercial Bank Lending.
Approximately 75 pages.   Monthly.   1918-
ISSN: 0021-986X   LCCN: 75-648976
Availability: $12.25 to members, $24.50 to non-members from the issuing source.

Monthly journal on the commercial bank lending industry for the United States includes an annual statistical analysis of finance company ratios. Provides data on composite ratios for installment sales finance, consumer finance companies and diversified finance companies. Most data cover a one year period. Contains approximately 3 tables. Title varies.
Data from private sources.
Description based on 1983 imprint covering 1982 data.

A0850
Morris, Robert Associates.
RMA ('year) Annual Statement Studies.
Approximately 390 pages.   Annual.   1923-
ISSN: 0080-3340   LCCN: 72-626355
Availability: $5.00 to members, $22.20 to non-members from the issuing source.

Provides composite financial and operating data for approximately 300 industries for the United States including assets, liabilities, income and performance ratios for companies with less than $50 million in assets. Most data cover a one fiscal year period. Includes data by industry/sector for the following: construction, finance, manufacturing, and wholesale and retail trade. Contains approximately 5 tables. Issuing source varies.
Data from private sources.
Description based on 1982 imprint covering FY1981 data.

A0860
Mortgage Bankers Association of America.
Mortgage Banking.
Approximately 90 pages.   Monthly.   1939-
ISSN: 0730-0212   LCCN: 81-649698
Availability: $25.00 per year from the issuing source.

Monthly journal on the mortgage banking industry for the United States includes monthly statistical feature, "Mortgage Market Trends". Provides data on the construction and finance industries including housing sales, interest rate and yields, new loans and loans closed. Most data cover a one year period. Includes data by unit type. Contains approximately 16 tables. Title varies.
Data from federal and private sources.
Description based on 1984 imprint covering 1983 data.

A0870
Motor Vehicle Manufacturers Association of the U.S.
MVMA Motor Vehicle Facts and Figures ('year).
Approximately 100 pages.   Annual.   1920-
ISSN: 0272-3395   LCCN: SN80-13685
Availability: $7.50 from the issuing source.

Provides data on the motor vehicle industry for the United States including employment, production, sales, imports, exports, registration, ownership, usage and operating expenses, auto loans, fuel and materials consumption, motor vehicle taxes, theft, accidents and safety, and related data on highways and transportation. Most data cover a one year period; select long term trends are included. Includes data by model year and state. Provides select comparisons to foreign data. Contains approximately 135 tables. Title and issuing source vary.
Data from federal and private sources.
Description based on 1984 imprint covering 1983 data.

A0880
Motor Vehicle Manufacturers Association of the U.S.
World Motor Vehicle Data, (year).
Approximately 350 pages.   Annual.   1964-
ISSN: 0085-8307   LCCN: 73-640507
Availability: $35.00 from the issuing source.

Provides data on the world motor vehicle industry including production/assembly, sales, imports, exports, diesel vehicles, registration and vehicles retired from circulation. Most data cover a two year period; select projections and long term trends are included. Includes data by manufacturer, region and country. Contains approximately 800 tables.
Data from federal, foreign and private sources.
Description based on 1983 imprint covering 1981-1982 data.

A0890
Motorcycle Industry Council.
(year) Motorcycle Statistical Annual.
Approximately 50 pages.   Annual.   1977-
ISSN: 0149-3027   LCCN: 77-643309
Availability: Free to members, $25.00 to non-members, $10.00 to educational institutions, students and motorcycle dealers from Research and Statistics Department.

Provides data on the motorcycle industry for the United States including data on production, sales, registration, imports, usage and ownership. Most data cover a three year period; select trends are included. Includes data by region and state. Contains approximately 35 tables.
Data from federal and private sources.
Description based on 1984 imprint covering 1981-1983 data.

A0900
National Association for State Information Systems.
Information Systems Technology in State Government.
Approximately 420 pages.   Annual.   1970-
Availability: $50.00 from the issuing source.

Provides data on computers in state government including coordination and control of computer systems, inventory, financing, employment, employee training, contractual services, utilization of software and security measures. Most data cover a five year period; select trends and projections are included. Includes data by computer size, region and state. Contains approximately 21 tables.
Data from survey of state governments.
Description based on 1985 imprint covering 1979-1984 data.

A0910
National Association of Broadcasters.
(year) Radio Financial Report.
Approximately 120 pages.   Annual.
                                          LCCN: SN85-19744
Availability: $10.00 to members, $30.00 to non-members from the issuing source.

Provides data on the radio broadcasting industry for the United States including revenues, expenses, profits, employment and advertising. Most data cover a one year period. Includes data by type of station, market size, revenue size and format. Contains approximately 120 tables.
Data from survey of approximately 1,700 commercial stations.
Description based on 1983 imprint covering 1982 data.

A0920
National Association of Broadcasters.
(year) Television Financial Report.
Approximately 80 pages.   Annual.
Availability: $10.00 to members, $30.00 to non-members from the issuing source.

Provides data on the television broadcasting industry for the United States including revenues, expenses, profits, employment and advertising. Most data cover a one year period. Includes data by type of station, ADI (Area Dominant Influence) market, revenue size and region. Contains approximately 105 tables.
Data from survey of approximately 450 commercial stations.
Description based on 1983 imprint covering 1982 data.

A0930
National Association of Business Economists.
NABE News.
Approximately 5 pages.   Bimonthly.   1977-
ISSN: 0745-3205   LCCN: SN82-8405
Availability: $5.00 per issue from the issuing source.
Bimonthly publication includes recurring statistical feature in its November issue. Feature provides data on business and economic conditions including forecasts and

views on the economy from business economists. Most data are four year projections; select longer term projections are included. Includes data by region. Contains approximately 7 tables.
Data from survey of approximately 200 members.
Description based on 1982 imprint covering 1982-1985 data.

A0940
National Association of Hosiery Manufacturers.
Hosiery Statistics.
Approximately 65 pages.   Annual.   1934-
                                 LCCN: 45-52616
Availability: $35.00 from the issuing source.

Provides data on the hosiery industry for the United States including production, shipments, stocks, consumption, foreign trade, plants and employment. Most data cover a one year period; select trends are included. Includes data by hosiery type. Contains approximately 44 tables.
Data from federal and private sources.
Description based on 1983 imprint covering 1982 data.

A0950
National Association of Real Estate Investment Trusts.
REIT Fact Book.
Approximately 35 pages.   Annual.   1974-
ISSN: 0095-1374   LCCN: 74-647976
Availability: $40.00 from the issuing source.

Provides data on the real estate investment trust industry for the United States including performance, assets, dividends, investments, loans by REITs, construction loans, ownership of property, sources of funds. Most data cover a two year period; select trends are included. Contains approximately 12 tables. Title varies.
Data from federal and private sources.
Description based on 1982 imprint covering 1981-1982 data.

A0960
National Association of Realtors.
Existing Home Sales.
Approximately 15 pages.   Annual.   1972-
ISSN: 0161-5882   LCCN: 78-641508
Availability: $36.00 per year to members, $45.00 per year to non-members (with monthly updates), $10.00 as a separate from the issuing source.

Provides data on the real estate industry for the United States and sales of existing single family homes including volume and value of sales, price range and select characteristics of homes. Most data cover a one year period; select trends are included. Includes data by region. Contains approximately 16 tables. Title varies.
Data from private sources.
Description based on 1984 imprint covering 1983 data.
Includes *Existing Home Sales* (monthly) which provides updated data.

A0970

National Association of Realtors.
Outlook for the Economy and Real Estate.
Approximately 5 pages.   Monthly.   1979-
Availability: Free from the issuing source.

Provides data on business and economic conditions for the United States of relevance to the real estate industry including employment, personal income, money stocks, investment, home sales, imports and exports, Gross National Product or other measures of production, and data for the construction industry. Most data cover a seven year period with actual figures for one year and six year projections; select long term projections are included. Contains approximately 5 tables/charts.
Data from federal and private sources.
Description based on 1985 imprint covering 1984-1990 data.

A0980

National Association of Securities Dealers.
NASDAQ Securities Fact Book, (year).
Approximately 110 pages.   Annual.   1976-
ISSN: 0741-0921   LCCN: SC83-1846
Availability: Free from the issuing source.

Provides data on market price and volume performance of approximately 2,600 NAS-DAQ-traded securities including share volume, trading volume, number of companies and issues traded by NASDAQ, market value of securities and performance indexes. Most data cover a one year period; select trends are included. Contains approximately 20 tables. Title varies.
Data from private sources.
Description based on 1984 imprint covering 1983 data.

A0990

National Association Of State Budget Officers.
Fiscal Survey of the States (years).
Approximately 30 pages.   Annual.   1977-
ISSN: 0198-6562   LCCN: 80-641033
Availability: $4.00 from the issuing source.

Provides data on state government finances and operations for the United States including revenues, expenditures and balances. Most data cover a three fiscal year period with actual figures for two years and one year projections. Includes data by state. Contains approximately 12 tables/charts. Produced cooperatively with the National Governors' Association Title varies.
Data from survey of state budget officers.
Description based on 1984 imprint covering FY1983-1985 data.

A1000

National Association of State Racing Commissions.
Pari-mutuel Racing, (year).
Approximately 20 pages.   Annual.   1974-
Availability: $7.50 from the issuing source.

Provides data on the pari-mutuel horse and greyhound racing industry in the U.S. including total revenues, revenues to states, total races/games, attendance and purse distribution. Also provides data for jai lai. Most data cover a one year period; select trends are included. Includes data by state. Contains approximately 17 tables.
Data from private sources.
Description based on 1984 imprint covering 1983 data.

A1010
National Association of Wheat Growers.
Wheat Grower.
Approximately 10 pages.   Monthly.   1978-
Availability: $3.50 from the issuing source.

Monthly journal has recurring statistical feature "(year) Wheat Facts" in its August issue. Provides data on the wheat sector of the agriculture industry for the United States including production, supply, disappearance, prices received, costs, income, imports and exports. Most data cover a three year period; select trends and projections are included. Includes data by state. Provides select comparisons to foreign data. Contains approximately 28 tables/charts.
Data from federal and private sources.
Description based on 1984 imprint covering 1981-1983 data.

A1020
National Automobile Dealers Association.
NADA Data for (year).
Approximately 20 pages.   Annual.   1979-
Availability: Free from the issuing source.

Provides data on the new car and truck franchise sales industry for the United States including financial and operating data for the average dealership, profit expectations, advertising expenditures, sales volume and data for parts and service departments. Also, motor vehicle registration and select data on scrapping and used car sales by franchised new car dealers. Most data cover a six year period; select long term trends and projections are included. Includes data by state. Contains approximately 45 tables.
Data from federal and private sources.
Description based on 1984 imprint covering 1978-1983 data.

A1030
National Business Aircraft Association.
Business Flying: Business Aviation Statistics.
Approximately 10 pages.   Annual.   1959-
Availability: Free from the issuing source.

Annual statistical compilation is one of three annual reports in the Business Flying series. Provides data on the aviation industry for the United States including number and type of aircraft, hours flown, avionics equipment, active pilots and licensing, fuel consumption and airport facilities. Most data cover a five year period; select projections are included. Includes data by type of aircraft. Contains approximately 20 tables.
Data from federal and private sources.
Description based on 1984 imprint covering 1979-1983 data.

A1040
National Coal Association.
Coal Data.
Approximately 120 pages.   Annual.   1948-
ISSN: 0145-417X   LCCN: 76-648911
Availability: Free to members, $50.00 to non-members, $35.00 to non-profit organizations from the issuing source.

Provides data on the bituminous coal and lignite industries for the U.S. including employment, personal income, Producer Price Index, production, consumption, reserves, imports, exports, and ranking of the fifty largest coal mines in the U.S. Most data cover a five year period. Includes data by census division and state. Provides select comparisons to other fuels. Contains approximately 120 tables. Title varies.
Data from federal and private sources.
Description based on 1983 imprint covering 1978-1982 data.
Also publishes world data in *International Coal* (annual) and *International Coal Review* (semimonthly).

A1050
National Cotton Council of America.
Cotton Counts Its Customers.
Approximately 110 pages.   Annual.   1937-
                         LCCN: 60-51185
Availability: Free to members, $50 to non-members, 40% discount to public and educational institutions and libraries from the issuing source.

Provides data on the cotton textile industry for the United States including consumption and production. Most data cover a three year period. Includes data by end-use product category for approximately ninety detailed end-use categories in apparel, home furnishings, and industrial uses. Contains approximately 4 lengthy tables.
Data from federal and private sources.
Description based on 1984 imprint covering 1981-1983 data.

A1060
National Cotton Council of America.
Economic Outlook for U.S. Cotton, (year).
Approximately 90 pages.   Annual.   1963-
Availability: Free from the issuing source.

Provides data on business and economic conditions for the United States of relevance to the cotton industry including unemployment, personal income, Consumer Price Index, Producer Price Index, Gross National Product or other measures of production, and the following data for the textile industry: employment, personal income, inventory, shipments, unfilled orders, mill fiber consumption, textile production, imports, exports, cotton acreage, production, fiber prices, and data on cottonseed and cottonseed products. Most data cover a ten year period; select trends are included. Includes data by fiber type and state. Provides select comparisons to foreign data. Contains approximately 70 tables.
Data from federal, international and private sources.
Description based on 1985 imprint covering 1975-1984 data.

A1070
National Council of Savings Institutions.
(year) National Fact Book.
Approximately 60 pages.   Annual.   1960-
Availability: $15.00 from the issuing source.

Provides data on savings institutions for the United States including organization and structure, employment, assets and liabilities, deposits and reserves, capital market investments, income and expenses. Most data cover a one year period; select trends are included. Includes data by state. Provides select comparisons to other financial institutions. Contains approximately 55 tables. Title and issuing source vary.
Data from federal and private sources.
Description based on 1983 imprint covering 1982 data.

A1080
National Council of the Churches of Christ in the U.S.A.
Yearbook of American and Canadian Churches.
Approximately 300 pages.   Annual.   1916-
ISSN: 0084-3644   LCCN: 16-5726
Availability: $17.95 from Abingdon Press.

Provides data on approximately 220 religious bodies for the United States including number of churches, membership, clergy, and contributions, church finances and benevolence. Most data cover a one year period. Includes data by religion. Contains approximately 20 tables. Title varies.
Data from private sources.
Description based on 1984 imprint covering 1982 data.

A1090
National Education Association.
Estimates of School Statistics.
Approximately 40 pages.   Annual.   1942-
ISSN: 0077-4278   LCCN: 59-914
Availability: $4.00 to members, $9.00 to non-members from the issuing source.

Provides data on public education for the United States including estimated enrollment and attendance, staff and finances. Most data cover a one school year period; select short term trends are included. Includes data by state and district. Contains approximately 11 tables. This report provides interim data for use prior to issuance of official NCES figures.
Data from private and state sources.
Description based on 1984 imprint covering 1983-1984 data.

A1100
National Education Association.
Rankings of the States (years).
Approximately 70 pages.   Annual.   1959-
ISSN: 0077-4332   LCCN: 74-176052
Availability: $6.00 to members, $14.95 to non-members from the issuing source.

Provides data on public education for the United States including state rankings for population, enrollment, attendance, faculty, finances, revenues and operating expenditures. Most data cover a two year period; select long term trends are included. Contains approximately 130 tables. Title varies.

Data from federal and private sources.

Description based on 1984 imprint covering 1982-1983 data.

A1110

National Federation of Independent Business.
NFIB Quarterly Economic Report for Small Business.
Approximately 40 pages.   Quarterly.   1974-
ISSN: 0362-3548   LCCN: 76-642389
Availability: Free from the issuing source.

Provides data on business and economic conditions of relevance to small business firms for the United States including net earnings, employee compensation, job openings, sales volume, price fluctuations, capital expenditures, inventories, interest rates and loan availability. Also, provides data on small businessmen's perceptions of the single most important problem faced by small business. Most data cover a three year period; select short term projections are included. Includes data by region. Contains approximately 35 tables/charts. Title varies.

Data from survey.

Description based on 1984 imprint covering 1981-1983 data.

A1120

National Food Processors Association.
Canned Food Pack Statistics (years).
Approximately 75 pages.   Annual.   1935-
ISSN: 0069-018X   LCCN: 55-40089
Availability: $20.00 from the issuing source.

Provides data on food canning industry for the United States including canned vegetables, fruit and seafood. Includes data on production, shipment, carryover and consumption. Most data cover a ten year period; select long term trends are included. Includes data by commodity/sector, state and area. Contains approximately 120 tables. Title and issuing source vary.

Data from federal and private sources.

Description based on 1984 imprint covering 1973-1982 data.

A1130

National Funeral Directors Association of the U.S.
Statistical Abstract of Funeral Service Facts and Figures in the U.S.
Approximately 110 pages.   Annual.
Availability: $50.00 from the issuing source.

Provides data on the funeral home industry for the United States including finances and operations of funeral home operators and service prices. Most data cover a one year period. Includes data by region and state. Contains approximately 50 tables. Title varies.

Data from survey of approximately 1,000 funeral home operators.

Description based on 1984 imprint covering 1983 data.

A1140
National LP-Gas Association.
(year) LP-Gas Market Facts.
Approximately 25 pages.   Annual.   1950-
ISSN: 0075-9759
Availability: $3.00 to members, $6.00 to non-members from the issuing source.

Provides data on the liquefied petroleum gas (LPG) industry for the United States including production, storage, shipments, imports, exports, and uses. Most data cover a one year period; select trends are included. Includes data by LPG type, state, and district. Provides select comparisons to Canadian data. Contains approximately 35 tables.
Data from federal, foreign, private and state sources.
Description based on 1983 imprint covering 1982 data.

A1150
National Machine Tool Builders' Association.
(years) Economic Handbook of the Machine Tool Industry.
Approximately 320 pages.   Annual.   1969-
ISSN: 0070-8550   LCCN: 73-646105
Availability: $20.00 to members, $35.00 to non-members from the issuing source.

Provides data on the machine tool industry for the United States including production, imports, exports, employment, and financial and operating data. Most data cover a one year period; select trends are included. Provides select comparisons to foreign data. Contains approximately 260 tables.
Data from federal, foreign and private sources.
Description based on 1984 imprint covering 1983 data.

A1160
National Paperbox and Packaging Association.
Annual Financial Survey of the Rigid Paper Box Industry.
Approximately 30 pages.   Annual.   1926-
Availability: $25.00 to members, $50.00 to non-members from the issuing source.

Provides data on the rigid paper box industry for the United States including financial and operating ratios, sales, price indexes, billings, and production. Most data cover a one year period; select short term trends are included. Includes data by company size and region. Contains approximately 17 tables.
Data from survey and federal sources.
Description based on 1984 imprint covering 1983 data.

A1170
National Restaurant Association.
Restaurant Industry Operation Report.
Approximately 80 pages.   Annual.   1974-
ISSN: 0739-1439   LCCN: 83-644232
Availability: $12.50 to members, $25.00 to non-members from the issuing source.

Provides data on the restaurant industry finances and operations for the United States including income, expenses, sales volume and employment. Most data cover a one year

period. Contains approximately 42 tables. Title varies.
Data from survey of approximately 830 member restaurants.
Description based on 1984 imprint covering 1982 data.

A1180
National Retail Merchants Association.
Department and Specialty Store Merchandising and Operating Results of (year).
Approximately 200 pages.   Annual.   1924-
ISSN: 0271-5015   LCCN: 72-626565
Availability: $37.50 to members, $69.50 to non-members from the issuing source.

Provides data on the retail trade industry for the United States including price indexes,
and merchandising and operating ratios for department and specialty stores such as
mark-on, markdown, stock shortages, gross margin, stock turnover. Most data cover a
one year period. Includes data by merchandise type and stores sales volume. Contains
approximately 2 lengthy tables. Title varies.
Data from federal and private sources.
Description based on 1984 imprint covering 1983 data.

A1190
National Retail Merchants Association. Financial Executives Division.
Financial and Operating Results of Department and Specialty Stores of (year).
Approximately 125 pages.   Annual.   1974-
ISSN: 0547-8804   LCCN: 72-92812
Availability: $37.50 to members, $69.50 to non-members from the issuing source.

Provides data on the department and specialty store industry for the United States
including average sales, earnings, expenses by division, return on assets, and gross
margin. Most data cover a one year period; select trends are included. Includes data by
division and store sales volume. Contains approximately 100 tables.
Data from survey of approximately 210 companies and private sources.
Description based on 1982 imprint covering 1981 data.

A1200
National Safety Council.
Accident Facts, (year).
Approximately 100 pages.   Annual.   1921-
                             LCCN: 28-14389
Availability: $8.50 to members, $10.75 to non-members from the issuing source.

Provides data on accidental death and injury for the United States including accidents
in the work place, accidents in public areas, traffic accidents and farm accidents. Most
data cover a one year period. Includes data by accident type, city and state. Provides
select comparisons to foreign data. Contains approximately 95 tables.
Data from federal and private sources.
Description based on 1983 imprint covering 1982 data.

A1210
Newspaper Advertising Bureau.
(year) Daily Newspaper Readership Demographic Tables for Total U.S., Top One Hundred Metros and Top One Hundred DMAs.
Approximately 35 pages.   Annual.
Availability: $3.00 from the issuing source.

Provides data on newspaper readership for the United States including socioeconomic characteristics of daily newspaper readers. Most data cover a one year period. Includes data by region. Contains approximately 12 tables. Title varies.
Data from private sources.
Description based on 1984 imprint covering 1984 data.

A1220
Newspaper Advertising Bureau.
(year) Sunday/Weekend Readership Demographic Tables for Total U.S., Top One Hundred Metros and Top One Hundred DMAs.
Approximately 35 pages.   Annual.
Availability: $3.00 from the issuing source.

Provides data in newspaper readership for the United States including socioeconomic characteristics of weekend and Sunday newspaper readers. Most data cover a one year period. Includes data by region. Contains approximately 12 tables.
Data from private sources.
Description based on 1984 imprint covering 1984 data.

A1230
Newsprint Information Committee.
Newspaper and Newsprint Facts at a Glance (years).
Approximately 30 pages.   Annual.   1958-
Availability: Free to research organizations, $2.50 to others from the issuing source.

Provides data on the newsprint and newspaper industry for the United States including newsprint capacity, production, consumption and prices. Most data cover a one year period. Provides select comparisons to foreign data. Contains approximately 25 tables. Title varies.
Data from federal and private sources.
Description based on 1984 imprint covering 1984 data.

A1240
North American Electric Reliability Council.
Electric Power Supply and Demand (years).
Approximately 175 pages.   Annual.   1979-
ISSN: 0737-1845   LCCN: 83-641820
Availability: Free from the issuing source.

Provides data on the electric utility industry for the United States including forecasts of electric power supply and demand, generating capacity, planned additional generating units and annual energy generation. Most data cover a ten year period with actual data

for one year and nine year projections. Includes data by fuel, season and region. Contains approximately 23 tables. Title varies.
Data from private sources.
Description based on 1984 imprint covering 1984-1993 data.

A1250
Northeast-Midwest Institute.
State of the Region (year).
Approximately 110 pages.   Biennial.   1979-
Availability: $6.00 from from the issuing source.

Provides data on business and economic conditions for the United States including population, education, employment, unemployment, personal income, financial and operating data for state and federal governments, and the following industries: agriculture, construction, energy, and manufacturing. Most data cover an eleven year period. Includes data by state and region. Contains approximately 27 tables.
Data from federal sources.
Description based on 1983 imprint covering 1970-1980 data.

A1260
Pacific Area Travel Association.
Annual Statistical Report, (year).
Approximately 105 pages.   Annual.   1968-
Availability: $35.00 to members, $60.00 to non-members from the issuing source.

Provides data on the transportation and tourism industries for the Pacific region including mode of travel, country of residence and purpose of visit for Pacific region visitors. Also provides data on hotel rooms and occupancy, visitor expenditures and average length of stay. Most data cover a one year period; select trends are included. Includes data by country. Contains approximately 30 tables.
Data from federal and foreign sources.
Description based on 1983 imprint covering 1982 data.

A1270
Population Reference Bureau.
(year) World Population Data Sheet of the Population Reference Bureau.
Approximately 2 pages.   Annual.   1962-
ISSN: 0085-8315   LCCN: SC77-838
Availability: $1.00 from the issuing source.

Provides data on world population including size, characteristics and Gross National Product or other measures of production. Most data cover a thirty-seven year period with estimated figures for one year and thirty-six year projections. Includes data by region and country. Contains approximately 1 table/chart.
Data from federal and foreign sources.
Also publishes U.S. data in *U.S. Population Data Sheet* (annual).

49

A1280
Produce Marketing Association.
Produce Marketing Almanac.
Approximately 275 pages.　　　Annual.　　　　1958-
Availability: $25.00 to members, $35.00 to non-members from the issuing source.

Provides data on the food marketing industry for the United States with an emphasis on fruit and vegetables including Consumer Price Index for food items, grocery store sales, market share, select data for the restaurant industry, U.S. produce imports and exports, produce arrivals and unloads, production and consumption of produce items. Most data cover a three year period; select short term trends are included. Includes data by commodity, food item, region and city. Provides select comparisons to Canadian data. Contains approximately 70 tables. Title and issuing source vary.
Data from federal and private sources.
Description based on 1985 imprint covering 1981-1983 data.

A1290
Public Securities Association
Statistical Yearbook of Municipal Finance.
Approximately 130 pages.　　　Annual.　　　　1979-
ISSN: 0740-5790　　　　　LCCN: SC83-7396
Availability: $35.00 to members, $45.00 to non-members from the issuing source.

Provides data on the municipal securities market for the United States including long- and short-term volume, sales by use and proceeds, yield, ratio of tax-exempt to taxable bonds, and underwriting activity. Most data cover a two year period; select trends are included. Includes data by region and type of security. Contains approximately 100 tables. Title varies.
Data from original research by the SUNYA Municipal Finance Study Group.
Description based on 1983 imprint covering 1981-1982 data.

A1300
Radio Advertising Bureau.
Radio Facts (year).
Approximately 45 pages.　　　Annual.　　　　1960-
Availability: Free from issuing source.

Provides data on the commercial radio industry for the United States including radio ownership, sales, advertising, revenues, and radio station format. Most data cover a four year period; select trends are included. Contains approximately 45 tables/charts.
Data from federal and private sources.
Description based on 1984 imprint covering 1980-1983 data.

A1310
Regional Airline Association.
Annual Report: Regional/Commuter Airline Industry.
Approximately 135 pages.　　　Annual.　　　　1975-
　　　　　　　　　LCCN: SC83-2285
Availability: $15.00 to members, $25.00 to non-members from the issuing source.

Provides data on the regional/commuter airline industry for the United States including air traffic, passengers, aircraft operated, top regional airlines, airports receiving regional service, aircraft inventories and production. Most data cover a six year period; select long term trends and projections are included. Includes data by carrier, manufacturer and state. Contains approximately 25 tables/charts.
Data from private sources.
Description based on 1984 imprint covering 1978-1983 data.

A1320
Scientific Manpower Commission.
Professional Women and Minorities: A Manpower Data Resource Service.
Approximately 280 pages.   Annual.   1975-
ISSN: 0190-1796   LCCN: 75-324671
Availability: $70.00 from the issuing source.

Provides data on the characteristics of the scientific workforce for the United States including number of women and minorities, higher education enrollment and degrees. Most data cover a ten year period; select trends and projections are included. Includes data by field of study, profession and sector for the general, academic and federal workforces. Provides select comparisons to other professions. Contains approximately 330 tables.
Data from federal and private sources.
Description based on 1983 imprint covering 1973-1982 data.

A1330
Scientific Manpower Commission.
Salaries of Scientists, Engineers and Technicians.
Approximately 200 pages.   Biennial.   1965-
ISSN: 0146-5015   LCCN: 77-641787
Availability: $30.00 from the issuing source.

Provides data on salaries paid for scientists, engineers and technicians for the United States including starting and advanced salaries in industry, government and education, and numbers employed. Most data cover a two year period; select trends are included. Includes data by field, degree level, level of experience, type of employer, census division and state. Provides select comparisons to other professions. Contains approximately 165 tables.
Data from federal and private sources.
Description based on 1983 imprint covering 1982-1983 data.

A1340
Securities Industry Association.
Securities Industry Yearbook (years).
Approximately 600 pages.   Annual.   1980-
ISSN: 0730-5796   LCCN: 83-647551
Availability: $35.00 to members, $50.00 to non-members from the issuing source.

Provides data on the securities brokerage industry for the United States including firms assets, number of offices, employment, account ownership, industry revenues and

expenditures, return on equity, market activity and indexes, interest, profit to earnings ratios, and yields. Most data cover a one year period. Includes data by firm. Contains approximately 30 tables.
Data from survey of member firms.
Description based on 1983 imprint covering 1983 data.
Also publishes updated data on market activity in *Securities Industry Trends* (7-8 per year).

A1350
Silver Institute.
Mine Production of Silver (year) with Projections for (years).
Approximately 10 pages.   Annual.   1975-
Availability: Free from the issuing source.

Provides data on the world silver mining industry including production figures. Most data cover a five year period with actual figures for one year and four year projections. Includes data by country for approximately fifty-eight silver-producing countries. Provides select comparisons to world data. Contains approximately 5 tables.
Data from federal and private sources.
Description based on 1984 imprint covering 1983-1987 data.
Also publishes updated data in *Silver Institute Letter* (bimonthly).

A1360
Silver Institute.
Modern Silver Coinage (year).
Approximately 40 pages.   Annual.   1972-
ISSN: 0149-7707   LCCN: 78-640559
Availability: $10.00 from the issuing source.

Provides data on world silver coinage including coin and issue values, silver content and physical characteristics. Most data cover a one year period. Includes data by country for approximately one hundred countries. Contains 1 lengthy table.
Data from federal and foreign sources.
Description based on 1984 imprint covering 1983 data.

A1370
Society of Industrial Realtors.
Industrial Real Estate Market Survey.
Approximately 200 pages.   Semiannual.   1980-
ISSN: 0730-0131   LCCN: 81-64990
Availability: $7.50 to members, $10 to non-members from the issuing source.

Provides data on the industrial real estate industry for the United States including market condition and outlook. Most data cover a one year period; select trends are included. Includes data by city and metropolitan region. Provides select comparisons to foreign data. Contains approximately 750 tables.
Data from survey of 100 specialists.
Description based on 1984 imprint covering 1984 data.

A1380
Southern Regional Education Board.
Fact Book on Higher Education in the South (years).
Approximately 100 pages.   Biennial.   1960-
ISSN: 0191-1643   LCCN: 79-642573
Availability: $4.00 from the issuing source.

Provides data on higher education for the South including population, educational attainment, personal income, tax revenues, enrollment and institutions, degrees, finances and faculty. Most data cover a one school year period. Includes data by state for fourteen Southern states: Alabama, Arkansas, Florida, Georgia, Kentucky, Louisiana, Mississippi, Missouri, North Carolina, South Carolina, Tennessee, Texas, Virginia and West Virginia. Provides select comparisons to national data. Contains approximately 62 tables.
Data from federal, private and state sources.
Description based on 1984 imprint covering 1983-1984 school year data.
Also publishes updated data in *Comparative Information on Higher Education* (annual).

A1390
Tax Foundation.
Facts and Figures on Government Finance.
Approximately 364 pages.   Biennial.   1941-
ISSN: 0071-3678   LCCN: 44-7109
Availability: $15.00 to members, $20.00 to non-members + $1.00 P/H from the issuing source.

Provides data on federal, state and local government finances for the United States including revenues, expenditures, taxation, assets, and debt. Also, provides select data on business and economic conditions for the United States including employment, unemployment, Consumer Price Index, Producer Price Index, interest rates, and Gross National Product or other measures of production. Most data cover a one fiscal year period; select trends and projections are included. Contains approximately 285 tables.
Title varies.
Data from federal, private and state sources.
Description based on 1983 imprint covering FY1981 data.

A1400
Television Bureau of Advertising.
TV Basics.
Approximately 10 pages.   Annual.   1958-
Availability: $0.25 from the issuing source.

Provides data on the television industry for the United States including TV ownership, sales, use, perceived credibility, advertising investment, number of stations, viewing habits and cable operations. Most data cover a one year period; select trends are included. Contains approximately 25 tables.
Data from private sources.
Description based on 1984 imprint covering 1983 data.

A1410
U.S. Brewers Association.
Brewers Almanac (year).
Approximately 105 pages.   Annual.   1940-
                                  LCCN: 45-51432
Availability: Free to members, $50.00 to non-members from the issuing source.

Provides data on the brewing industry for the United States including production, consumption, inventories, withdrawals, shipments, imports, exports, taxes, and financial and operating data. Most data cover a one year period; select trends are included. Includes data by state and area. Contains approximately 75 tables.
Data from federal sources.
Description based on 1982 imprint covering 1981 data.

A1420
U.S. Conference of Mayors.
Federal Budget and the Cities.
Approximately 100 pages.   Annual.   1973-
                                  LCCN: SN82-20657
Availability: $10.00 from the issuing source.

Provides data on business and economic conditions for the United States and the potential impact of proposed budget on urban areas including Gross National Product or other measures of production, Consumer Price Index, interest rates, education, employment, unemployment, tax collection, the aging, the arts and humanities, community development, housing, science and technology, and the energy and defense-related industries. Most data cover a six fiscal year period with actual figures for five years and one year projections. Contains approximately 20 tables.
Data from federal sources.
Description based on 1984 imprint covering FY1980-1985 data.

A1430
U.S. League of Savings Institutions.
Homeownership.
Approximately 150 pages.   Biennial.   1977-
Availability: $20.00 from the issuing source.

Provides data on the real estate industry for the United States including socioeconomic characteristics of home buyers, the housing market, type and location of home purchased, and financing. Most data cover a one year period. Includes data by region and metropolitan area size. Contains approximately 50 tables. Issuing source varies.
Data from survey of approximately 13,000 conventional single family home mortgages.
Description based on 1984 imprint covering 1983 data.

A1440
U.S. League of Savings Institutions.
(year) Savings Institutions Sourcebook.
Approximately 80 pages.   Annual.   1954-
ISSN: 0731-0935   LCCN: 82-640552
Availability: Free from the issuing source.

Provides data on the banking and savings industry for the United States including savings accounts and deposits, yield, mortgage lending and interest rates, and financial and operating data for savings institutions. Also, provides related data on household budgets, personal income and the construction and real estate industries. Most data cover a five year period; select long term trends are included. Includes data by type of institution and state. Contains approximately 100 tables. Title and issuing source vary.
Data from federal and private sources.
Description based on 1984 imprint covering 1979-1983 data.

A1450
U.S. Telephone Association.
Statistics of the Independent Telephone Industry (year).
Approximately 200 pages in two volumes.   Annual.   1955-
                              LCCN: 59-19815
Availability: Volume One: $5.00; Volume Two: $10.00 to members, $35.00 to non-members from the issuing source.

Provides data on the telephone industry in the United States including access lines, operating company exchanges, investments, revenues and income, employment and balance sheets. Volume One provides aggregate data. Volume Two provides data by company. Most data cover a one year period. Includes data for individual firms and data by state. Contains approximately 30 tables. Issuing source varies.
Data from private sources.
Description based on 1984 imprint covering 1983 data.
Also publishes the following annuals: **Holding Company Report** and brief summary **Phone Facts ('year).**

A1460
U.S. Travel Data Center.
(years) Economic Review of Travel in America.
Approximately 75 pages.   Annual.   1981-
ISSN: 0733-642X   LCCN: 82-644321
Availability: $45.00 from the issuing source.

Provides data on the transportation and tourism industries for the United States including Gross National Product or other measures of production, personal income, employment, volume of travel, travel related expenditures, and receipts and employment. Most data cover a two year period. Provides select comparisons to foreign data. Contains approximately 50 tables/charts.
Data from federal and private sources.
Description based on 1984 imprint covering 1982-1983 data.
Also publishes **Travel Printout** (quarterly) and **National Travel Survey** (annual with quarterly updates).

A1470
U.S. Travel Data Center.
Impact of Travel on State Economies, (year).
Approximately 50 pages.   Annual.   1974-
ISSN: 0730-9813   LCCN: 81-644365
Availability: $45.00 from the issuing source.

Provides data on the transportation and tourism industries for the United States including travel related expenditures, receipts, tax receipts, payroll and employment. Most data cover a one year period. Includes data by state. Contains approximately 12 tables.
Data from federal and private sources.
Description based on 1984 imprint covering 1982 data.

A1480
Western Wood Products Association.
(year) Statistical Yearbook of the Western Lumber Industry.
Approximately 75 pages.   Annual.   1968-
ISSN: 0195-931X   LCCN: 82-640405
Availability: $12.50 from the issuing source.

Provides data on the forest products industry for the western United States including lumber production, sawmill operations, lumber industry import and exports. Most data cover a two year period; select trends are included. Data by species cut. Also, by state and county for the twelve western lumber region states: Arizona, California, Colorado, Idaho, Montana, Nevada, Oregon, South Dakota, Utah, Washington and Wyoming. Also includes select data for Alaska and Hawaii. Provides select comparisons to U.S. and foreign data. Contains approximately 25 tables. Title varies.
Data from federal and private sources.
Description based on 1984 imprint covering 1982-1983 data.

A1490
Zinc Institute.
Annual Review of the U.S. Zinc and Cadmium Industry Including Statements from Other Countries, (year).
Approximately 40 pages.   Annual.   1967-
ISSN: 0731-2711   LCCN: 81-646247
Availability: Free from the issuing source.

Provides data on the zinc and cadmium industries for the United States including production, stocks, consumption, imports and exports. Most data cover a two year period; select trends are included. Includes data by end product. Provides select comparisons to foreign data. Contains approximately 45 tables. Title and issuing source vary.
Data from federal, foreign and private sources.
Description based on 1982 imprint covering 1980-1981 data.

PUBLICATIONS OF THE FEDERAL GOVERNMENT

F0010
Board of Governors of the Federal Reserve System (U.S.).
Annual Statistical Digest, (year).
Approximately 265 pages.　　Annual.　　　　1975-
ISSN: 0148-4338　　　　　LCCN: 77-641499
SUDOCS: FR1.59:(year)
Availability: $6.50 from Publications Section, Division of Administrative Services.

Provides data on business and economic conditions for the United States including employment, unemployment, personal income, Gross National Product or other measures of production, imports and exports, and data on the finance industry and monetary system including the money aggregate, the credit aggregate, interest rates and mortgages, the stock market, the federal budget and debt, and assets and liabilities of savings and loan associations, mutual savings banks, life insurance companies and credit unions. Most data cover a one year period and serve to cumulate tables found in the *Federal Reserve Bulletin* [FR1.3:(vol)/(nos)]. Includes data by industry/sector. Contains approximately 95 tables. 1980 imprint provides data for the period 1970-1979. There are plans to provide data for the period 1980-1984 in 1985. Thereafter, every five years, *Annual Statistical Digest* will provide data for a five or ten year period; in intervening years the *Digest* will provide data for the previous year only.
Data from federal and private sources.
Description based on 1983 imprint covering 1982 data.
Also provides historic data in *Banking and Monetary Statistics, (years)* [FR1.2:B22/5:(year), FR1.2:B22/5/suppl/ (years), FR1.3/a:B225/14:(years)] which provides data for the period 1914-1973.

F0020
Board of Governors of the Federal Reserve System (U.S.).
Federal Reserve Bulletin.
Approximately 165 pages.　　Monthly.　　　1915-
ISSN: 0014-9209　　　　　LCCN: 15-26318
SUDOCS: FR1.3:(vol)/(nos)　　　ITEM NO: 433-C
Availability: $20.00 per year from Publications Section, Division of Administrative Services.

Monthly journal on business and economic conditions for the United States includes recurring statistical features. Provides data on employment, unemployment, personal income, Gross National Product or other measures of production, Consumer Price Index, the construction industry, and data on the finance industry and monetary system including assets and liabilities of Federal Reserve Banks and commercial banks, the money aggregate, the credit aggregate, the stock market, and interest rates. Most data

cover a one year period; select short term trends are included. Provides select comparison to foreign data. Contains approximately 3 tables. Data provided in the *Federal Reserve Bulletin* is also cumulated in the *Annual Statistical Digest* [FR1.59:(year)].
Data from federal and private sources.
Description based on 1984 imprint covering 1984 data.

F0030
Board of Governors of the Federal Reserve System (U.S.).
Federal Reserve Chart Book.
Approximately 100 pages.   Quarterly.   1976-
ISSN: 0277-5476   LCCN: 80-642313
SUDOCS: FR1.30:(date)   ITEM NO: 443-D
Availability: $7.00 per year from Publications Section, Division of Administrative Services.

Provides data on business and economic conditions for the United States including employment, unemployment, personal income, Consumer Price Index, Producer Price Index, Gross National Product or other measures of production, the manufacturing, and retail trade industries and data on the finance industry and monetary system including the money aggregate, federal, state and local government finance, corporate and household finance, mortgage debt, assets and liabilities of financial institutions, the stock market and interest rates. Most data cover a nine year period. Includes data by industry/sector. Provides select comparisons to foreign data. Contains approximately 75 charts. Title varies.
Data from federal, foreign and private sources.
Description based on 1984 imprint covering 1976-1984 data.
Includes annual *Historical Chart Book* [FR1.30/2:(date)] which provides data for the period 1920-(year).

F0040
Center for Disease Control (U.S.).
MMWR: Morbidity and Mortality Weekly Report.
Approximately 15 pages.   Weekly.   1952-
ISSN: 0149-2195   LCCN: 83-644022
SUDOCS: HE20.7009:(vol)/(nos) ITEM NO: 508-A
Availability: $77.00 per year from Superintendent of Documents.

Weekly journal on morbidity and mortality for the United States. Subject coverage and statistical content vary from issue to issue but the journal provides data on incidence of infectious diseases, injury and death. Includes data by city, county, state and region. Contains approximately 5 tables. Title and issuing source vary.
Data from federal and state sources.
Description based on 1984 imprint covering 1984 data.
Includes the following annual supplements: *Health Information for International Travel, (year)* and *Reported Morbidity and Mortality in the U.S., Annual Summary, (year)*.

F0050

Federal Aviation Administration.
FAA Statistical Handbook of Aviation, (year).
Approximately 180 pages.   Annual.   1944-
ISSN: 0566-9618
SUDOCS: TD4.20:(year)   ITEM NO: 431-C-14
Availability: $6.00 from Superintendent of Documents.

Provides data on the general aviation industry for the United States including air traffic
and airway mileage, accidents, FAA facilities, airports, air carriers, commuters, aircraft
production, imports and exports, and the Civil Air Carrier Fleet including financial and
operating data, and employment. Most data cover a one year period; select trends are
included. Includes data by state and region. Contains approximately 102 tables. Title
and issuing source vary.
Data from federal, local and private sources.
Description based on 1983 imprint covering 1983 data.

F0060

Federal Deposit Insurance Corporation.
(year) Statistics on Banking.
Approximately 85 pages.   Annual.   1981-
ISSN: 0740-6649   LCCN: 83-646106
SUDOCS: Y3.F31/8:
Availability: Free from Corporate Communications.

Provides data on the banking industry for the United States including number of banks
and branches, assets and liabilities of banks, and income of insured banks. Most data
cover a one year period; select trends are included. Includes data by class of bank, bank
asset size and state. Contains approximately 20 tables. Provides data formerly published
in the Federal Deposit Insurance Corporation *Annual Report* [Y3.F31/8:1/(year)].
Data from federal and private sources.
Description based on 1983 imprint covering 1982 data.

F0070

Federal Highway Administration.
Highway Statistics, (year).
Approximately 180 pages.   Annual.   1945-
ISSN: 0095-344X   LCCN: 74-648854
SUDOCS: TD2.23:(year)   ITEM NO: 265-B
Availability: $6.00 from Superintendent of Documents.

Provides data on the transportation industry for the United States with an emphasis on
highways and motor vehicles including fuel consumption, rates and revenues, vehicle
registration, rates and revenues, drivers licensing, highway financing including federal
aid for highways and user taxation. Most data cover a two year period. Includes data by
unit of government at the local, county and state level. Contains approximately 108
tables. Issuing source varies.
Data from federal, local and state sources.
Description based on 1983 imprint covering 1982-1983 data.

Also provides historic data in *Highway Statistics Summary to (year)* [TD2.110/2:(year)] which provides coverage for the period 1919-(year).

F0080
Federal Reserve Bank of Atlanta.
Economic Review.
Approximately 60 pages.   Monthly.   1916-
Availability: Free from Research Department.

Monthly journal on business and economic conditions for the United States and the Sixth Federal Reserve District region includes recurring statistical supplement. Provides data on employment, unemployment, personal income, and the agriculture, construction and finance industries. Most data cover a one year period. Includes data by state for the Sixth Federal Reserve District states: Alabama, Florida, Georgia, Louisiana, Mississippi and Tennessee. Contains approximately 4 tables. Title varies.
Data from federal and private sources.
Description based on 1984 imprint covering 1984 data.

F0090
Federal Reserve Bank of Boston.
New England Economic Indicators.
Approximately 30 pages.   Monthly.   1969-
ISSN: 0548-4448   LCCN: 71-10551
Availability: Free from Bank and Public Information Center.

Provides data on business and economic conditions for the United States and the First Federal Reserve District region including employment, unemployment, personal income, Consumer Price Index and the following industries: energy, finance, manufacturing and retail trade. Most data cover a one month period with the most current figures available; select trends are included. Includes data by industry/sector, city and state for the First Federal Reserve District states: Connecticut, Maine, Massachusetts, New Hampshire, Rhode Island and Vermont. Contains approximately 80 tables/charts.
Data from federal, private and state sources.
Description based on 1983 imprint covering 1983 data.

F0100
Federal Reserve Bank of Boston.
New England Economic Almanac.
Approximately 105 pages.   Irregular.   1957-
ISSN: 0545-106X   LCCN: SC82-7553
Availability: Free from Bank and Public Information Center.

Provides data on business and economic conditions for the First Federal Reserve District region including population, employment, unemployment, personal income, Consumer Price Index, Gross State Product or other measures of production, federal, state and local government finances, and the following industries: construction, energy, finance, fishing, manufacturing, select service industries, transportation, wholesale and retail trade . Most data cover a five year period; select projections and long term trends are included. Includes data by industry/sector, city, S.M.S.A. and state for the First Federal

Reserve District states: Connecticut, Maine, Massachusetts, New Hampshire, Rhode Island and Vermont. Provides select comparisons to U.S. data. Contains approximately 60 tables.
Data from federal, private, and state sources.
Description based on 1982 imprint covering 1976-1980.

F0110
Federal Reserve Bank of Chicago.
Midwest Update.
Approximately 4 pages.   Monthly.   1982-
Availability: Free from Publications Division.

Provides data on business and economic conditions for the United States and the Seventh Federal Reserve District region including Consumer Price Index, Gross National Product or other measures of production, and data for the agricultural and finance industries. Most data cover a three year period. Includes data by industry/sector, select city and state for the Seventh Federal Reserve District states: Illinois, Indiana, Iowa, Michigan, Wisconsin. Contains approximately 1 table.
Data from federal and private sources.
Description based on 1984 imprint covering 1982-1984 data.

F0120
Federal Reserve Bank of Chicago.
Seventh District Economic Data, (year).
Approximately 90 pages.   Irregular.   1982-
Availability: Free from Publications Division.

Provides data on business and economic conditions for the United States and the Seventh Federal Reserve District region including population, employment, personal income and the following industries: agriculture, construction, finance, and manufacturing. Most data cover a twenty-two year period. Includes data by industry/sector, S.M.S.A. and state for the Seventh Federal Reserve District states: Illinois, Indiana, Iowa, Michigan, and Wisconsin. Contains approximately 70 tables. Title varies.
Data from federal and private sources.
Description based on 1982 imprint covering 1960-1981 data.

F0130
Federal Reserve Bank of Cleveland.
Economic Trends.
Approximately 25 pages.   Monthly.   1981-
ISSN: 0748-2922   LCCN: SN84-8790
Availability: Free from Research Department.

Provides data on business and economic conditions for the United States including employment, unemployment, personal income, Gross National Product or other measures of production, Consumer Price Index, Producer Price Index, the money aggregate, and the construction, manufacturing, and retail trade industries. Statistical content varies from issue to issue. Most data cover a three year period; select trends are included.

Provides select comparisons to the Fourth Federal Reserve District states: Kentucky, Ohio, Pennsylvania and West Virginia. Contains approximately 75 tables/charts.
Data from federal, private and state sources.
Description based on 1984 imprint covering 1982-1984 data.

F0140
Federal Reserve Bank of Kansas City.
Tenth District Depository Institutions and Commercial Bank Statistics.
Approximately 12 pages.   Monthly.   1946-
Availability: Free from Research Department with their *Financial Letter.*

Provides data on the banking industry for the United States and the Tenth Federal Reserve District region including assets and liabilities, loans outstanding and deposits. Most data cover a two year period. Includes data by city and state for the Tenth Federal Reserve District states: Colorado, Kansas, Missouri, Nebraska, New Mexico, Oklahoma, Wyoming. Contains approximately 2 tables. Title varies.
Data from private sources.
Description based on 1984 imprint covering 1983-1984 data.

F0150
Federal Reserve Bank of Richmond.
Business Forecasts, (year).
Approximately 80 pages.   Annual.   1972-
ISSN: 0164-0801   LCCN: SN83-2270
Availability: Free from Public Service Department.

Provides data on published forecasts of business and economic conditions for the United States. Subject coverage varies from issue to issue. Most data cover a five quarter period with the actual figures for the most current quarterly available and one year projections. Contains approximately 30 tables.
Data from a wide variety of forecasting sources.
Description based on 1984 imprint covering 1984-1985 data.

F0160
Federal Reserve Bank of Richmond.
Cross Sections: A Review of Business and Economic Developments Published Quarterly by the Federal Reserve Bank of Richmond.
Approximately 8 pages.   Quarterly.   1984-
Availability: Free from Public Service Department.

Provides data on business and economic conditions for the United States and the Fifth Federal Reserve District region including employment, unemployment, personal income, and data for the construction and finance industries. Most data cover a one year period. Includes data by state for the Fifth Federal Reserve District states: District of Columbia, Maryland, North Carolina, South Carolina, and Virginia. Contains approximately 1 table.
Data from federal and private sources.
Description based on 1984 imprint covering 1983 data.

F0170
Federal Reserve Bank of St. Louis.
Annual U.S. Economic Data.
Approximately 20 pages.   Annual.   1953-
ISSN: 0091-8334   LCCN: 73-645502
Availability: Single copies free from Research and Public Information Department.

Provides data on the finance industry and monetary system for the United States including money stock, savings deposits, loans and investments, and federal government finances including the budget and debt. Most data cover a nineteen year period. Contains approximately 35 tables. Title varies.
Data from federal and private sources.
Description based on 1984 imprint covering 1965-1983 data.

F0180
Federal Reserve Bank of St. Louis.
International Economic Conditions.
Approximately 60 pages.   Quarterly.   1977-
Availability: Single copy subscriptions free from Research and Public Information Department.

Provides data on world business and economic conditions including employment, consumer prices, wholesale prices, Gross National Product or other measures of production, imports and exports, and data on world finance industry and monetary systems including exchange rates, relative rates of inflation, and money supply for Belgium, Canada, France, Italy, Japan, Netherlands, Sweden, Switzerland, the United Kingdom, the United States and West Germany. Most data cover a six month period. Includes data by country. Contains approximately 15 tables.
Data from federal, international and private sources.
Description based on 1984 imprint covering 1984 data.

F0190
Federal Reserve Bank of St. Louis.
Monetary Trends.
Approximately 15 pages.   Monthly.   1967-
ISSN: 0430-1978   LCCN: 79-1197
Availability: Single copy subscriptions free from Research and Public Information Department.

Provides data on the finance industry and monetary system for the United States including aggregate money supply, credit, interest rates and federal government finances including the budget and debt. Most data cover a one month period with the most current figures available. Contains approximately 30 tables/charts.
Data from federal sources.
Description based on 1984 imprint covering 1984 data.

F0200
Federal Reserve Bank of St. Louis.
National Economic Trends.
Approximately 20 pages.   Monthly.   1967-
ISSN: 0430-1986   LCCN: SF79-10609
Availability: Single copy subscriptions free from Research and Public Information Department.

Provides data on business and economic conditions for the United States including employment, unemployment, personal income, Gross National Product or other measures of production, Consumer Price Index, Producer Price Index, and the retail trade industry. Most data cover a one month or one quarterly period with the most current figures available. Contains approximately 30 charts/tables.
Data from federal and state sources.
Description based on 1984 imprint covering 1984 data.

F0210
Federal Reserve Bank of St. Louis.
United States Financial Data.
Approximately 10 pages.   Weekly.   1968-
                             LCCN: SF82-6583
Availability: Single copy subscriptions free from Research and Public Information Department.

Provides data on the finance industry and monetary system for the United States including monetary aggregate, stock market, interest rates, deposits and loans. Most data cover a one month period with the most current figures available; select data for the previous quarter. Contains approximately 22 tables/charts.
Data from federal sources.
Description based on 1984 imprint covering 1984 data.

F0220
National Center for Education Statistics.
Condition of Education: Volume One: Statistical Report.
Approximately 230 pages.   Annual.   1975-
ISSN: 0098-4572   LCCN: 75-643861
SUDOCS: ED1.109:(year)   ITEM NO: 461-A-12
Availability: $8.50 from Superintendent of Documents.

Provides data on education for the United States including enrollment, dropout rate, academic performance and degrees conferred, employment outlook, and financial data on expenditures per pupil and teacher salaries. Most data cover a thirteen year period including actual figures for three years and ten year projections. Includes data by level of education and state. Contains approximately 70 charts/tables.
Data from federal, private and state sources.
Description based on 1984 imprint covering 1970-1993 data.
Also publishes more detailed data in *Digest of Education Statistics* [ED1.113:(year)].

F0230
National Center for Education Statistics.
Digest of Education Statistics, (year).
Approximately 210 pages.   Annual.   1962-
ISSN: 0502-4102   LCCN: SC82-5029
SUDOCS: ED1.113:(year)   ITEM NO: 460-A-10
Availability: $6.50 from Superintendent of Documents.

Provides data on education for the United States including enrollment, degrees conferred, expected lifetime earnings by education level, number and level of institutions, educators by subject, expenditures per pupil. Most data cover a two year period; select trends are included. Includes data by level of education and state. Contains approximately 175 tables. Issuing source varies.
Data from federal, private and state sources.
Description based on 1984 imprint covering 1980-1981 data.
Also publishes more general data in *Condition of Education* [ED1.109:(year)].

F0240
National Center for Education Statistics.
Library Statistics of Colleges and Universities, (year).
Approximately 150 pages.   Triennial.   1960-
                    LCCN: 72-627021
SUDOCS: ED1.310/2:(nos)   ITEM NO: 466-A-13 [ERIC]
SUDOCS: ED1.122:(year)   ITEM NO: 460-A-15 (mf)
Availability: $3.25 from Superintendent of Documents.

Provides data on libraries in institutions of higher learning including staff, hours, holdings, acquisitions, receipts, expenses, circulation and interlibrary loan. Most data cover a one school year period; select short term trends are included. Includes data by category of institution and state. Contains approximately 65 tables.
Data from survey of approximately 3,300 college and university libraries.
Description based on 1984 imprint covering 1981-1982 school year data.
Institutional data from this survey is published as *Library Statistics of Colleges and Universities, (year) Institutional Data* by the Association of College and Research Libraries ($12.00 to members, $16.00 to non-members).

F0250
National Center for Education Statistics.
Projections of Education Statistics to (years): Volume One: Analytical Report.
Approximately 120 pages.   Biennial.   1965-
                    LCCN: 67-627767
SUDOCS: ED1.120:(years)/(vol. 1) ITEM NO: 460-A-10
Availability: $4.75 from Superintendent of Documents.

Provides data on education for the United States including school age population, birth, enrollment, graduation or earned degrees, expenditures for elementary, secondary and higher education, and employment in education. Most data cover a twenty-one year period with actual figures for twelve years and nine year projections. Includes data by state. Contains approximately 78 tables/charts. Issuing source varies.
Data from federal and state sources.
Description based on 1982 imprint covering 1970-1990 data.

F0260
National Center for Education Statistics.
Public Elementary and Secondary Education in the U.S. (years): A Statistical Compendium.
Approximately 110 pages.   Annual.   1979-
ISSN: 0735-6617   LCCN: 82-646584
SUDOCS: ED1.112/2:(years)   ITEM NO: 460-B-1
Availability: $5.50 from Superintendent of Documents.

Provides data on public elementary and secondary education for the United States including number of districts, enrollment, graduation, employment, revenues and expenditures. Most data cover a one school year period. Includes data by state. Contains approximately 51 tables.
Data from federal and state sources.
Description based on 1984 imprint covering 1982-1983 school year data.

F0270
National Center for Education Statistics.
Statistics of Public Libraries.
Approximately 130 pages.   Quadrennial   1955-
                                LCCN: 82-603387
SUDOCS: ED1.122/2:   ITEM NO: 460-B-2 (mf)
SUDOCS: ED1.310/2:(nos)   ITEM NO: 466-A-3 [ERIC]
Availability: $6.50 from Superintendent of Documents.
Provides data on public libraries for the United States including population served, receipts and expenditures, facilities, staff, circulation and holdings. Most data cover a two year period; select short term trends are included. Includes data by library, S.M.S.A. and state. Contains approximately 45 tables. Title and issuing source vary.
Data from survey of approximately 8,500 public libraries, federal and private sources.
Description based on 1983 imprint covering 1977-1978 data.

F0280
National Center for Health Statistics (U.S.).
Health: U.S., (year).
Approximately 190 pages.   Annual.   1975-
ISSN: 0361-4468   LCCN: 76-641496
SUDOCS: HE20.6223:(year)   ITEM NO: 483-A-8
Availability: $8.50 from Superintendent of Documents.

Provides data on population, birth, death and the health care services industry for the United States including determinants and measures of health, utilization of health care resources, expenditures for health care services and health care personnel, employment, and facilities. Most data cover a nine year period; select trends and projections are included. Includes data by state. Contains approximately 120 tables/charts.
Data from federal, international and private sources.
Description based on 1984 imprint covering 1973-1981 data.

F0290
National Center for Health Statistics (U.S.).
Monthly Vital Statistics Report: Provisional Data.
Approximately 40 pages.   Monthly.   1938-
ISSN: 0364-0396   LCCN: 66-51898
SUDOCS: HE20.6217:(vol)/(nos) ITEM NO: 508-B
Availability: Free from the issuing source.

Provides data on birth, death, marriage and divorce for the United States. Most data
cover a one month period; select annual data are included. Includes data by state and
region. Contains approximately 20 tables. Title varies.
Data from federal sources.
Description based on 1984 imprint covering 1984 data.
Includes the following annual supplements: *Advance Report of Final Mortality Statistics,*
(year), *Advance Report of Final Divorce Statistics, (year)*, *Advance Report of Final*
Marriage Statistics, (year), *Births of Hispanic Parentage, (year)*, and *Annual Summary*
of Birth, Deaths, Marriages and Divorces: United States, (year).
Updates data provided in *Vital Statistics of the U.S.* [HE20.6210:(year)/(vol)/(pt)].

F0300
National Center for Health Statistics (U.S.).
Vital Statistics of the U.S. (year).
Approximately 1,800 pages in four volumes.   Annual.   1900-
ISSN: 0083-6710   LCCN: 40-26272
SUDOCS: HE20.6210:(year)/(vol)/(pt)   ITEM NO: 510
Availability: Volume One: $15.00; Volume Two, Parts A and B: $19.00 each; Volume
Three: $9.00 from Superintendent of Documents.

Provides data on population, birth, death, marriage and divorce for the United States.
Volume One provides data on birth; Volume Two Part A provides general mortality
data; Volume Two Part B provides geographic mortality data; Volume Three provides
data on marriage and divorce. Most data cover a one year period; select trends are
included. Includes data by place, city, S.M.S.A., county and state, and metropolitan and
non-metropolitan area. Contains approximately 300 tables.
Data from federal and state sources.
Description based on 1984 imprint covering 1979 data.
Also publishes provisional updated data in *Monthly Vital Statistics Report: Provisional*
Data [HE20.6217:(vol)/(nos)] and its supplements.

F0310
National Institute of Mental Health. (U.S.)
Mental Health, U.S., (year).
Approximately 150 pages.   Annual.   1983-
                              LCCN: 83-603453
SUDOCS: HE20.8137:(year)
Availability: $5.50 from Superintendent of Documents.

Provides data on mental health and the mental health care industry for the United States
including patients, facilities, services and personnel. Most data cover a five year period;

select trends are included. Includes data by occupation. Contains approximately 96 tables.

Data from federal and private sources.

Description based on 1983 imprint covering 1978-1982 data.

F0320
National Science Foundation (U.S.).
Science and Engineering Personnel: A National Overview.
Approximately 65 pages.   Biennial.   1980-
ISSN: 0278-9620   LCCN: 81-649996
SUDOCS: NS1.42:(year)   ITEM NO: 834-C-4
Availability: Free from Division of Science Resources Studies.

Provides data on scientific and engineering personnel for the United States including employment, unemployment and personal income. Most data cover a four year period; select trends are included. Includes data by discipline and educational level. Contains approximately 80 tables/charts.

Data from federal sources.

Description based on 1982 imprint covering 1976-1980 data.

F0330
National Science Foundation (U.S.). National Science Board.
Science Indicators.
Approximately 350 pages.   Biennial.   1972-
ISSN: 0092-315X   LCCN: 82-641819
SUDOCS: NS1.28:(nos)   ITEM NO: 834-Z (mf)
Availability: $9.50 from Superintendent of Documents.

Provides data on scientific activity for the United States including research and development activity, expenditures, federal support, literature, patents, royalties and fees, international cooperation, scientific imports and exports, and employment, unemployment and personal income of scientists in academics and industry. Most data cover a three year period; select trends are included. Provides select comparisons to foreign data. Contains approximately 320 tables/charts. Title varies.

Data from federal, foreign and private sources.

Description based on 1984 imprint covering 1979-1981 data.

F0340
Social Security Administration.
Social Security Bulletin.
Approximately 80 pages.   Monthly.   1938-
ISSN: 0037-7910   LCCN: 40-29327
SUDOCS: HE3.3:(vol)/(nos)   ITEM NO: 523
Availability: $29.00 per year from Superintendent of Documents.

Provides data on personal income and income maintenance programs for the United States including employment, unemployment, personal income, Consumer Price Index, Gross National Product or other measures of production, and benefit payments, contributions or tax collections for income maintenance programs. Programs covered include

Social Security Trust Funds, Old Age and Survivors Insurance, Disability Insurance, Black Lung Benefits and medical insurance programs. Also provides select data on state unemployment insurance programs. Most data cover an eight year period; select long term trends are included. Includes data by benefit program and state. Contains approximately 42 tables. Issuing source varies.
Data from federal and state sources.
Description based on 1984 imprint covering 1967-1984 data.
Includes *Social Security Bulletin: Annual Statistical Supplement* [HE3.3/3:(year)] which provides historic data for the period 1937-(year).

F0350
U.S. Armed Forces Information Service.
Defense.
Approximately 50 pages.   Monthly.   1978-
ISSN: 0737-1217   LCCN: 83-641923
SUDOCS: D2.15/3:(year)/(nos) ITEM NO: 312-B
Availability: $23.00 per year from Superintendent of Documents.

Monthly journal on the armed forces for the United States includes recurring statistical feature as its September issue: *Defense ('year) Almanac*. Provides data on major weapons and combat forces including active and reserve forces, personnel functions, skills, location and rank, compensation, military training loads, the Department of Defense budget and defense contractors, major weapon systems, foreign military sales and military assistance programs. Most data cover a two year period; select trends and projections are included. Includes data by branch of service, state and country. Contains approximately 20 tables. Title varies.
Data from federal sources.
Description based on 1983 imprint covering 1982-1983 data.

F0360
U.S. Arms Control and Disarmament Agency.
World Military Expenditures and Arms Transfers, (years).
Approximately 120 pages.   Annual.   1964-
                    LCCN: 78-645925
SUDOCS: AC1.16:(years)   ITEM NO: 125-A-8
Availability: $4.25 from Superintendent of Documents.

Provides data on world population, Gross National Product or other measures of production, military expenditures, armed forces and arms transfers. Most data cover an eleven year period. Includes data by organization, region and country. Contains approximately 4 lengthy tables. Title varies.
Data from federal and international sources.
Description based on 1984 imprint covering 1972-1982 data.

F0370
U.S. Bureau of Economic Analysis.
Business Conditions Digest.
Approximately 120 pages.   Monthly.   1968-
ISSN: 0146-7735   LCCN: 72-621004
SUDOCS: C59.9:(vol)/(nos)   ITEM NO: 131-A
Availability: $55.00 per year from Superintendent of Documents.

Provides data on business and economic conditions for the United States including
employment, unemployment, personal income, Consumer Price Index, Producer Price
Index and Gross National Product or other measures of production. Most data cover a
three year period. Provides select comparisons to foreign data. Contains approximately
106 tables. Title and issuing source vary.
Data from federal and private sources.
Description based on 1984 imprint covering 1982-1984 data.

F0380
U.S. Bureau of Economic Analysis.
Business Statistics: (year).
Approximately 280 pages.   Biennial.   1931-
ISSN: 0083-2545   LCCN: SC78-1633
SUDOCS: C59.11/3:(year)   ITEM NO: 228
Availability: $8.00 from Superintendent of Documents.

Provides data on business and economic conditions for the United States including
employment, unemployment, personal income, Consumer Price Index, Producer Price
Index, and the following industries: construction, energy, finance, forest products,
manufacturing, transportation, and and wholesale and retail trade. Most data cover a
four year period; select trends are included. Includes data by industry/sector. Contains
130 approximately tables. This series is a supplement to the *Survey of Current Business*
[C59.11:(vol)/(nos)]. Title and issuing source vary.
Data from federal and private sources.
Description based on 1983 imprint covering 1979-1982 data.

F0390
U.S. Bureau of Economic Analysis.
Local Area Personal Income, (years).
Approximately 1,200 pages in nine volumes.   Annual.   1969-
                        LCCN: 80-641946
SUDOCS: C59.18:(years)/(vol) ITEM NO: 130-D-4
Availability: Price per volume varies ($3.00-$13.00 each) from Superintendent of
Documents.

Provides data on personal income for the United States. Volume One provides summary
data for the United States; Volume Two provides data for the New England Region;
Volume Three provides data for the Mideast Region; Volume Four provides data for
the Great Lakes Region; Volume Five provides data for the Plains Region; Volume Six
provides data for the Southeast Region; Volume Seven provides data for the Southwest
Region; Volume Eight provides data for the Rocky Mountain Region; Volume Nine
provides data for the Far West, Alaska and Hawaii. Most data cover a six year period.

Includes data by type of income, industry/sector, county, state, region and metropolitan and non-metropolitan area. Contains approximately 5 lengthy tables per volume.
Data from federal and state sources.
Description based on 1985 imprint covering 1978-1983 data.

F0400
U.S. Bureau of Economic Analysis.
National Income and Product Accounts of the U.S. (years): Statistical Tables.
Approximately 440 pages.   Irregular.   1929-
SUDOCS: C59.11/4:In2:(years) ITEM NO: 228
Availability: $10.00 from Superintendent of Documents.

Data on business and economic conditions for the United States including employment, unemployment, personal income and expenditures, federal government finances including receipts and expenditures, Gross National Product or other measures of production, and data on the finance industry. Most data cover a forty-six year period. Contains approximately 160 tables. Title and issuing source vary. This series is a supplement to *Survey of Current Business* [C59.11:(vol)/(nos)].
Data from federal and private sources.
Description based on 1981 imprint covering 1929-1976 data.

F0410
U.S. Bureau of Economic Analysis.
Survey of Current Business.
Approximately 80 pages.   Monthly.   1921-
ISSN: 0039-6222   LCCN: 21-26819
SUDOCS: C59.11:(vol)/(nos)   ITEM NO: 228
Availability: $50.00 per year from Superintendent of Documents.

Provides data on business and economic conditions for the United States including employment, unemployment, personal income, Consumer Price Index, Producer Price Index, Gross National Product or other measures of production, and the following industries: agriculture, construction, finance, manufacturing, transportation and wholesale and retail trade. Most data cover a one year period. Includes data by industry/sector. Contains approximately 130 tables. Title and issuing source vary.
Data from federal and private sources.
Description based on 1983 imprint covering 1982 data.
Also publishes the following supplements to this series: *Business Statistics: (year)* [C59.11/3:(year)] and *National Income and Product Account Statistics of the U.S.: Statistical Tables* [C59.11/4:In2:(years)].

F0420
U.S. Bureau of Indian Affairs. Phoenix Area Office.
Information Profiles of Indian Reservations in Arizona, Nevada and Utah.
Approximately 175 pages.   Irregular.   1976-
SUDOCS: I20.2:R31/4:(year)   ITEM NO: 627
Availability: Free from the issuing source.

Provides data on Native Americans for Arizona, Nevada, and Utah including population, housing, employment, personal income, education, health, resource development and

industrial development of Indian lands. Most data cover a one year period. Includes data by reservation, Indian colony and community. Contains approximately 50 tables.
Data from federal sources.
Description based on 1981 imprint covering 1980 data.

F0430
U.S. Bureau of Industrial Economics.
Construction Review.
Approximately 60 pages.   Bimonthly.   1945-
ISSN: 0010-6917   LCCN: 56-41035
SUDOCS: C62.10:(vol)/(nos)   ITEM NO: 219
Availability: $17.00 per year from Superintendent of Documents.

Provides data on the construction and real estate industries for the United States including construction cost indexes, interest rates, value of new construction, housing starts and completions, sales of new and existing homes, building permits and contract awards, employment and production, shipment and stock of construction materials. Also provides data on mobile homes. Most data cover a two year period; select trends are included. Includes data by type of construction, metropolitan and non-metropolitan area, and region. Contains approximately 40 tables. Title and issuing source varies.
Data from federal and private sources.
Description based on 1984 imprint covering 1982-1983 data.

F0440
U.S. Bureau of Industrial Economics.
(year) U.S. Industrial Outlook.
Approximately 485 pages.   Annual.   1960-
ISSN: 0078-2671   LCCN: 84-645436
SUDOCS: C62.17:(year)   ITEM NO: 215-L
Availability: $11.00 from Superintendent of Documents.

Provides data on business and economic conditions for the United States including number of business establishments, value of shipments, receipts, value added, employment, imports and exports, and Producer Price Index for the following industries: construction, energy, finance, forest products, manufacturing, minerals, select service industries, transportation, wholesale and retail trade. Most data cover a thirteen year period with actual figures for twelve years and one year projections. Includes data by industry/sector. Contains approximately 75 tables. Title and issuing source vary.
Data from federal sources.
Description based on 1984 imprint covering 1972-1984 data.

F0450
U.S. Bureau of Justice Statistics.
Sourcebook of Criminal Justice Statistics, (year).
Approximately 675 pages.   Annual.   1973-
                              LCCN: 74-601963
SUDOCS: J29.9:(nos)   ITEM NO: 968-H-6
Availability: $10.00 from Superintendent of Documents.

Provides data on crime and criminal justice for the United States including known offenses, arrests, judicial processing of defendants, correctional supervision, and criminal justice agencies, workload, expenditures and employment. Also, provides data on public attitudes toward crime and criminal justice. Most data cover a one year period; select trends are included. Contains approximately 545 tables/charts.
Data from federal, private and state sources.
Description based on 1983 imprint covering 1981 data.

F0460
U.S. Bureau of Labor Statistics.
Area Wage Survey.
Approximately 400 pages in seventy-seven volumes.   Irregular.   1950-
ISSN: 0360-3431
SUDOCS: L2.3/2:(nos)   ITEM NO: 768-B-(nos)
Availability: $88.00 per year from Superintendent of Documents.

Provides data on personal income for the United States including hourly earnings and supplemental benefits in approximately seventy-seven Labor Market Areas. Most data cover a one year period. Includes data by occupation and area. Contains approximately 550 tables.
Data from survey.
Description based on 1984 imprint covering 1983 data.
Also publishes *Area Wage Survey: Selected Metropolitan Areas* [L2.3/2:(nos)] which provides summary data.

F0470
U.S. Bureau of Labor Statistics.
CPI Detailed Report.
Approximately 110 pages.   Monthly.   1953-
ISSN: 0095-926X   LCCN: 75-641423
SUDOCS: L2.38/3:(date)   ITEM NO: 768-F
Availability: $25.00 per year from Superintendent of Documents.

Provides data on Consumer Price Index for the United States including aggregate rate of change in consumer prices, and rates of change for specific expenditure categories, commodities and cities. Most data cover a one month or bimonthly period with the most current figures available; select annual data and short term trends are included. Includes data by expenditure category, commodity and city. Contains approximately 30 tables.
Title varies.
Data from federal sources.
Description based on 1984 imprint covering 1984 data.
Also publishes updated data in *CPI Mailgram* (available from N.T.I.S.) which provides data within twenty-four hours of its release.

F0480
U.S. Bureau of Labor Statistics.
Employment and Earnings.
Approximately 150 pages.   Monthly.   1923-
ISSN: 0013-6840   LCCN: 83-645868
SUDOCS: L2.41/2:(vol)/(nos) ITEM NO: 768-B
Availability: $39.00 per year from Superintendent of Documents.

Provides data on employment, unemployment and personal income for the United
States. Most data cover a one month or quarterly period with the most current figures
available. Includes data by area and state. Contains approximately 160 tables. Title
varies.
Data from federal sources including Current Population Survey.
Description based on 1984 imprint covering 1984 data.
Includes annual *Supplement to Employment and Earnings, Revised Establishment
Data* [L2.41/2:(vol)/suppl] which provides historic data covering a ten year period.

F0490
U.S. Bureau of Labor Statistics.
Employment and Wages: Annual Averages, (year).
Approximately 525 pages.   Annual.   1975-
ISSN: 0748-5336   LCCN: 84-645713
SUDOCS: L2.104/2:(year)   ITEM NO: 768-D
Availability: $16.00 from Superintendent of Documents.

Provides data on employment and personal income for the United States. Most data cover
a two year period. Includes data by industry/sector and state. Contains approximately 8
lengthy tables.
Data from federal, local, private and state sources.
Description based on 1984 imprint covering 1981-1982 data.

F0500
U.S. Bureau of Labor Statistics.
Handbook of Labor Statistics.
Approximately 450 pages.   Irregular.   1924-
ISSN: 0082-9056   LCCN L27-328
SUDOCS: L2.3/5:(nos)   ITEM NO: 768-C-3
Availability: $9.50 from Superintendent of Documents.

Provides data on business and economic conditions for the United States including
population, employment, unemployment, personal income, Consumer Price Index,
Producer Price Index, Gross National Product or other measures of production, import
and export price indexes, and consumer expenditures. Most data cover an eight year
period; select trends from the 1940s and 1950s are included. Includes data by industry/
sector, state and region. Provides select comparisons to foreign data. Contains approximately 150 tables.
Data from federal sources including the Current Population Survey.
Description based on 1983 imprint covering 1975-1982 data.

F0510
U.S. Bureau of Labor Statistics.
Labor Force Statistics Derived from the Current Population Survey: A Databook.
Approximately 1500 pages in three volumes.   Irregular.   1982-
LCCN: 81-607902
SUDOCS: L2.3:2096-(nos)   ITEM NO: 768-A-1
Availability: Volume One: $14.00; Volume Two: $12.00; Supplement: $5.50 from
Superintendent of Documents.

Provides data on population, employment, unemployment, and personal income for the
United States. Most data cover a seventeen year period; select long term trends are
included. Includes data by industry/sector, metropolitan and non-metropolitan area.
Contains approximately 172 tables.
Data from the Current Population Survey.
Description based on 1982 and 1984 imprints covering 1967-1983 data.

F0520
U.S. Bureau of Labor Statistics.
Monthly Labor Review.
Approximately 100 pages.   Monthly.   1915-
ISSN: 0098-1818   LCCN: 15-26485
SUDOCS: L2.6:(vol)/(nos)   ITEM NO: 770
Availability: $24.00 per year from Superintendent of Documents.

Monthly journal on employment for the United States includes recurring statistical
feature. Provides data on business and economic conditions including employment,
unemployment, personal income, Consumer Price Index, Producer Price Index, and
Gross National Product or other measures of production. Most data cover a two year
period. Includes data by industry/sector, commodity and state. Contains approximately
40 tables. Title varies.
Data from federal and private sources.
Description based on 1984 imprint covering 1982-1983 data.

F0530
U.S. Bureau of Labor Statistics.
National Survey of Professional, Administrative, Technical and Clerical Pay, (year).
Approximately 90 pages.   Annual.   1960-
ISSN: 0501-7041   LCCN: l61-4
SUDOCS: L2.3:(nos)   ITEM NO: 768-A-1
Availability: $4.00 from Superintendent of Documents.

Provides data on personal income for the United States including salary and wage data
for professional, administrative, technical and clerical workers. Most data cover a
one year period. Includes data by occupation, industry/sector and S.M.S.A. Contains
approximately 15 lengthy tables.
Data from sample survey.
Description based on 1984 imprint covering 1984 data.

F0540
U.S. Bureau of Labor Statistics.
Occupational Outlook Handbook.
Approximately 385 pages.   Biennial.   1949-
SUDOCS: L2.3/4:(years)   ITEM NO: 768-C-2
Availability: $9.50 from Superintendent of Documents.

Primarily narrative work provides data on occupational characteristics, training or educational requirements, and outlook for approximately two hundred occupations. Statistical content and coverage vary but may include data on population, education, employment, unemployment and personal income with emphasis on occupational supply and demand. Most data cover a fifteen year period with actual figures for two years and thirteen year projections. Includes data by industry/sector and occupation. Contains approximately 150 tables/charts.
Data from federal sources.
Description based on 1984 imprint covering 1981-1995 data.
Also publishes updated data in *Occupational Outlook Quarterly* [L2.70/4:(vol)/(nos)] and a biennial supplement to this series, *Occupational Projections and Training Data, (year)* [L2.3:(nos)] which provides ten year projections.

F0550
U.S. Bureau of Labor Statistics.
Occupational Projections and Training Data, (year).
Approximately 120 pages.   Biennial.   1971-
ISSN: 0273-382X   LCCN: 80-649629
SUDOCS: L2.3:(nos)   ITEM NO: 768-A-1
Availability: $4.00 from Superintendent of Documents.

Primarily narrative work provides data on employment and unemployment for the United States including current and projected employment, and annual job openings due to growth and replacement for approximately fifty-five occupational categories. Most data cover an eleven year period with actual figures for one year and ten year projections. Includes data by occupation. Contains approximately 95 tables. This series is a *Statistical and Research Supplement to Occupational Outlook Handbook.*
Data from state and federal sources.
Description based on 1982 imprint covering 1980-1990 data.

F0560
U.S. Bureau of Labor Statistics.
Producer Price Indexes.
Approximately 175 pages.   Monthly.   1947-
ISSN: 1061-7311   LCCN: 78-643627
SUDOCS: L2.61:(date) and L2.61:(date)/(suppl) ITEM NO: 771-B
Availability: $29.00 per year from Superintendent of Documents.

Provides data on Producer Price Indexes for the United States including aggregate rate of change in producer prices, and rates of change for specific commodities and industries. Most data cover a one month period with the most current figures available. Includes data by commodity, industry/sector and region. Contains approximately 20 tables. Title varies.

Data from federal sources.
Description based on 1985 imprint covering 1985 data.
Includes annual *Supplement to Producer Price Indexes* [L2.61:(date)/(suppl)] which provides cumulative data for the year.
Also publishes updated data in a brief monthly press release *Producer Price Indexes* [L2.61/10:(date)].

F0570
U.S. Bureau of Labor Statistics.
Productivity Measures for Selected Industries, (years).
Approximately 280 pages.   Annual.   1975-
                                LCCN: 83-640507
SUDOCS: L2.3:(nos)   ITEM NO: 768-A-1
Availability: $7.50 from Superintendent of Documents.

Provides data on employment and productivity for the United States including indexes which represent change in output per employee hour for approximately 130 industries. Most data cover a thirty year period. Includes data by industry/sector. Contains approximately 390 tables/charts. Title varies.
Data from federal sources.
Description based on 1985 imprint covering 1954-1983 data.

F0580
U.S. Bureau of Labor Statistics.
U.S. Department of State Indexes of Living Costs Abroad, Quarters Allowances and Hardship Differentials.
Approximately 5 pages.   Quarterly.   1977-
SUDOCS: L2.101:(date)   ITEM NO: 768-M
Availability; $10.00 per year from Superintendent of Documents.

Provides data on comparative cost of living for approximately 130 countries including exchange rates and relative cost of living measures, U.S. Department of State quarters allowances and hardship differentials. Most data are derived from the most current figures available. Includes data by city and country. Contains approximately 3 tables. Title varies.
Data from federal, foreign and private sources.
Description based on 1984 imprint covering 1983 data.

F0590
U.S. Bureau of Labor Statistics.
U.S. Import and Export Price Indexes.
Approximately 15 pages.   Quarterly.   1971-
ISSN: 0091-1658
SUDOCS: L2.60/3:(date)
Availability: Free from Information Office.

Provides data on business and economic conditions for the United States including changes in import and export prices. Most data cover a one year period. Includes data by category of goods. Contains approximately 3 tables.

Data from federal sources.
Description based on 1984 imprint covering 1984 data.

F0600
U.S. Bureau of Land Management.
Public Land Statistics, (year).
Approximately 220 pages.   Annual.   1958-
ISSN: 0082-9110   LCCN: 79-647223
SUDOCS: I53.1/2:(year)   ITEM NO: 633-C
Availability: $6.50 from Superintendent of Documents.

Provides data on Federal land holdings for the United States including land disposition and use, fires, trespass operations and collections, public land surveys, and Federal receipts and payments to state and local governments. Most data cover a two fiscal year period; select trends are included. Contains approximately 115 tables. Incorporates data published in *Statistical Appendix to the Annual Report of the Director* [I53.1:(year)] from 1958-1961.
Data from federal sources.
Description based on 1984 imprint covering FY1982-FY1983 data.

F0610
U.S. Bureau of Mines.
Mineral Commodity Summaries, (year).
Approximately 185 pages.   Annual.   1964-
ISSN: 0160-5151   LCCN: 78-640742
SUDOCS: I28.148:(year)   ITEM NO: 639-B-1
Availability: Free from Publications Distribution Section.

Provides data on the minerals industries for the United States including U.S. and world production, consumption, reserves, prices, imports and exports for approximately ninety non-fuel commodities. Most data cover a three year period with the most current estimates available. Includes data by commodity/sector. Contains approximately 90 tables. Title varies.
Data from federal and private sources.
Description based on 1985 imprint covering 1982-1984 data.

F0620
U.S. Bureau of Mines.
Mineral Facts and Problems.
Approximately 1,100 pages.   Quinquennial.   1956-
SUDOCS: I28.3:(nos)   ITEM NO: 636
Availability: $23.00 from Superintendent of Documents.

Provides data on the world minerals industries including production capacity, reserves, prices, supply and demand for approximately eighty mineral commodities. Most data cover a two year period; select trends and projections are included. Includes data by commodity/sector. Provides select comparisons to U.S. production and reserve data. Contains approximately 1,200 tables.
Data from federal sources.

Description based on 1980 imprint covering 1978-1979 data.
Also publishes updated data in *Mineral Facts and Problems Chapter Preprints* [I28.3/
C:(CT)].

F0630
U.S. Bureau of Mines.
Minerals and Materials: A Bimonthly Survey.
Approximately 35 pages.   Bimonthly.   1979-
ISSN: 0363-9622   LCCN: 76-647389
SUDOCS: I28.149:(date)   ITEM NO: 638-C(mf)
Availability: Free from Publications Distribution Section.

Provides data on the minerals industries for the United States including production,
consumption, inventories, prices, imports and exports for approximately thirteen strategic
mineral commodities. Most data cover a six year period. Includes data by commodity/
sector. Provides select comparisons to foreign data. Contains approximately 15 tables.
Data from federal and international sources.
Description based on 1984 imprint covering 1979-1984 data.

F0640
U.S. Bureau of Mines.
Minerals Yearbook.
Approximately 3,000 pages in three volumes.   Annual.   1882-
ISSN: 0076-8952   LCCN: 33-26551
SUDOCS: I28.37:(year)   ITEM NO: 639
Availability: Volume One and Volume Two: $16.00 each; Volume Three: $22.00 from
Superintendent of Documents.

Provides data on the world minerals industries including production, consumption,
prices, imports and exports, and reserves for approximately seventy-five mineral commodities. Volume One provides data by commodities; Volume Two provides domestic data
by state; Volume Three provides data by country. Most data cover a two year period.
Includes data by commodity/sector, state and country. Contains approximately 1,800
tables. Title and issuing source vary.
Data from federal, foreign and state sources.
Description based on 1984 imprint covering 1981-1983 data.
Also publishes updated data in *Minerals Yearbook Chapter Preprints* [I28.27/a2:(CT)/
(year)].

F0650
U.S. Bureau of the Census.
Congressional District Data Book.
Approximately 550 pages.   Irregular.   1963-
                         LCCN: A63-7725
SUDOCS: C3.134/2:C76/(year)   ITEM NO: 151
Availability: $14.00 from Superintendent of Documents.

Provides data on population, housing, education, employment, unemployment and
personal income for the United States. Most data cover a one year period. Includes data

by industry, Congressional District and state. Contains approximately 50 tables providing 303 data items in 17 categories. This series is a supplement to the *Statistical Abstract of the U.S.* [C3.134:(year)].
Data derived from the Census of Population and Housing.
Description based on 1973 imprint covering 1970 data.

F0660
U.S. Bureau of the Census.
County Business Patterns.
Approximately 5,300 pages in fifty-three volumes.   Annual.   1946-
                        LCCN: 49-45747
SUDOCS: C3.204:(year)/(nos)   ITEM NO: 133-A-(nos)
Availability: Price per volume varies, most are under $5.00 from Superintendent of Documents.

Provides data on employment, unemployment and personal income for the United States. One volume provides summary data for the U.S.; fifty-two volumes provide data for the states, District of Columbia and Puerto Rico. Most data cover a one year period. Includes data by industry/sector and state. Contains approximately 15 lengthy tables. Title and issuing source vary.
Data from federal sources, primarily Internal Revenue Service and Bureau of the Census sources including the Annual Company Organization Survey.
Description based on 1984 imprint covering 1982 data.

F0670
U.S. Bureau of the Census.
County and City Data Book, (year).
Approximately 1,000 pages.   Irregular.   1949-
ISSN: 0082-9455   LCCN: 52-4576
SUDOCS: C3.134/2:C83/2/(year) ITEM NO: 151
Availability: $24.00 from Superintendent of Documents.

Presents a broad range of social and economic data for the United States. Data on population, birth, death, marriage, divorce, housing, education, employment, unemployment, personal income, and the following industries: agriculture, construction, finance, manufacturing, and wholesale and retail trade. Most data cover a one year period with the most current enumerative data available; select short term trends are included. Includes data by industry/sector, place (for places with a population of 2,500 or more), city (for cities with a population of 25,000 or more), county and state. Contains approximately 4 lengthy tables. This series is a supplement to the *Statistical Abstract of the U.S.* [C3.134:(year)].
Data are primarily from Bureau of the Census sources and other federal and private sources.
Description based on 1983 imprint covering 1977, 1978 and 1980 data.

F0680
U.S. Bureau of the Census.
Historical Statistics of the United States, Colonial Times to (year).
Approximately 1,200 pages in two volumes.   Irregular.   1949-
                              LCCN: 75-38832
SUDOCS: C3.134/2:H62/(years) ITEM NO: 151
Availability: $35.00 per set from Superintendent of Documents.

Presents a broad range of social and economic data for the United States. Provides
data on population, housing, birth, death, marriage, divorce, education, employment,
unemployment, personal income, Consumer Price Index, Gross National Product or
other measures of production and the following industries: agriculture, construction,
energy, finance, fishing, forest products, manufacturing, minerals, tourism, and transportation. Most data cover the broadest possible time span; colonial and pre-federal data
are included. Includes data by industry/sector, time period, state and region. Contains
approximately 850 tables. This series is a supplement to the *Statistical Abstract of the*
U.S. [C3.134:(year)]
Data from colonial, federal, pre-federal private, and state sources.
Description based on 1975 imprint covering approximately 1789-1970 data.

F0690
U.S. Bureau of the Census.
State and Metropolitan Area Data Book, (year).
Approximately 600 pages.   Biennial.   1979-
ISSN: 0276-6566   LCCN: 80-600018
SUDOCS: C3.134/5:(year)   ITEM NO: 150
Availability: $15.00 from Superintendent of Documents.

Presents a broad range of social and economic data for the United States. Provides data
on population, housing, birth, death, marriage, divorce, education, crime, employment,
unemployment, federal, state and local government finances and operations, and the
following industries: manufacturing, select service industries, and wholesale and retail
trade. Most data cover an eleven year period. Includes data by industry/sector, city,
S.M.S.A., county, and state. Contains approximately 3 tables presenting 320 data items
for 318 S.M.S.A.s, 73 data items for 429 cities and 2,018 data items for the U.S., states
and census regions and divisions. This series is a supplement to the *Statistical Abstract*
of the U.S. [C3.134:(year)].
Data from federal sources.
Description based on 1982 imprint covering 1970-1980 data.

F0700
U.S. Bureau of the Census.
Statistical Abstract of the U.S., (year).
Approximately 1,000 pages.   Annual.   1878-
ISSN: 0081-4741   LCCN: 04-18089
SUDOCS: C3.134:(year)   ITEM NO: 150
Availability: $24.00 from Superintendent of Documents.

Presents a broad range of social and economic data for the United States. Provides data on population, birth, death, marriage, divorce, education, employment, unemployment, personal income, Gross National Product or other measures of production, Consumer Price Index, Producer Price Index, crime, national defense, federal, state and local government finances and operations, and the following industries: agriculture, construction, energy, finance, fishing, forest products, manufacturing, minerals, select service industries, transportation, and wholesale and retail trade. Most data cover a fifteen year period; select long term trends and projections are included. Includes data by industry/sector, city, S.M.S.A., state and region. Provides select comparisons to foreign data. Contains approximately 1,515 tables. Issuing source varies.

Data from federal, international, private and state sources.

Description based on 1985 imprint covering 1970-1984 data.

Includes brief supplement *U.S.A. Statistics in Brief* [C3.134:2/St2] which provides summary data.

Also publishes the following supplements to the *Statistical Abstract of the U.S.: Congressional District Data Book* [C3.134/2:C76/(year)], *County and City Data Book* [C3.134/2:C83/2/(year)], *Historical Statistics of the United States, Colonial Times to (year)* [C3.134/2: H62/(years)] and *State and Metropolitan Area Data Book, (year)* [C3.134/5:(year)].

F0710
U.S. Bureau of the Census.
World Population: (year) Recent Demographic Estimates for the Countries and Regions of the World.
Approximately 590 pages.   Biennial.   1973-
ISSN: 0099-1139   LCCN: 74-60016
SUDOCS: C3.205/3:WP-(year) ITEM NO: 146-F
Availability: $13.00 from Superintendent of Documents.

Provides data on world population, birth and death. Most data cover a thirty-six year period with actual figures for thirty-four years and two year projections. Includes data by continent, region, subregion and country for approximately 200 countries with a population of 5,000 or more. Contains approximately 250 tables/charts. Issuing source varies.

Data from federal, foreign, international and private sources including national censuses and vital event registrations.

Description based on 1983 imprint covering 1950-1985 data.

F0720
U.S. Bureau of the Mint.
Annual Report of the Director of the Mint, Fiscal Year Ended (date).
Approximately 40 pages.   Annual.   1872-
                                LCCN: 09-34686
SUDOCS: T28.1:(year)   ITEM NO:965
Availability: $4.50 from Superintendent of Documents.

Provides data on coinage for the United States including U.S. and foreign coins and medals manufactured by the U.S. Mint, U.S. Mint inventories, shipments, numismatic programs, and transactions involving gold, silver and other monetary metals. Most data cover a one fiscal year period. Includes data by mint office and denomination. Contains approximately 15 tables. Issuing source varies.

Data from federal sources.

Description based on 1984 imprint covering FY1983 data.

Also publishes historic data in *Domestic and Foreign Coins Manufactured by Mints of the U.S., (years)* [T28.1/A:C666/2:(years)] which provides coverage for the period 1793-1980.

F0730

U.S. Central Intelligence Agency.
Handbook of Economic Statistics, (year).
Approximately 235 pages.   Annual.   1980-
ISSN: 0195-9018   LCCN: 79-644495
SUDOCS: PREX3.10/7:CPASS(nos) ITEM NO: 856-A-4
Availability: $14.00 from Superintendent of Documents.

Presents a broad range of world social and economic data. Provides data on population, education, employment, unemployment, Gross National Product or other measures of production, national government finances including debt and defense expenditures, imports and exports, and the following industries: agriculture, energy, finance, forest products, manufacturing, minerals, and transportation. Most data cover a twenty-four year period. Includes data by country for approximately 200 countries. Contains approximately 200 tables. Issuing source varies.

Data from federal, foreign and international sources.

Description based on 1984 imprint covering 1960-1983 data.

F0740

U.S. Central Intelligence Agency.
World Factbook, (year).
Approximately 270 pages.   Annual.   1975-
ISSN: 0277-1527   LCCN: 81-641760
SUDOCS: PREX3.15:(year)   ITEM NO: 856-A-7
Availability: $11.00 from Superintendent of Documents.

Presents a broad range of world social and economic data including population, education, employment, unemployment, personal income, Gross National Product or other measures of production, imports and exports, national government finances including budgets and defense expenditures, and the finance and transportation industries. Most data cover a one year period. Includes data by country for approximately 200 countries. Contains approximately 190 tables. Issuing source varies.

Data from federal, foreign and international sources.

Description based 1984 imprint covering 1984 data.

F0750

U.S. Coast Guard.
Boating Statistics, (year).
Approximately 35 pages.   Annual.   1959-
SUDOCS: TD5.11:(year)   ITEM NO: 941-A
Availability: Free from Commandant (G-BP).

Provides data on recreational boating for the United States including boat numbering

or registration, accidents, injuries, fatalities and property damage. Most data cover a five year period; select long term trends are included. Includes data by class of boat and state. Contains approximately 18 tables.
Data from federal sources.
Description based on 1984 imprint covering 1979-1983 data.

F0760
U.S. Congress. Joint Economic Committee.
Economic Indicators.
Approximately 40 pages.   Monthly.   1948-
ISSN: 0013-0125   LCCN: 48-46615
SUDOCS: Y4.EC7:EC7/(year)/(nos)   ITEM NO: 997
Availability: $25.00 per year from Superintendent of Documents.

Provides data on business and economic conditions for the United States including employment, unemployment, personal income and expenditures, Consumer Price Index, Gross National Product or other measures of production, and data on the construction, finance and manufacturing industries. Most data cover a twelve year period; select long term trends are included. Includes data by industry/sector. Provides select comparisons to international data. Contains approximately 45 tables.
Data from federal and private sources.
Description based on 1984 imprint covering 1972-1983 data.
Also publishes historical data in *Supplement to Economic Indicators* (irregular) [Y4.Ec7:Ec7/suppl/(year)] which provides coverage for the period 1929 to the present.

F0770
U.S. Congressional Budget Office.
Analysis of the President's Budgetary Proposals for Fiscal Year (fy).
Approximately 180 pages.   Annual.   1978-
                 LCCN: 82-601473
SUDOCS: Y10.2:B85/8/(year)   ITEM NO: 1005-C
Availability: Free from Office of Intergovernmental Relations.

Provides data on business and economic conditions for the United States with an emphasis on the impact of the proposed federal budget including revenues and outlays, deficit, and Gross National Product or other measures of production. Most data are five fiscal year projections; select trends are included. Includes data by major budget category. Provides select comparisons of administration and Congressional Budget Office projections and economic assumptions. Contains approximately 50 tables.
Data from federal sources.
Description based on 1984 imprint covering FY1985-FY1989 data.

F0780
U.S. Department of Agriculture.
Agricultural Statistics, (year).
Approximately 550 pages.   Annual.   1926-
ISSN: 0082-9714   LCCN: AGR36-465
SUDOCS: A1.47:(year)   ITEM NO: 1
Availability: $13.00 from Superintendent of Documents.

Provides data on the agriculture industry for the United States including production figures and prices from crops, livestock, dairy and poultry. Also provides data on the finance, fishing and forest products industries. Most data cover a one year period; select trends are included. Includes data by commodity/sector and state. Contains approximately 740 tables. Title varies (prior to 1936, data is contained in the *Yearbook of Agriculture*).
Data from federal, private and state sources including U.S.D.A. sources and the U.S. Bureau of the Census's *Census of Agriculture.*
Description based on 1983 imprint covering 1982 data.
Also publishes more general data in *Factbook of United States Agriculture, (year)* [A1.38:1063/(nos)], and updated and detailed data in *Crop Production*, monthly with annual summary [A92.24:(year)/(nos) and A92.24/4:(year)], and *Agricultural Prices*, monthly with annual summary [A92.16:(year)/(nos) and A 92.16:(year)].

F0790
U.S. Department of Agriculture.
Factbook of United States Agriculture, (year).
Approximately 125 pages.   Annual.   1962-
ISSN: 0501-9273   LCCN: SN85-20489
SUDOCS: A1.38:1063/(nos)   ITEM NO: 13-A(mf)
Availability: $4.00 from Superintendent of Documents.

Provides data on the agriculture industry for the United States including production figures and prices for crops, livestock, dairy and poultry. Also provides data on the finance industry and farm credit. Most data cover a one year period; select trends are included. Includes data by commodity/sector and state. Contains approximately 25 tables.
Data from federal sources.
Description based on 1983 imprint covering 1982 data.
Also publishes more detailed data in *Agricultural Statistics, (year)* [A1.47:(year)].

F0800
U.S. Department of Agriculture.
Handbook of Agricultural Charts.
Approximately 100 pages.   Annual.   1963-
ISSN: 0501-9060   LCCN: 64-62697
SUDOCS: A1.76:(nos)   ITEM NO: 3
Availability: $5.00 from Superintendent of Documents.

Provides data on the agriculture industry for the United States including production figures and prices. Also provides data on population, food consumption and the finance industry and farm credit. Most data cover a five year period; select trends are included. Provides select comparisons to foreign data. Contains approximately 275 charts/tables.
Data from federal sources.
Description based on 1983 imprint covering 1978-1982 data.

F0810
U.S. Department of Agriculture. Economic Research Service.
Agricultural Finance Statistics, (year).
Approximately 55 pages.   Biennial.   1938-
ISSN: 0091-3502   LCCN: 73-643425
SUDOCS: A1.34:(nos)
Availability: $2.25 from Superintendent of Documents.

Provides data on the agriculture and finance industries for the United States with an
emphasis on farm financial statistics including outstanding farm debt for real estate and
non-real estate and interest rates on loans. Most data cover a twenty-four year period.
Includes data by lender and state. Contains approximately 52 tables.
Data from federal and private sources.
Description based on 1984 imprint covering 1960-1983 data.

F0820
U.S. Department of Agriculture. Economic Research Service.
Food Consumption, Prices and Expenditures, (years).
Approximately 110 pages.   Annual.   1972-
                                 LCCN: 82-603692
SUDOCS: A1.34:(nos)   ITEM NO: 15(mf)
Availability: $4.00 from Superintendent of Documents.

Provides data on the agriculture industry and food consumption for the United States
including population, Consumer Price Index, Producer Price Index, farm-to-retail price
spreads, marketing costs, food consumption, prices and expenditures. Most data cover a
twenty-one year period. Includes data by food group and city. Contains approximately
91 tables.
Data from federal and private sources.
Description based on 1984 imprint covering 1963-1984 data.

F0830
U.S. Department of Education.
Digest of Data on Persons with Disabilities.
Approximately 175 pages.   Irregular.   1979-
SUDOCS: ED1.2:D26/(edition) ITEM NO: 455-B-2
Availability: $5.50 from Superintendent of Documents.

Provides data on disabled persons for the United States including prevalence and
severity of disabilities, living arrangements, health care services utilization, employment,
unemployment, personal income and federal programs relevant to disabled persons.
Most data cover a two year period; select trends are included. Includes data by disability
and state. Contains approximately 52 tables. Issuing source varies.
Data from survey, federal, private and state sources.
Description based on 1984 imprint covering 1979-1980 data.

F0840
U.S. Department of Energy.
Statistical Data for the Uranium Industry.
Approximately 80 pages.   Annual.
SUDOCS: E1.28:GJO-100(year)
Availability: $11.50 from Bendix Field Engineering Corporation, Technical Library.

Provides data on the world uranium industry including resources, reserves, production, exploration, drilling, employment, and financial and operating data. Most data cover a one year period; select trends are included. Includes data by state and country. Contains approximately 116 tables/charts.
Data from federal, foreign and private sources.
Description based on 1983 imprint covering 1983 data.

F0850
U.S. Department of Energy.
Electric Power Supply and Demand for the Contiguous United States, (years).
Approximately 220 pages.   Annual.   1978-
                             LCCN: SC82-7389
SUDOCS: E1.90:(nos)
Availability: $19.00 for paper, $4.50 for microfiche from N.T.I.S.

Provides data on the electric utility industry for the United States with emphasis on winter and summer electric power demand and generating capacity. Most data are ten year projections; select short term trends are included. Includes data by season and area for nine Regional Electric Reliability Council areas and twenty-six electric regions. Contains approximately 26 tables. Title varies.
Data from EP-411 reports of the Regional Electric Reliability Councils.
Description based on 1984 imprint covering 1984-1993 data.

F0860
U.S. Department of Health and Human Services. Health Care Financing Administration.
Health Care Financing Program Statistics: The Medicare and Medicaid Data Book.
Approximately 160 pages.   Annual.   1981-
SUDOCS: HE22.19/4-2:D26/(year)   ITEM NO: 512-A-14
Availability: $4.75 from Superintendent of Documents.

Provides data on the health care services industry for the United States with emphasis on financing programs including enrollments and recipients, expenditures and benefits for Medicare and Medicaid. Most data cover a two year period; select trends are included. Contains approximately 100 tables/charts.
Data from federal sources.
Description based on 1983 imprint covering 1979-1980 data.
Also publishes updated data in *Health Care Financing Review* [HE22.18:(vol)/(nos)].

F0870
U.S. Department of Health and Human Services. Health Resources and Services Administration.
Report to the President and Congress on the Status of Health Professions in the U.S.
Approximately 550 pages in two volumes.   Biennial.   1978-
SUDOCS: HE20.9310:(year)/(vol) ITEM NO: 507-J-12(mf)
Availability: Free from the Bureau of Health Professions, Office of Data Analysis and Management.

Provides data on health care services industry personnel for the United States including supply, demand and distribution of health care services workers. Also provides data on students and educational institutions for select health care occupations. Most data cover a five year period; select trends and projection to the year 2000 are included. Includes data by occupation. Contains approximately 160 tables.
Data from federal and private sources.
Description based on 1984 imprint covering 1978-1982 data.

F0880
U.S. Department of Health and Human Services. Health Resources and Services Administration.
Statistics on Hospital Personnel, from the American Hospital Association's (year) Annual Survey of Hospitals.
Approximately 70 pages.   Annual.   1983-
SUDOCS: HE20.9302:H79   ITEM NO: 507-J-1
Availability: Free from the Bureau of Health Professions, Office of Data Analysis and Management.

Provides data on hospital personnel for the United States including full-time employment, part-time employment and vacancy rates for approximately thirty categories of hospital personnel. Most data cover a one year period. Includes data by job category, hospital size and specialty, state and region. Contains approximately 11 tables.
Data from American Hospital Association survey of approximately 7,000 hospitals.
Description based on 1983 imprint covering 1980 data.

F0890
U.S. Department of Labor. Women's Bureau.
(year) Handbook on Women Workers.
Approximately 190 pages.   Irregular.   1948-
ISSN: 0083-3622   LCCN: SC80-671
SUDOCS: L36.103:(nos)   ITEM NO: 781
Availability: Free from the issuing source.

Provides data on employment for the United States with an emphasis on women in the work force including population, education, employment, unemployment, personal income and family status. Most data cover a two year period; select trends are included. Includes data by industry/sector and occupation. Contains approximately 110 tables/charts.
Data from federal sources.
Description based on 1983 imprint covering 1981-1982 data.

F0900
U.S. Department of State. Bureau of International Organizations.
United States Contributions to International Organizations, (edition) Annual Report to Congress for (fy).
Approximately 130 pages.   Annual.   1952-
ISSN: 0499-1583   LCCN: 53-60235
SUDOCS: S1.70:(nos)   ITEM NO: 882-B
Availability: Free from Bureau of Public Affairs.

Provides data on United States' contributions to international, intergovernmental organizations including the United Nations and its specialized agencies and programs, inter-American organizations, regional and other intergovernmental organizations including dollar amount of contributions and percentage of total organizational budget. Most data cover a one fiscal year period; select long term trends are included. Includes data by organization. Provides select comparisons to contributions of foreign nations. Contains approximately 50 tables.
Data from federal sources.
Description based on 1984 imprint covering FY1983 data.

F0910
U.S. Department of the Treasury.
Treasury Bulletin.
Approximately 150 pages.   Quarterly.   1939-
ISSN: 0041-2155   LCCN: 39-26387
SUDOCS: T1.3:(date)/(nos)   ITEM NO: 926-A
Availability: $20.00 per year from Superintendent of Documents.

Provides data on the finance industry for the United States including federal government finances and Treasury Department operations including federal debt, U.S. Savings Bonds and other Treasury securities. Most data cover a one year period. Provides select comparisons to foreign data. Contains approximately 90 tables. Title varies.
Data from federal sources.
Description based on 1984 imprint covering 1984 data.

F0920
U.S. Department of Transportation.
National Transportation Statistics.
Approximately 235 pages.   Annual.   1974-
ISSN: 0161-8628   LCCN: 78-643715
SUDOCS: TD10.9:(year)   ITEM NO: 982-K-1(mf)
Availability: $6.50 from Superintendent of Documents.

Provides data on the transportation industry for the United States including employment, energy consumption, inventory and financial and operating data. Most data cover an eleven year period. Includes data by sector for the following sectors of the transportation industry: air carrier, automobile, bus, general aviation, local transit, oil and natural gas pipelines, rail, truck, and water. Contains approximately 80 tables. Title varies.
Data from federal and private sources.
Description based on 1984 imprint covering 1972-1982 data.

F0930
U.S. Department of Transportation. Urban Mass Transportation Administration.
National Urban Mass Transportation Statistics: (year) Section 15 Annual Report.
Approximately 450 pages.   Annual.   1979-
ISSN: 0737-2981   LCCN: 83-641959
SUDOCS: TD7.11:(nos)   ITEM NO: 982-H-8
Availability: Free from Information Services, Office of Technical Assistance.

Provides data on public urban mass transportation finances and operation for the United
States including revenues, expenses, performance, transit maintenance, transit mileage,
energy consumption, employment, services supplied and consumed. Most data cover a
one fiscal year period. Includes data for individual systems and data by mode of transit.
Contains approximately 105 tables.
Data from reports submitted by approximately 320 transit systems.
Description based on 1983 imprint covering FY1982 data.

F0940
U.S. Energy Information Administration.
Annual Energy Outlook, (year), with Projections to (year).
Approximately 350 pages.   Annual.   1977-
ISSN: 0740-4190   LCCN: 83-645822
SUDOCS: E3.1/4:(year)   ITEM NO: 429-J-1
Availability: $6.50 from Superintendent of Documents.

Provides data on the energy industry for the United States including supply and price
projections based on several different scenarios. Most data cover a twelve year period
with actual figures for one year and eleven year projections; select long term trends and
projections are included. Includes data by fuel type or form of energy. Provides select
comparisons to foreign data. Contains approximately 58 tables/charts. Title varies.
Data from federal sources.
Description based on 1985 imprint covering 1984-1995 data.
Also publishes updated short term data in *Short Term Energy Outlook* (quarterly)
[E3.31:(nos)] which provides detailed two year projections.

F0950
U.S. Energy Information Administration.
Annual Energy Review, (year).
Approximately 250 pages.   Annual.   1977-
ISSN: 0740-3909   LCCN: 83-645824
SUDOCS: E3.1/2:(year)   ITEM NO: 429-J-1
Availability: $6.50 from Superintendent of Documents.

Provides data on the energy industry for the United States including production,
consumption, prices, and imports and exports. Most data cover a ten year period; select
long term trends are included. Includes data by fuel type or form of energy. Provides
select comparisons to foreign data. Contains approximately 110 tables. Title varies.
Data from federal and private sources.
Description based on 1984 imprint covering 1974-1983 data.
Also publishes updated data in *Monthly Energy Review* [E3.9:(date)].

F0960
U.S. Energy Information Administration.
Financial Statistics of Selected Electric Utilities.
Approximately 810 pages. Annual.   1966-
ISSN: 0747-7635   LCCN: 84-644324
SUDOCS: E3.18/4:(year) ITEM NO: 435-E-1
Availability: $16.00 from Superintendent of Documents.

Provides data on electric utility industry finances and operations for the United States including income, sales, earnings, and expenses for approximately 200 publicly and privately owned companies. Most data cover a ten year period. Includes data by company. Contains approximately 60 tables. Title and issuing source vary.
Data from federal and private sources.
Description based on 1985 imprint covering 1974-1983 data.

F0970
U.S. Energy Information Administration.
(year) International Energy Annual.
Approximately 110 pages. Annual.   1963-
ISSN: 0731-5341   LCCN: 82-64118
SUDOCS: E3.11/20:(year) ITEM NO: 435-H
Availability: $5.00 from Superintendent of Documents.

Provides data on the world energy industry including production, consumption, reserves, imports, exports, and prices. Most data cover a two year period; select trends are included. Includes data by type of fuel, form of energy and country for approximately 190 countries. Contains approximately 31 tables. Issuing source varies.
Data from federal, foreign, international and private sources.
Description based on 1984 imprint covering 1982-1983 data.

F0980
U.S. Energy Information Administration.
Typical Electric Bills, (date).
Approximately 320 pages. Annual.   1935-
ISSN: 0499-3977   LCCN: 59-64187
SUDOCS: E3.22:(year) ITEM NO: 429-T-32
Availability: $7.50 from Superintendent of Documents.

Provides data on the energy industry for the United States including typical electric utility bills, national and regional averages, lowest and highest bills, and rates for specific amounts of electricity in residential, commercial and industrial service. Most data cover a one year period. Includes data by public or private utility, city, state and region. Contains approximately 42 tables. Issuing source varies.
Data from survey of approximately 1,200 electric utilities.
Description based on 1984 imprint covering 1984 data.

F0990
U.S. Federal Bureau of Investigation.
Uniform Crime Reports: Crime in the U.S. (year).
Approximately 380 pages.   Annual.   1930-
ISSN: 0082-7592   LCCN: 30-27005
SUDOCS: J1.14/7:(year)   ITEM NO: 722
Availability: $7.00 from Superintendent of Documents.

Provides data on crime for the United States including incidence of crime, crimes
cleared by arrest and law enforcement personnel. Most data cover a five year period.
Includes data by type of crime, urban, non-urban or suburban area, and region. Contains
approximately 98 tables/charts.
Data from federal sources.
Description based on 1984 imprint covering 1979-1983 data.

F1000
U.S. Federal Communications Commission.
Statistics of Communications Common Carriers, (year).
Approximately 190 pages.   Annual.   1939-
ISSN: 0161-5173   LCCN: 41-50610
SUDOCS: CC1.35:(year)   ITEM NO: 228(mf)
Availability: $8.00 from Superintendent of Documents.

Provides financial and operating data for approximately sixty telephone companies, eight
telegraph companies and thirteen controlling companies for the United States including
number of phones, telephone development, telephone traffic, employment, revenues,
expenses and rates. Also, provides financial and operating data for the Communications
Satellite Communications Corporation. Most data cover a one year period. Includes data
by state and large exchange area. Provides select comparisons to foreign data. Contains
approximately 55 tables.
Data from reports submitted by carriers.
Description based on 1984 imprint covering 1982 data.

F1010
U.S. Federal Home Loan Bank Board.
Savings and Home Financing Source Book, (year).
Approximately 75 pages.   Annual.   1952-
                            LCCN: 53-63519
SUDOCS: FHL1.11:(year)   ITEM NO: 597-A-1
Availability: Free from Office of Communications.

Provides data on the finance industry for the United States with an emphasis on
the real estate sector including savings and mortgage activity, mortgage loans held,
foreclosures and delinquent loans of Federal Home Loan Banks, and savings and loan
associations. Most data cover a one year period; select long term trends are included.
Includes data by type of institution, S.M.S.A., state and Federal Home Loan Bank
District. Contains approximately 44 tables. Issuing source varies.
Data from federal and private sources.
Description based on 1984 imprint covering 1983 data.

F1020
U.S. Federal Housing Administration.
FHA Homes, (year).
Approximately 460 pages in two volumes.   Annual.   1977-
Volume One:
ISSN: 0091-4932   LCCN: 73-644270
Volume Two:
ISSN: 0275-1267   LCCN: 80-649620
SUDOCS: HH2.24/4:(year) and HH2.24/4-2:(year)
                         ITEM NO: 593-F(mf)
Availability: $3.50 per volume from Management Information Systems Division.

Provides data on the real estate industry for the United States with emphasis on FHA administered loans for single family homes insured under Sec 203(b) and 245 of the National Housing Act including financial data for mortgages, characteristics of property, structure and site, and mortgagee/mortgagor characteristics. Most data cover a one year period. Includes data by S.M.S.A. and state. Contains approximately 180 tables. Issuing source varies.
Data from federal sources.
Description based on 1984 imprint covering 1983 data.
Also publishes *Characteristics of FHA Single-Family Mortgages* (annual) [HH2.24/7:(year)] which provides summary data for homes covered by Sec 203(b), Sec 221(d)(2), Sec 223(e), Sec 244, Sec 235(i) and Sec 245 of the National Housing Act.

F1030
U.S. Forest Service.
U.S. Timber Production, Trade, Consumption and Price Statistics, (years).
Approximately 80 pages.   Annual.   1950-
SUDOCS: A1.38:1424   ITEM NO: 13-A
Availability: Free from the issuing source.

Provides data on the forest products industry for the United States including Producer Price Index, production, consumption, imports, exports, employment and prices for the following product categories: logs, lumber, paper-, board- and woodpulp, particle board and associated products, plywood and veneer, pulpwood, and turpentine and rosin. Most data cover a thirty-two year period. Includes data by product category, state and region. Provides select comparisons to foreign data. Contains approximately 70 tables/charts. Title varies.
Data from federal, private and state sources.
Description based on 1983 imprint covering 1950-1981 data.

F1040
U.S. Internal Revenue Service.
Economic, Demographic and Related Tax Statistics: Districts, Regions and Service Centers.
Approximately 40 pages.   Annual.   1966-
SUDOCS: T22.2:Ec7/3/(year)   ITEM NO: 956
Availability: Free from Office of Public Affairs.

Provides data on population, employment, personal income, tax collections, and corporate and personal income tax returns. Most data cover a nineteen year period with actual figures for an eleven year period and eight year projections. Includes data by I.R.S. District and Region. Contains approximately 36 tables/charts. This series is Internal Revenue Service *Document 6011*.

Data from federal sources.

Description based on 1983 imprint covering 1972-1990 data.

F1050
U.S. Internal Revenue Service.
Statistics of Income.
Approximately 700 pages in four volumes.   Annual.   1916-
ITEM NO: 964
Individual Returns:
LCCN: 60-37567   SUDOCS: T22.35/2:IN2/(year)
Sole Proprietorship Returns:
LCCN: 81-649972   SUDOCS: T22.35/2:P94/(year)
Corporate Returns:
LCCN: 61-37568   SUDOCS: T22.35/2:C81/(years)
Partnership Returns:
                                 SUDOCS: T22.35/2:P25/(year)
Availability: $5.50 per volume from Superintendent of Documents.

Provides data on federal income tax returns filed for the United States including number of returns filed, sources of income, adjustments to income, assets and liabilities of corporations, exemptions, deductions, tax credits, and taxes withheld and paid. Most data cover a one year period. Includes data by industry/sector. Contains approximately 120 tables/charts. Title and issuing source vary.

Data from federal sources.

Description based on *Sole Proprietorship Returns*, 1983 imprint, *Individual Returns*, 1983 imprint, *Corporate Returns*, 1984 imprint, all covering 1981 data, and *Partnership Returns*, 1982 imprint covering 1978 data.

Also publishes preliminary and supplemental data in *Statistics of Income Bulletin* (quarterly) [T22.35/4:(vol)/(nos)].

F1060
U.S. International Trade Administration.
International Economic Indicators.
Approximately 75 pages.   Quarterly.   1975-
ISSN: 0149-1873   LCCN: 80-643653
SUDOCS: C61.14:(vol)/(nos)   ITEM NO: 231-B-6
Availability: $18.00 per year from Superintendent of Documents.

Provides data on world business and economic conditions including the following comparative economic indicators for Canada, Federal Republic of Germany, Italy, Japan, Netherlands, the United Kingdom and the United States: employment, unemployment, Producer Prices, Consumer Price Index, Gross National Product or other measures of production, imports and exports, and the finance industry and monetary systems including data on the money supply and foreign investment. Most data cover a four year

period; select short term trends are included. Includes data by country. Contains approximately 50 tables. Title and issuing source vary.
Data from federal and international sources.
Description based on 1984 imprint covering 1981-1984 data.

F1065
U.S. International Trade Administration.
U.S. Trade Performance in (year) and Outlook.
Approximately 140 pages.   Annual.   1983-
                                LCCN: 84-646615
SUDOCS: C61.28:(year)   ITEM NO: 231-B-14
Availability: $9.00 from Superintendent of Documents.

Provides data on world merchandise trade including Gross National Product or other measures of production, currency exchange rates, employment, unemployment and labor costs, merchandise imports, exports and balance of trade. Most data cover a five year period; select trends are included. Includes data by product category, country and world region. Contains approximately 125 tables/charts.
Data from federal, international and private sources.
Description based on 1985 imprint covering 1980-1984 data.

F1070
U.S. Interstate Commerce Commission.
Transport Statistics in the U.S.
Approximately 200 pages in four volumes.   Annual.   1888-
SUDOCS: IC1.25:(year/part)   ITEM NO: 699
Availability: Free from Office of the Secretary, Publications Room.

Provides data on the transportation industry for the United States including traffic, financial and operating data and employment for carriers subject to the Interstate Commerce Act. Part One provides data on the railroad sector (in two releases). Part Two provides data on the motor carrier industry (in two releases). Most data cover a one year period. Includes data by industry/sector and district. Contains 60 tables. Title varies.
Data from federal and private sources.
Description based on 1985 imprint covering 1983 data.

F1080
U.S. Maritime Administration.
Domestic Waterborne Trade of the United States, (years).
Approximately 250 pages.   Annual.   1958-
                                LCCN: 79-641307
SUDOCS: TD11.19:(year)   ITEM NO: 233-B(mf)
Availability: $8.50 from Superintendent of Documents.

Provides data on the waterborne sector of the transportation industry for the United States including vessels, commodities transported, freight charges and employment. Most data cover a one year period; select trends are included. Includes data by port and state. Contains approximately 120 tables. Title varies.
Data from federal and private sources.
Description based on 1984 imprint covering 1982 data.

F1090
U.S. National Credit Union Administration.
National Credit Union Administration, (year) Year End Statistics.
Approximately 30 pages.   Annual.   1970-
ISSN: 0278-4025   LCCN: 81-643959
SUDOCS: NCU1.9/2:(year)   ITEM NO: 527-F(mf)
Availability: Free from Office of Public Information.

Provides data on credit unions for the United States including assets, liabilities, operating
expenses and loans outstanding for federally insured credit unions. Most data cover a
one year period. Includes data by asset size, age, type of membership and state. Contains
approximately 45 tables. Title varies.
Data from statements filed by federally insured credit unions.
Description based on 1985 imprint covering 1984 data.
Also publishes updated data in *National Credit Union Administration, (year) Mid-Year
Statistics* (semiannual) [NCU1.9/3:(year)].

F1100
U.S. National Marine Fisheries Service.
Fisheries of the United States, (year).
Approximately 130 pages.   Annual.   1952-
SUDOCS: C55.309/2:(nos)   ITEM NO: 610-A
Availability: Free from Public Affairs.

Provides preliminary data on the fishing industry for the United States including fish
landings, supply, production of processed fish products, consumption, employment,
imports and exports, and prices. Most data cover a two year period; select trends are
included. Includes data by type of product and region. Provides select comparisons to
foreign data. Contains approximately 75 tables.
Data from federal, international and state sources.
Description based on 1985 imprint covering 1983-1984 data.
Also publishes final data in *Fishery Statistics of the U.S.* [C55.316:(nos)].

F1110
U.S. National Park Service.
National Park Statistical Abstract, (year).
Approximately 40 pages.   Annual.   1940-
ISSN: 0028-1328   LCCN: 81-643329
SUDOCS: I29.2:ST2/8/(year)   ITEM NO: 648
Availability: Free from Office of Public Affairs.

Provides data on national park usage for the United States including visits and overnight
stays. Most data cover a one year period; select trends and projections are included.
Includes data by state and National Park Service Region. Contains approximately 11
tables. Title varies.
Data from federal sources.
Description based on 1984 imprint covering 1983 data.

F1120
U.S. Office of Management and Budget.
Historical Tables of the Budget of the U.S. Government, (fy).
Approximately 390 pages.   Annual.   1985-
SUDOCS: PrEx2.8/8:(year)   ITEM NO: 853
Availability: $9.00 from Superintendent of Documents.

Provides data on federal government finances for the United States including receipts,
outlays, appropriations, balances and federal debt. Most data cover a fifty-one fiscal year
period with actual figures for forty-six years and five year projections. Includes data by
source of funds, agency, function and subfunction. Contains approximately 47 tables.
Data from federal sources.
Description based on 1985 imprint covering FY1940-1990 data.

F1130
U.S. Office of Management and Budget.
U.S. Budget in Brief, (fy).
Approximately 85 pages.   Annual.   1963-
                               LCCN: 70-611022
SUDOCS: PREX2.8/2:(year)   ITEM NO: 855-A
Availability: $2.50 from Superintendent of Documents.

Provides data on federal government finances and the proposed budget including
receipts, outlays, appropriations, federal debt and credit. Most data cover a thirteen fiscal
year period with actual figures for ten years and three year projections; select long term
trends are included. Includes data by agency, function and subfunction. Contains
approximately 35 tables/charts. Title and issuing source vary. Data from federal sources.
Description based on 1985 imprint covering FY1976-FY1988 data.
Also publishes *Special Analyses, Budget of the U.S. Government, (fy)* (annual series of
eleven reports) [PREX2.8/5:(year)] which provides detailed analyses of federal outlays
for economic programs and activities including historic data and projections.

F1140
U.S. Organization of the Joint Chiefs of Staff.
U.S. Military Posture, (fy).
Approximately 95 pages.   Annual.   1978-
SUDOCS: D5.19:(year)   ITEM NO: 315-C-2
Availability: $4.50 from Superintendent of Documents.

Provides data on the world balance of power with an emphasis on the United States and
the U.S.S.R. Provides data on population, employment, technology levels, Gross National
Product or other measures of production, weapons production, military expenses, nuclear
and conventional forces, and minerals resources. Most data cover a one year period;
select trends and short term projections are included. Includes data by branch of service
and world region. Contains approximately 50 tables/charts. Issuing source varies.
Data from federal sources.
Description based on 1984 imprint covering 1984 data.

F1150
U.S. President.
Economic Report of the President Transmitted to Congress (date).
Approximately 350 pages.   Annual.   1947-
                                    LCCN: 47-32975
SUDOCS: PR40.9:(year)   ITEM NO: 848
Availability: $8.00 from Superintendent of Documents.

Narrative report on the administration view of business and economic conditions for the United States includes lengthy statistical appendix. Provides data on population, employment, unemployment, personal income and expenditures, Consumer Price Index, Producer Price Index, Gross National Product or other measures of production, imports and exports, and data on the following industries: construction, the finance industry and monetary system, and wholesale and retail trade. Also provides data on government and corporate finances. Most data cover a nineteen year period; select long term trends are included. Provides select comparisons to foreign data. Contains approximately 110 tables.
Data from federal sources.
Description based on 1985 imprint covering 1967-1984 data.

F1160
U.S. President.
Report of the President of the United States on the Trade Agreements Program.
Approximately 220 pages.   Annual.   1957-
SUDOCS: PR40.11:(years)   ITEM NO: 848-E
Availability: $13.00 from Superintendent of Documents.

Provides data on world business and economic conditions with an emphasis on the international trading system and United States trade relations including imports and exports, exports of selected states and industries, export share of Gross National Product, and national debt. Most data cover a two year period; select trends are included. Data by industry, state and country for select foreign countries. Provides select comparisons to the European Community, Nonmarket Economy Countries and world regions. Contains approximately 70 tables.
Data from federal, international and private sources.
Description based on 1982 imprint covering 1980-1981 data.

F1170
U.S. Securities and Exchange Commission.
SEC Monthly Statistical Review.
Approximately 40 pages.   Monthly.   1940-
ISSN: 0272-7846   LCCN: 80-648272
SUDOCS: SE1.20:(vol)/(nos)   ITEM NO: 908-A
Availability: $22.00 per year from Superintendent of Documents.

Provides data on the securities industry with an emphasis on stock market activity including market value and volume of equity sales, options, primary stock offering and securities registrations. Most data cover a three year period. Includes data by industry/sector and stock exchange. Contains approximately 25 tables/charts. Title varies.

Data from federal and private sources.
Description based on 1984 imprint covering 1982-1984 data.
Also publishes *Annual Report* [SE1.1:(year)] which provides historic data.

F1180
U.S. Small Business Administration.
State of Small Business: A Report of the President, Transmitted to Congress (date)
Together with the Annual Report of the Small Business Administration.
Approximately 485 pages.   Annual.   1982-
ISSN: 0735-1437   LCCN: 83-647757
SUDOCS: SBA 1.1/2:(year)   ITEM NO: 901-A
Availability: $13.00 from Superintendent of Documents.

Provides data on business and economic conditions for the United States with an
emphasis on the effects of economic conditions on small business including finances
and employment in small business firms, foreign trade, minority- and women-owned
small businesses and Federal procurement. Most data cover twenty-three year period.
Includes data by size of firm. Contains approximately 200 tables/charts.
Data from federal and private sources.
Description based on 1984 imprint covering 1960-1983 data.

F1190
U.S. Travel and Tourism Administration.
International Travel to and From the U.S.: (year) Outlook.
Approximately 15 pages.   Annual.
Availability: Free from the issuing source.

Provides data on the world transportation and tourism industries including currency
exchange rates, foreign arrivals to the United States, U.S. departures, and Travel and
Traveler Balances. Most data cover a three year period with actual figures for one year
and two year projections; select trends and additional projections are included. Contains
approximately 13 tables/charts. Issuing source varies.
Data from federal sources.
Description based on 1984 imprint covering 1983-1985 data.

F1200
U.S. Travel and Tourism Administration.
Recap of International Travel to and from the U.S. in (year).
Approximately 10 pages.   Annual.   1961-
SUDOCS: C47.2:T69/5:(year)
Availability: Free from the issuing source.

Provides data on the world transportation and tourism industries including foreign
arrivals and expenditures in the United States, U.S. travel abroad by country of
destination, and U.S. travelers' expenditures overseas including U.S. Travel Account
and Travel Dollar Account balances. Most data cover a one year period. Includes data
by country. Contains approximately 10 tables. Title and issuing source.
Data from federal sources.
Description based on 1984 imprint covering 1983 data.

PUBLICATIONS OF STATE
GOVERNMENTS

S0010
Alabama. Crop and Livestock Reporting Service.
Alabama Agricultural Statistics (year) Revised, (year) Preliminary.
Approximately 50 pages.   Annual.   1948-
ISSN: 0270-2436   LCCN: 54-63111
Availability: Limited distribution from the issuing source.

Provides data on the agriculture industry for the state of Alabama including production figures and prices for crops, livestock and poultry. Crop data cover a five year period. Poultry and livestock data cover a ten year period. Includes select data by county. Contains approximately 80 tables.
Data from state and U.S.D.A. sources.
Description based on 1983 imprint covering 1978-1982 data.

S0020
Alabama. Department of Industrial Relations.
Annual Planning Information, State of Alabama.
Approximately 30 pages.   Annual.   1976-
ISSN: 0361-297X   LCCN: 76-640454
Availability: Free from Labor Market Analysis Unit.

Provides data on population, employment, unemployment and personal income for the state of Alabama. Most data are one year projections; select trends are included. Includes data by industry/sector, occupation and county. Provides select comparisons to U.S. data. Contains approximately 25 tables.
Data from federal and state sources.
Description based on 1983 imprint covering 1984 data.

S0030
Alabama. Office of State Planning and Federal Programs.
Alabama County Data Book, (year).
Approximately 90 pages.   Annual.   1976-
                    LCCN: 84-643971
Availability: $4.00 from State Planning Division.

Presents a broad range of social and economic data for the state of Alabama. Provides data on population, housing, birth, death, education, employment, unemployment, personal income, and the following industries: energy, forest products, minerals, retail trade, select service industries, and transportation. Most data cover a one year period;

population data cover a forty year period with actual figures for a twenty year period and twenty year projections. Includes data by industry/sector, city and county. Contains approximately 55 tables.

Data from federal, private and state sources.

Description based on 1983 imprint covering 1980 data.

S0040
Alabama. Office of State Planning and Federal Programs.
Alabama Economic Outlook, (year).
Approximately 30 pages.   Annual.   1978-
                                 LCCN: 84-645499
Availability: $10.00 from State Planning Division.

Provides data on business and economic conditions for the state of Alabama including population, employment, personal income, Gross State Product or other measures of production, and the energy and retail trade industries. Most data are nine year projections; select trends are included. Provides select comparisons to U.S. data. Contains approximately 65 tables.

Data from state sources.

Description based upon 1983 imprint covering 1983-1991 data.

S0050
Alabama. Vital Statistics Bureau.
Alabama's Vital Events for (year).
Approximately 260 pages.   Annual.   1972-
ISSN: 0095-3431   LCCN: 74-648227
Availability: $10.00 from Special Services Administration.

Provides data on population, birth, death, marriage and divorce for the state of Alabama. Most data cover a one year period; select long term trends are included. Includes data by city, county and Public Health Area. Provides select comparisons to U.S. data. Contains approximately 110 tables.

Data from federal and state sources.

Description based on 1983 imprint covering 1982 data.

S0060
Alaska. Bureau of Vital Records.
Alaska Vital Statistics, (year).
Approximately 70 pages.   Annual.   1977-
ISSN: 0277-6200   LCCN: 81-642531
Availability: Free from Department of Health and Social Services, Information Systems Office, Statistical Support Section.

Provides data on population, birth, death, marriage and divorce for the state of Alaska. Most data cover a one year period. Includes data by census division and Health Services Area. Contains approximately 22 tables. Title varies.

Data from state sources.

Description based on 1983 imprint covering 1981 data.

S0070
Alaska. Crop and Livestock Reporting Service.
Alaska Agricultural Statistics, (year).
Approximately 30 pages.   Annual.   1960-
                         LCCN: 79-640359
Availability: $5.00 from the issuing source.

Provides data on the agriculture industry for the state of Alaska including production
figures and prices for crops, livestock, dairy and poultry. Most data cover a three year
period; select trends are included. Includes data by commodity/sector and district.
Contains approximately 30 tables. Title and issuing source vary.
Data from state and U.S.D.A. sources.
Description based on 1983 imprint covering 1980-1982 data.

S0080
Alaska. Department of Labor.
Annual Statewide Planning Information.
Approximately 85 pages.   Annual.   1980-
                         LCCN: 80-647796
Availability: Free from Research and Analysis Section.

Provides data on population, employment, unemployment, personal income, Consumer
Price Index and cost of living for the state of Alaska. Most data cover a one year period;
select long term trends and short term projections are included. Includes data by
community for select Alaska communities. Contains approximately 40 tables. Title
varies.
Data from federal and state sources.
Description based on 1984 imprint covering 1983 data.
Also publishes updated data in *Alaska Economic Trends* (monthly).

S0090
Alaska. Management and Budget Office.
Alaska Statistical Review, (year).
Approximately 240 pages in two volumes.   Biennial.   1968-
ISSN: 0360-5957   LCCN: SN81-1443
Availability: Free from the issuing source.

Presents a broad range of social and economic data for the state of Alaska. Volume One
provides data on population, birth, death, Consumer Price Index, cost of living and
the following industries: construction, finance, fishing, forest products, minerals, and
transportation. Volume Two provides data on population and personal income. Volume
One covers a one year period; Volume Two covers a five year period. Includes data by
industry/sector. Provides select comparisons to U.S. data. Contains approximately 60
tables. Issuing source varies.
Data from federal and state sources.
Description based on 1983 imprint; Volume One covers 1982 data; Volume Two covers
1975-1980 data.
Also plans to publish data on business and economic conditions in *Alaska Economic
Review and Outlook* (annual) (expected in late 1985 or early 1986).

S0100
Arizona State University. Bureau of Business and Economic Research.
Arizona Business.
Approximately 40 pages.   Quarterly.   1954-
ISSN: 0093-0717   LCCN: 74-640105
Availability: Free from the issuing source.

Quarterly journal on business and economic conditions for the state of Arizona includes several recurring statistical features. Provides data on Consumer Price Index and the construction, energy and retail trade industries. Most data cover a one year period. Includes data by S.M.S.A. Contains approximately 10 tables. Title varies.
Data from original research, federal, private and state sources.
Description based on 1983 imprint covering 1983 data.

S0110
Arizona. Crop and Livestock Reporting Service.
(year) Arizona Agricultural Statistics.
Approximately 110 pages.   Annual.   1867-
ISSN: 0570-9954
Availability: Free from the Agricultural Statistician.

Provides data on the agriculture industry for the state of Arizona including production figures and prices for crops, livestock, dairy and poultry. Most data cover a one year period; select short term trends and projections are included. Includes data by county. Contains approximately 150 tables. Title varies.
Data from state sources.
Description based on 1983 imprint covering 1982 data.

S0120
Arizona. Department of Economic Security.
Annual Planning Information, Arizona (fy).
Approximately 200 pages.   Annual.   1972-
                          LCCN: 82-640185
Availability: Free from Labor Market Information, Publications.

Provides data on population, employment, and unemployment for the state of Arizona. Most data are one fiscal year projections; select additional projections are included. Includes data by county and reservation. Contains approximately 35 tables. Title varies.
Data from federal and state sources.
Description based on 1984 imprint covering FY1985 data.
Also publishes updated data in *Arizona Labor Market Newsletter* (monthly).

S0130
Arizona. Department of Health Services.
(year) Arizona Vital Health Statistics.
Approximately 45 pages.   Annual.   1974-
ISSN: 0160-9610   LCCN: 78-642237
Availability: Free from Vital Records and Information Services Bureau, Research and Analysis Section.

Provides data on population, birth, death, marriage and divorce for the state of Arizona. Most data cover a one year period; select trends are included. Includes data by county. Provides select comparisons to U.S. data. Contains approximately 45 tables.
Data from federal and state sources.
Description based on 1983 imprint covering 1982 data.

S0140
Arkansas. Crop and Livestock Reporting Service.
(year) Agricultural Statistics for Arkansas.
Approximately 55 pages.   Annual.   1917-
                                  LCCN: 59-63340
Availability: Free from the issuing source.

Provides data on the agriculture industry for the state of Arkansas including production figures and prices for crops, livestock, dairy and poultry. Most data cover a one year period; select trends are included. Includes data by commodity/sector, county and district. Contains approximately 62 tables. Title and issuing source vary.
Data from state and U.S.D.A. sources.
Description based on 1984 imprint covering 1983 data.

S0150
Arkansas. Division of Health Statistics.
Arkansas Vital Statistics, (year).
Approximately 80 pages.   Annual.   1970-
ISSN: 0364-0728   LCCN: 76-647425
Availability: Free from the issuing source.

Provides data on population, birth, death, marriage and divorce for the state of Arkansas. Most data cover a one year period. Includes data by county and Health Services Area. Contains approximately 70 tables. Title varies.
Data from state sources.
Description based on 1983 imprint covering 1981 data.

S0160
Arkansas. Employment Security Division. Research and Analysis Section.
Annual Planning Information, State of Arkansas (fy).
Approximately 220 pages.   Annual.   1979-
                                  LCCN: 80-643449
Availability: Free from the issuing source.

Provides data on population, employment, unemployment, and personal income for the state of Arkansas. Most data are one fiscal year projections; select trends are included. Includes data by industry/sector, occupation, S.M.S.A. and Service Delivery Area. Contains approximately 200 tables. Title varies.
Data from federal and state sources.
Description based on 1984 imprint covering FY1984 data.

S0170
Ball State University. Bureau of Business Research.
Statistical Abstract of East-Central Indiana: (year).
Approximately 140 pages.   Irregular.   1983-
Availability: $6.00 from the issuing source.

Presents a broad range of social and economic data for East-Central Indiana. Provides
data on population, housing, birth, death, education, employment, unemployment,
personal income, and the following industries: agriculture, construction, finance, manufacturing, and minerals industries. Most data cover a three year period; select trends are
included. Includes data by industry/sector and county for twelve East-Central Indiana
counties. Contains approximately 53 tables.
Data from federal and private sources.
Description based on 1983 imprint covering 1980-1982 data.

S0180
Belo, A.H., Corporation.
(years) Texas Almanac and State Industrial Guide.
Approximately 700 pages.   Biennial.   1857-
ISSN: 0363-4248   LCCN: 10-3390
Availability: $12.95 for hardback, $7.95 for paperback from the issuing source.

A general interest narrative work arranged by broad subject category. Provides statistical
data for the state of Texas including data on population, education, employment,
unemployment, personal income, imports and exports, and the following industries:
agriculture, construction, energy, finance, forest products, manufacturing, minerals, and
transportation. Most data cover a six year period; select trends and projections are
included. Includes data by industry/sector, city, county, and region. Contains approximately 150 tables. Title varies.
Data from federal, private and state sources.
Description based on 1983 imprint covering 1978-1983 data.

S0190
California. Crop and Livestock Reporting Service.
California Principal Crop and Livestock Commodities (year).
Approximately 20 pages.   Annual.   1975-
ISSN: 0276-2439   LCCN: SC80-1304
Availability: $1.50 from the issuing source.

Provides data on the agriculture industry in the state of California including production
figures and prices for crops, livestock and poultry. Most data cover a one year period;
select trends are included. Includes data by commodity/sector, county and district.
Contains approximately 15 tables.
Data from private, state and U.S.D.A. sources.
Description based on 1983 imprint covering 1982 data.
Also publishes the following detailed annual reports: *California Livestock Statistics,*
California Fruit and Nut Acreage, California Vegetable Crop Statistics.

S0200
California. Department of Finance.
California Statistical Abstract, (year).
Approximately 230 pages.   Annual.   1958-
ISSN: 0575-6200   LCCN: 58-63807
Availability: $5.00 from Finance Research Section.

Presents a broad range of social and economic data for the state of California. Provides data on population, birth, death, marriage, divorce, education, employment, unemployment, personal income, Consumer Price Index and the following industries: agriculture, construction, energy, finance, fishing, forest products, manufacturing, minerals, retail trade, select service industries, and transportation. Most data cover a one year period; select trends are included. Includes data by industry/sector, city, S.M.S.A. and county. Contains approximately 165 tables. Issuing source varies.
Data from federal, private and state sources.
Description based on 1984 imprint covering 1983 data.
Also publishes updated data on business and economic conditions in *California Economic Indicators* (bimonthly).

S0210
California. Department of Health Services.
Vital Statistics of California, (years).
Approximately 500 pages.   Annual.   1965-
ISSN: 0094-0356   LCCN: 74-636455
Availability: Free from Center for Health Statistics, Health Demographics Unit.

Provides data on population, birth, death, marriage and divorce for the state of California. Most data cover a two year period; select trends are included. Includes data by county. Provides select comparisons to U.S. data. Contains approximately 90 tables.
Data from federal and state sources.
Description based on 1983 imprint covering 1980-1981 data.

S0220
California. Employment Data Research Division.
Annual Planning Information, California (years).
Approximately 130 pages.   Annual.   1972-
                            LCCN: 79-643631
Availability: Free from Labor Market Information Section.

Provides data on population, employment, unemployment and personal income for the state of California. Most data cover a one year period; select trends and projections are included. Includes data by industry/sector, occupation and county. Contains approximately 45 tables. Title varies.
Data from federal and state sources.
Description based on 1983 imprint covering 1980 data.
Also publishes updated data in *California Labor Market Bulletin* (monthly).

S0230
California. Governor.
Economic Report of the Governor (year).
Approximately 150 pages.   Annual.   1963-
ISSN: 0527-009X
Availability: Free from Department of Finance, Finance Research Section.

Provides data on business and economic conditions for the state of California including population, employment, unemployment, personal income, Consumer Price Index and the following industries: agriculture, construction, energy, finance, forest products, tourism, and transportation. Most data cover a one year period; select trends and projections are included. Includes data by industry/sector and S.M.S.A. Provides select comparisons to U.S. data. Contains approximately 70 tables.
Data from federal, private and state sources.
Description based on 1983 imprint covering 1982 data.

S0240
Colorado. Crop and Livestock Reporting Service.
(year) Colorado Agriculture Statistics.
Approximately 95 pages.   Annual.   1922-
                             LCCN: 52-62059
Availability: Free from the issuing source.

Provides data on the agriculture industry in the state of Colorado including production figures and prices for crops, livestock, dairy and poultry. Most data cover a two year period; select trends are included. Includes data by commodity/sector, county and district. Provides select comparisons to U.S. data. Contains approximately 125 tables.
Data from state and U.S.D.A. sources.
Description based on 1983 imprint covering 1981-1982 data.

S0250
Colorado. Department of Health. Health Statistics Section.
Annual Report of Vital Statistics, Colorado, (year).
Approximately 85 pages.   Annual.   1967-
ISSN: 0588-456X   LCCN: 75-646408
Availability: $2.00 from the issuing source.

Provides data on population, birth, death, marriage and divorce for the state of Colorado. Most data cover a one year period; select trends are included. Includes data by county and Health Service Area. Contains approximately 50 tables. Title varies.
Data from state sources.
Description based on 1983 imprint covering 1981 data.

S0260
Colorado. Division of Employment and Training.
Annual Planning Information Report, (fy), Colorado.
Approximately 230 pages.   Annual.   1980-
ISSN: 0749-7857   LCCN: SC84-1534
Availability: Free from Research and Development Section.

Provides data on population, employment, unemployment, and personal income for the state of Colorado. Most data cover a one fiscal year period; select trends and projection are included. Includes data by industry/sector, occupation and county. Contains approximately 70 tables.
Data from federal and state sources.
Description based on 1983 imprint covering FY1982 data.
Also publishes updated data in *Colorado Labor Force Review* (monthly).

S0270
Connecticut. Department of Agriculture.
(year) Connecticut Agriculture.
Approximately 40 pages.   Annual.   1959-
ISSN: 0749-1514   LCCN: 84-646415
Availability: Free from Marketing Division.

Provides data on the agriculture industry for the state of Connecticut including production figures and prices for crops, livestock, dairy and poultry. Most data cover a one year period; select trends are included. Includes data by commodity/sector. Contains approximately 60 tables. Title varies.
Data from state and U.S.D.A. sources.
Description based on 1983 imprint covering 1982 data.

S0280
Connecticut. Department of Economic Development.
Connecticut Market Data, (year).
Approximately 80 pages.   Irregular.   1958-
ISSN: 0573-665X   LCCN: 80-644586
Availability: Limited distribution from the issuing source.

Presents a broad range of social and economic data for the state of Connecticut. Provides data on population, housing, employment, personal income, and the following industries: finance, manufacturing, retail trade, and transportation for the state of Connecticut. Most data cover a two year period; select trends and long term projections are included. Includes data by industry/sector, S.M.S.A. and county. Contains approximately 40 tables. Issuing source varies.
Data from federal, private and state sources.
Description based on 1983 imprint covering 1981-1982 data.

S0290
Connecticut. Employment Security Division. Office of Research and Information.
Annual Planning Information for Connecticut, (fy).
Approximately 110 pages.   Annual.   1980-
                          LCCN: 81-641914
Availability: Free from the issuing source.

Provides data on population, employment, unemployment and personal income for the state of Connecticut. Most data cover a one fiscal year period; select trends and projections are included. Includes data by industry/sector and occupation. Contains approximately 25 tables.

Data from state sources.
Description based on 1983 imprint covering FY1982 data.
Also publishes updated data in *Connecticut Labor Situation* (monthly).

S0300
Connecticut. Governor.
Economic Report of the Governor, (years).
Approximately 140 pages.   Annual.   1980-
                           LCCN: 83-641293
Availability: Free from the issuing source.

Provides data on business and economic conditions for the state of Connecticut including population, employment, unemployment, personal income, Consumer Price Index, imports and exports and the following industries: energy and manufacturing. Most data cover a one year period; select trends and projections are included. Contains approximately 74 tables/charts.
Data from federal and state sources.
Description based on 1985 imprint covering 1984 data.

S0310
Connecticut. State Department of Health Services.
Registration Report of Births, Marriages, Deaths for the Year Ended (date).
Approximately 65 pages.   Annual.   1800s-
                           LCCN: 83-643327
Availability: $10.00 from Health Statistics Division, Statistics and Demographics Unit.

Provides data on population, birth, death, marriage and divorce for the state of Connecticut. Most data cover a one year period; select long term trends are included. Includes data by city and county. Contains approximately 15 tables. Title varies.
Data from state sources.
Description based on 1983 imprint covering 1980 data.

S0320
County Supervisors Association of California.
California County Fact Book.
Approximately 215 pages.   Annual.   1960-
ISSN: 0590-0158
Availability: $10.60 from the issuing source.

Presents a broad range of social and economic data for the state of California. Provides data on population, birth, death, marriage, education, employment, unemployment and the following industries: agriculture, construction, energy, forest products, minerals, and transportation. Most data cover a two year period; select trends and projections are included. Includes data by industry/sector, S.M.S.A. and county. Contains approximately 75 tables.
Data from federal, private and state sources.
Description based on 1983 imprint covering 1980-1981 data.

S0330
Delaware. Bureau of Disease Control.
Delaware Monthly Surveillance Report.
Approximately 4 pages.   Monthly.   1901-
Availability: Free from the Division of Public Health.

Provides data on the incidence of disease and immunization for the state of Delaware.
Most data cover a one month period with the most current figures available. Includes
data by disease type and county. Contains approximately 7 tables. Title varies.
Data from state sources.
Description based on 1984 imprint covering 1984 data.
Also plans to publish a vital statistics compilation for the state of Delaware.

S0340
Delaware. Department of Labor.
Annual Planning Report, (fy), State of Delaware and Major Subareas.
Approximately 55 pages.   Annual.   1980-
Availability: Free from Planning, Research and Evaluation Office.

Provides data on population, employment and unemployment for the state of Delaware.
Most data are one fiscal year projections; select trends are included. Includes data by
industry/sector, occupation and county. Contains approximately 20 tables.
Data from federal and state sources.
Description based on 1982 imprint covering FY1983 data.
Also publishes updated data in *Delaware and Wilmington S.M.S.A. Labor Market
Trends (quarterly).*

S0350
Delaware. Development Office.
Delaware Data Book.
Approximately 130 pages.   Annual.   1982-
Availability: $25.00 from the issuing source.

Presents a broad range of social and economic data for the state of Delaware. Provides
data on population, education, employment, personal income, cost of living and the
finance, energy and transportation industries. Most data cover a one year period; select
trends are included. Includes data by industry/sector and city. Contains approximately
45 tables.
Data from federal, private and state sources.
Description based on 1984 imprint covering 1984 data.

S0360
District of Columbia. Department of Employment Services.
*(fy) Annual Planning Information Report: The District of Columbia and Washington
Metropolitan Area.*
Approximately 110 pages.   Annual.   1973-
Availability: Free from Labor Market Information Division.

Provides data on population, employment, unemployment, Consumer Price Index,
personal income and the retail trade industry for the District of Columbia. Most data

are three year projections; select trends are included. Data by industry/sector and occupation. Contains approximately 45 tables.

Data from district, federal, private and state sources.

Description based on 1982 imprint covering 1983-1985 data.

Also publishes updated data in *Metropolitan Washington, D.C., Area Labor Summary* (monthly).

S0370

District of Columbia. Department of Human Services. Research and Statistics Division.
Vital Statistics Summary, (year).
Approximately 100 pages.　　　　Annual.　　　　1954-
ISSN: 0419-4381　　　　　　　　LCCN: 74-640273
Availability: Free from the issuing source.

Provides data on population, birth and death for the District of Columbia. Most data cover a one year period; select trends are included. Includes data by Clinic Service Area, census tract and ward. Contains approximately 36 tables. Issuing source varies.

Data from district sources.

Description based on 1983 imprint covering 1979 data.

S0380

District of Columbia. Office of Policy and Program Evaluation.
Indices: A Statistical Index to District of Columbia Services.
Approximately 110 pages.　　　Annual.　　　　1984-
Availability: $5.00 from the issuing source.

Presents a broad range of social and economic data for the District of Columbia. Provides data on population, housing, education, employment, unemployment, personal income and the following industries: construction, finance, retail trade, select service industries and tourism. Most data cover a three year period. Includes data by industry/sector and ward. Contains approximately 26 tables.

Data from district sources.

Description based on 1984 imprint covering 1981-1983 data.

S0390

Florida. Crop and Livestock Reporting Service.
Florida Agricultural Statistics.
Approximately 210 pages in six volumes.　　　Annual.　　　　1963-
Volume One:
ISSN: 0428-6413　　　　　　　　LCCN: 74-644777
Volume Two:
　　　　　　　　　　　　　　　LCCN: A63-7731
Volume Three:
　　　　　　　　　　　　　　　LCCN: 76-645669
Volume Five:
ISSN: 0091-9985　　　　　　　　LCCN: SN79-9311
Volume Six:
ISSN: 0428-6421　　　　　　　　LCCN: 75-646842
Availability: $2.50 each, $12.50 for the series from the issuing source.

Provides data on the agriculture industry for the state of Florida including production figures and prices for crops, livestock, dairy and poultry. Volume One provides data on citrus fruits; Volume Two provides data on vegetables; Volume Three provides data on poultry; Volume Four provides data on livestock; Volume Five provides data on field crops; Volume Six provides data on dairy. Most data cover a ten year period; select long term trends are included. Includes data by commodity/sector and county. Provides select comparisons to U.S. data. Contains approximately 250 tables. Titles and issuing source vary.
Data from local, private, state and U.S.D.A. sources.
Description based on 1983 imprint covering 1973-1982 data.

S0400
Florida. Division of Employment Security.
Annual Planning Information, (year), State of Florida.
Approximately 110 pages.   Annual.   1982-
                              LCCN: 81-649671
Availability: Free from Research and Analysis Bureau.

Provides data on population, employment, unemployment and personal income for the state of Florida. Most data cover a two year period; select trends are included. Includes data by industry/sector and S.M.S.A. Contains approximately 25 tables.
Data from federal and state sources.
Description based on 1982 imprint covering 1981-1982 data.
Also publishes updated data in *Florida Employment Statistics* (quarterly).

S0410
Florida. Governor.
Economic Report of the Governor, (years).
Approximately 75 pages.   Annual.   1974-
ISSN: 0094-9647   LCCN: 74-646537
Availability: Limited distribution from Revenue and Economic Analysis Unit.

Provides data on business and economic conditions for the state of Florida including population, employment, personal income, imports and exports, and the construction and tourism industries. Most data cover a two year period; select trends and projections are included. Includes data by industry/sector. Contains approximately 11 tables.
Data from state sources.
Description based on 1982 imprint covering 1979-1980 data.

S0420
Florida. Public Health Statistics Section.
Florida Vital Statistics, (year).
Approximately 110 pages.   Annual.   1946-
                              LCCN: 83-643734
Availability: Free from the issuing source.

Provides data on population, birth, death, marriage and divorce for the state of Florida. Most data cover a one year period; select short term trends are included. Includes data by county. Contains approximately 80 tables.
Data from state sources.
Description based on 1982 imprint covering 1981 data.

S0430
Georgia State University: Economic Forecasting Project.
GSU Economic Forecasting Project Newsletter: Monthly Projections.
Approximately 15 pages.   Monthly.   1970s-
Availability: $50.00 per year from the issuing source.

Provides data on business and economic conditions for the United States including
employment, personal income, Consumer Price Index, Producer Price Index, Gross
National Product or other measures of production, the composite index of leading
economic indicators, and the construction, finance, and retail trade industries. Most data
are one year projections. Includes data by industry/sector. Contains approximately 10
tables.
Data based on original research.
Description based on 1983 imprint covering 1984 data.

S0440
Georgia State University: Economic Forecasting Project.
*Georgia State University Forecast: Volume One: Georgia and Atlanta; Volume Two:
The Nation.*
Approximately 35 pages in two volumes.   Quarterly.   1975-
Availability: $25.00 per year for each volume. from the issuing source.

Provides data on business and economic conditions for the United States including
personal income, Consumer Price Index, Producer Price Index, Industrial Production
Index, imports and exports, and Gross National Product or other measures of production.
Volume Two provides data for the United States; Volume One provides data for the
state of Georgia. Most data are two year projections. Volume One includes data by city
for Atlanta. Contains approximately 15 tables.
Data based on original research.
Description based on 1984 imprint covering 1984-1985 data.

S0450
Georgia. Crop Reporting Service.
Georgia Agricultural Facts (year) Edition.
Approximately 85 pages.   Annual.   1900-
Availability: Free from issuing source.

Provides data on the agriculture industry for the state of Georgia including production
figures and prices for crops, livestock dairy and poultry. Most data cover a one year
period; select short term trends are included. Includes data by commodity/sector and
county. Provides select comparisons to U.S. data. Contains approximately 55 tables.
Data published in University of Georgia Agricultural Experiment Station **Bulletins** from
1900-1956.
Data from state and U.S.D.A. sources.
Description based on 1983 imprint covering 1982 data.

S0460
Georgia. Division of Public Health.
Vital Statistics Data Book, (year), Georgia.
Approximately 200 pages.   Annual.   1947-
                                              LCCN: 83-643156
Availability: Free from the issuing source.

Provides data on population, birth, death, marriage and divorce for the state of Georgia. Most data cover a one year period. Includes data by city, S.M.S.A., county and district. Contains approximately 5 tables.
Data from state sources.
Description based on 1983 imprint covering 1981 data.

S0470
Georgia. Labor Information Systems.
Georgia Labor Market Trends.
Approximately 20 pages.   Monthly.   1976-
ISSN: 0147-9865   LCCN: 77-640866
Availability: Free from the issuing source.

Provides data on employment, unemployment and personal income for the state of Georgia. Most data cover a one month period with the most current figures available. Includes data by industry/sector, city and S.M.S.A. Provides select comparisons to U.S. data. Contains approximately 15 tables.
Data from state sources.
Description based on 1983 imprint covering 1983 data.

S0480
Georgia. Office of Planning and Budget.
Georgia Descriptions in Data, (year).
Approximately 260 pages.   Annual.   1982-
ISSN: 0741-0182   LCCN: 83-646614
Availability: $7.50 from State Data Center.

Presents a broad range of social and economic data for the state of Georgia. Provides data on population, housing, birth, death, education, employment, unemployment, personal income, Gross State Product or other measures of production, and the following industries: agriculture, energy, finance, fishing, minerals, select service industries, tourism, and transportation. Most data cover a one year period; select trends and long term projections are included. Content varies from issue to issue. Includes data by industry/sector and county. Contains approximately 80 tables.
Data from federal sources.
Description based on 1982 and 1983 imprints covering 1980 data.

S0490
Hawaii. Agricultural Reporting Service.
Statistics of Hawaiian Agriculture, (year).
Approximately 100 pages.   Annual.   1954-
Availability: Free from the issuing source.

Provides data on the agriculture industry for the state of Hawaii including production figures and prices for crops, livestock, dairy and poultry. Most data cover a five year period; select trends are included. Includes data by commodity/sector and island. Contains approximately 135 tables. Title and issuing source vary.
Data from state and U.S.D.A. sources.
Description based on 1983 imprint covering 1978-1982 data.

S0500
Hawaii. Department of Health.
Annual Report: Statistical Supplement, (year).
Approximately 250 pages.   Annual.   1948-
Availability: Free from Research and Statistics Office.

Provides data on population, birth, death, marriage and divorce for the state of Hawaii. Most data cover a one year period; select trends are included. Includes data by city, county and island. Contains approximately 70 vital statistics tables. Issuing source varies.
Data from state sources.
Description based on 1983 imprint covering 1982 data.

S0510
Hawaii. Department of Labor and Industrial Relations.
Labor Market Review, Hawaii, (year).
Approximately 35 pages.   Annual.   1980-
Availability: Free from Labor Market and Employment Service Research Section.

Provides data on population, employment, unemployment and personal income, Consumer Price Index and the tourism industry for the state of Hawaii. Most data cover a two year period. Includes data by industry/sector, S.M.S.A., and county. Contains approximately 10 tables.
Data from federal, private and state sources.
Description based on 1983 imprint covering 1981-1982 data.

S0520
Hawaii. Department of Planning and Economic Development.
State of Hawaii Data Book (year): A Statistical Abstract.
Approximately 600 pages.   Annual.   1962-
ISSN: 0073-1080   LCCN: 68-66724
Availability: $5.00 to state residents, $10.00 to others from Information Office.

Presents a broad range of social and economic data for the state of Hawaii. Provides data on population, birth, death, education, employment, unemployment, personal income, Consumer Price Index, cost of living, Gross State Product or other measures of production, and the following industries: agriculture, construction, energy, finance, fishing, forest products, minerals, select service industries, tourism, transportation, and wholesale and retail trade. Most data cover a fourteen year period; select projections and long term trends are included. Includes data by industry/sector, county and island. Contains approximately 620 tables. Title varies.
Data from federal, private and state sources.
Description based on 1983 imprint covering 1970-1983 data.
Also publishes updated data on business and economic conditions in **Quarterly Statistical and Economic Report, State of Hawaii.**

S0530
Idaho. Crop and Livestock Reporting Service.
Idaho Agricultural Statistics, (year).
Approximately 75 pages.   Annual.   1972-
ISSN: 0094-1271   LCCN: 74-642213
Availability: $5.00 from the issuing source.

Provides data on the agriculture industry for the state of Idaho including production
figures and prices for crops, livestock, dairy and poultry. Most data cover a one year
period; select long term trends are included. Includes data by commodity/sector and
county. Provides select comparisons to U.S. data. Contains approximately 100 tables.
Data from state and U.S.D.A. sources.
Description based on 1983 imprint covering 1982 data.

S0540
Idaho. Department of Employment. Research and Analysis Bureau.
Annual Planning Information Report (fy), Idaho.
Approximately 70 pages.   Annual.   1972-
                                   LCCN: 81-640212
Availability: Free from the issuing source.

Provides data on population, employment, unemployment and personal income for the
state of Idaho. Most data are one fiscal year projections; select trends are included.
Includes data by industry/sector, occupation and county. Contains approximately 45
tables. Title varies.
Data from federal and state sources.
Description based on 1984 imprint covering FY1985 data.

S0550
Idaho. Department of Employment. Research and Analysis Bureau.
The Labor Force in Idaho and Basic Economic Data for Idaho.
Approximately 85 pages.   Annual.   1982-
Availability: Free from the issuing source.

Provides data on population, employment, unemployment and personal income for the
state of Idaho. Most data cover a one year period; select short term trends are included.
Includes data by industry/sector, S.M.S.A. and county. Contains approximately 5 tables.
Formed by a merger of two separate publications: *The Labor Force in Idaho*, and *Basic
Economic Data for Idaho.*
Data from state sources.
Description based on 1982 imprint covering 1981-1982 data.

S0560
Idaho. Department of Health and Welfare.
(year) Annual Summary of Vital Statistics, Idaho.
Approximately 110 pages.   Annual.   1974-
ISSN: 0362-9279   LCCN: 76-644913
Availability: Free from Vital Statistics, Standards and Local Health Services Bureau.

Provides data on population, birth, death, marriage and divorce for the state of Idaho.

Most data cover a one year period; select trends are included. Includes data by city, county and Health District. Contains approximately 65 tables.
Data from federal and state sources.
Description based on 1983 imprint covering 1982 data.

S0570
Idaho. Division of Economic and Community Affairs.
(year) Census Profiles of Idaho Cities.
Approximately 400 pages.   Monograph.   1983.
Availability: Free from State Census Data Center.

Provides data on population and housing for the state of Idaho. Most data cover a one year period. Includes data by city. Contains approximately 24 tables for each Idaho city.
Data from U.S. Bureau of the Census *Summary Tape File One.*
Description based on 1983 imprint covering 1980 data.

S0580
Idaho. Division of Finance Management.
Idaho Economic Forecast.
Approximately 75 pages.   Quarterly.   1980-
                                   LCCN: 82-646815
Availability: $7.50 per year to state residents, $15.00 per year to others from the issuing source.

Provides data on business and economic conditions for the state of Idaho including population, employment, personal income, Gross State Product or other measures of production, and the construction industry. Most data cover a five year period with actual figures for three years and two year projections; select trends are included. Provides select comparisons to U.S. data. Contains approximately 10 tables.
Data from original research, federal and state sources.
Description based on 1983 imprint covering 1981-1985 data.

S0590
Illinois. Bureau of Employment Security. Research and Analysis Division.
Annual Planning Report, (fy).
Approximately 130 pages.   Annual.   1977-
                                   LCCN: 78-643579
Availability: Free from the issuing source.

Provides data on population, employment, unemployment and personal income for the state of Illinois. Most data cover an eight year period. Includes data by industry/sector and occupation. Contains approximately 20 tables. Title varies.
Data from federal and state sources.
Description based on 1983 imprint covering 1976-1983 data.

S0600
Illinois. Bureau of the Budget.
State of Illinois Statistical Abstract, (year).
Approximately 160 pages.   Annual.   1973-
ISSN: 0094-5188   LCCN: 74-645555
Availability: Free from Planning Office.

Presents a broad range of social and economic data for the state of Illinois. Provides data
on population, birth, death, marriage, divorce, education, employment, unemployment,
personal income, and the following industries: agriculture, energy, minerals, select
service industries, and transportation. Most data cover a four year period; select trends
and projections are included. Includes data by industry/sector and county. Contains
approximately 70 tables.
Data from federal and state sources.
Description based on 1981 imprint covering 1978-1981 data.

S0610
Illinois. Cooperative Crop Reporting Service.
Illinois Agricultural Statistics, (year).
Approximately 100 pages.   Annual.   1954-
ISSN: 0422-2562   LCCN: 51-62568
Availability: Free to state residents, $5.00 to others from the issuing source.

Provides data on the agriculture industry for the state of Illinois including production
figures and prices for crops, livestock, dairy and poultry. Most data cover a one year
period; select trends are included. Includes data by commodity/sector, county and
district. Contains approximately 145 tables.
Data from state and U.S.D.A. sources.
Description based on 1983 imprint covering 1982 data.

S0620
Illinois. Department of Commerce and Community Affairs.
Illinois State and Regional Economic Data Book.
Approximately 185 pages.   Biennial.   1970-
ISSN 0737-1543   LCCN: 83-641787
Availability: Free from the Office of Research.

Provides data business and economic conditions for the state of Illinois including
population, employment, unemployment, personal income, Gross State Product or other
measures of production, and the following industries: agriculture, manufacturing,
minerals, and transportation. Most data cover a ten year period. Includes data by
industry/sector and region for eight Illinois regions. Provides select comparisons to U.S.
data. Contains approximately 100 tables. Issuing source varies.
Data from federal and state sources.
Description based on 1982 imprint covering 1971-1980 data.
Also publishes updated data in *Illinois Monthly Economic Data Sheets* and *Illinois
Gross State Product* (quarterly).

S0630
Illinois. Department of Public Health. Bureau of Statistics.
Vital Statistics, Illinois, (year).
Approximately 150 pages.   Annual.   1958-
                                   LCCN: A60-9072
Availability: Free from Health Information and Evaluation Division.

Provides data on population, birth, death, marriage and divorce for the state of Illinois. Most data cover a one year period; select trends are included. Includes data by city, county and region. Contains approximately 155 tables. Title varies.
Data from state sources.
Description based on 1984 imprint covering 1981 data.

S0640
Indiana University. Graduate School of Business.
Indiana Business Review.
Approximately 5 pages.   Monthly.   1926-
ISSN: 0019-6541   LCCN: SF83-1130
Availability: Free to Indiana residents, limited distribution to others from the issuing source.

Monthly report on business and economic conditions for the state of Indiana includes recurring statistical feature. Provides data on employment, unemployment, personal income, Gross State Product or other measures of production, and the following industries: construction, energy, minerals, and retail trade. Also, includes a semiannual feature which provides data on forecasted economic conditions for the United States and the state of Indiana. Most data cover a one month period with the most current figures available. Includes data by industry/sector. Provides select comparisons to U.S. data. Contains approximately 3 tables.
Data from federal, private and state sources.
Description based on 1984 imprint covering 1984 data.

S0650
Indiana. Crop and Livestock Reporting Service.
Annual Crop and Livestock Summary, (year).
Approximately 140 pages.   Annual.   1971-
ISSN: 0148-1932   LCCN: 77-642270
Availability: $2.00 for 4th class, $4.00 for 1st class from the issuing source.

Provides data on the agriculture industry for the state of Indiana including production figures and prices for crops, livestock, dairy and poultry. Most data cover a one year period; select trends are included. Data by commodity/sector. Provides select comparisons to U.S. data. Contains approximately 100 tables. Title varies.
Data from state and U.S.D.A. sources.
Description based on 1983 imprint covering 1982 data.

S0660
Indiana. Employment Security Division.
Indiana Labor Market Trends.
Approximately 40 pages.   Quarterly.
Availability: Free from Research and Statistics Section.

Provides data on employment, unemployment and personal income for the state of
Indiana. Most data cover a two year period; select trends are included. Includes data by
industry/sector and county. Contains approximately 30 tables.
Data from state sources.
Description based on 1984 imprint covering 1983-1984 data.

S0670
Indiana. State Board of Health. Public Health Statistics Division.
Health Profile Report, (years), by State and County, Indiana.
Approximately 185 pages.   Biennial.   1968-
ISSN: 0193-9378   LCCN: 81-64421
Availability: Free from the issuing source.

Provides data on population, birth, death, marriage, divorce, employment, unemployment, personal income and the health services industry for the state of Indiana. Most
data cover a thirteen year period. Includes data by county. Contains approximately 12
tables.
Data from federal and state sources.
Description based on 1982 imprint covering 1968-1980 data.

S0680
Indiana. State Board of Health. Public Health Statistics Division.
Indiana Vital Health Statistics Summary, (year).
Approximately 60 pages.   Annual.   1959-
ISSN: 0445-8826   LCCN: 61-64187
Availability: Free from the issuing source.

Provides data on population, birth, death and marriage for the state of Indiana. Most
data cover a two year period; select trends are included. Includes data by city, county
and Health Services Area. Contains approximately 8 tables. Prior to 1959, Indiana's vital
statistics were published in individual tabular form, or as part of the *Indiana Year Book.*
Data from state sources.
Description based on 1983 imprint covering 1980-1981 data.

S0690
Iowa State University. World Food Institute.
World Food Trade and U.S. Agriculture, (years).
Approximately 75 pages.   Annual.   1981-
ISSN: 0733-2378   LCCN: 82-643729
Availability: Free from the issuing source.

Provides data on the world agriculture industry including production figures and prices
for crops, livestock and poultry. Most data covers a twenty-two year period. Includes
data by commodity and country. Contains approximately 45 tables.

Data from F.A.O. and U.S.D.A. sources.
Description based on 1983 imprint covering 1960-1982 data.

S0700
Iowa. Crop and Livestock Reporting Service.
Iowa Agricultural Statistics, (year).
Approximately 110 pages.   Annual.   1975-
ISSN: 0364-9040   LCCN: 76-646749
Availability: Free from the issuing source.

Provides data on the agriculture industry for the state of Iowa including production
figures and prices for crops, livestock, dairy and poultry. Most data cover a one year
period; select trends are included. Includes data by county and district. Contains
approximately 75 tables.
Data from state and U.S.D.A. sources.
Description based on 1983 imprint covering 1981 data.

S0710
Iowa. Department of Job Service. Audit and Analysis Department.
Resources Handbook of Facts and Figures.
Approximately 200 pages.   Annual.   1980-
                             LCCN: 80-623939
Availability: Free from the issuing source.

Provides data on population, employment, unemployment and personal income for the
state of Iowa. Most data cover a one year period; select trends are included. Includes
data by industry/sector. Provides select comparisons to U.S. data. Contains approximately
76 tables.
Data from federal and state sources.
Description based on 1982 imprint covering 1981 data.

S0720
Iowa. Development Commission.
Iowa Development Commission Digest.
Approximately 15 pages.   Monthly.   1972-
ISSN: 0193-8460   LCCN: SC79-3388
Availability: Free from the Communications Group.

Monthly report on business and economic conditions for the state of Iowa includes
recurring statistical features. Provides data on employment, unemployment, personal
income, stock market indexes, Gross State Product or other measures of production,
and the following industries: agriculture, construction, finance, and retail trade. Also
includes an annual feature which provides data on Iowa's new and expanding industries.
Most data cover a one month or one quarter period with the most current figures
available. Includes data by industry/sector. Provides select comparisons to U.S. data.
Contains approximately 17 tables.
Data from federal, private and state sources.
Description based on 1984 imprint covering 1984 data.

S0730
Iowa. Development Commission.
Statistical Profile of Iowa.
Approximately 125 pages.   Annual.   1969-
                              LCCN: 75-650016
Availability: Free from Research and Development Group.

Presents a broad range of social and economic data for the state of Iowa. Provides data on population, housing, education, employment, unemployment, personal income and the following industries: agriculture, construction, energy, finance, manufacturing, minerals, select service industries, tourism, transportation, and wholesale and retail trade. Most data cover a one year period; select trends and projections are included. Includes data by industry/sector and county. Provides select comparisons to U.S. data. Contains approximately 150 tables.
Data from federal and state sources.
Description based on 1983 imprint covering 1981 data.

S0740
Iowa. State Department of Health.
Vital Statistics of Iowa, (year).
Approximately 95 pages.   Annual.   1888-
ISSN: 0161-8695   LCCN: 79-644698
Availability: Free from Division of Records and Statistics, Statistics Services Unit.

Provides data on birth, death, marriage and divorce for the state of Iowa. Most data cover a one year period; select trends are included. Includes data by city and county. Contains approximately 40 tables. Title varies.
Data from state sources.
Description based on 1983 imprint covering 1981 data.

S0750
Kansas State University.
Kansas Economic Report, (date).
Approximately 30 pages.   Annual.   1964-
Availability: $1.00 from Office of University Relations.

Provides data on business and economic conditions for the state of Kansas including employment, unemployment, personal income, Consumer Price Index, and Gross State Product or other measures of production. Most data cover a two year period with actual figures for one year and one year projections; select trends are included. Includes data by industry, S.M.S.A and county. Provides select comparisons to U.S. data. Contains approximately 45 tables. Incorporates the data formerly provided by *Economic and Social Report of the Governor.* Produced in cooperation with University of Kansas.
Data from federal and state sources.
Description based on 1984 imprint covering 1983-1984 data.

S0760
Kansas. Bureau of Registration and Health Statistics.
Annual Summary of Vital Statistics Kansas, (year).
Approximately 150 pages.   Annual.   1949-
ISSN: 0364-2372   LCCN: 76-647679
Availability: Free from the issuing source.

Provides data on population, birth, death, marriage and divorce for the state of Kansas. Most data cover a one year period; select trends are included. Includes data by city and county. Contains approximately 41 tables. Title varies.
Data from state sources.
Description based on 1982 imprint covering 1981 data.

S0770
Kansas. Crop and Livestock Reporting Service.
Biennial Report and Farm Facts.
Approximately 275 pages.   Biennial.   1916-
ISSN: 0196-0954   LCCN: 79-644613
Availability: Free from State Board of Agriculture.

Provides data on the agriculture industry for the state of Kansas including production figures and prices for crops, livestock, dairy and poultry. Most data cover a two year period; select trends are included. Includes data by commodity/sector, county and district. Provides select comparisons to U.S. data. Contains approximately 190 tables. Title and issuing source vary.
Data from state and U.S.D.A. sources.
Description based on 1982 imprint covering 1980-1981 data.

S0780
Kansas. Department of Human Resources.
Kansas Annual Planning Information, (year).
Approximately 90 pages.   Annual.   1981-
Availability: Free from Division of Staff Services, Research and Analysis Section.

Provides data on population, employment, unemployment and personal income for the state of Kansas. Most data cover a one year period; select trends and projections are included. Includes data by S.M.S.A. Contains approximately 22 tables. Title varies.
Data from federal and state sources.
Description based on 1983 imprint covering 1982 data.

S0790
Kentucky. Council of Economic Advisors.
Kentucky Economy: Review and Perspective.
Approximately 15 pages.   Quarterly.   1977-
ISSN: 0270-1421   LCCN: 84-647089
Availability: Free from the issuing source.

Quarterly report on business and economic conditions for the state of Kentucky includes recurring statistical feature, "Selected Indicators of Economic Activity". Provides data on U.S. economic indicators including employment, unemployment, personal income,

Consumer Price Index, Producer Price Index, and Gross National Product or other measures of production. Also, provides data on business and economic conditions for the state of Kentucky including employment, unemployment, personal income and the following industries: construction, energy, finance, minerals industries, and retail trade. Most data covers a one quarter period with the most current figures available. Includes data by industry/sector. Contains approximately 2 tables.
Data from federal, private and state sources.
Description based on 1982 imprint covering 1982 data.

S0800
Kentucky. Crop and Livestock Reporting Service.
Kentucky Agricultural Statistics, (years).
Approximately 110 pages.   Annual.   1948-
                                LCCN: 50-63276
Availability: Free from the issuing source.

Provides data on the agriculture industry for the state of Kentucky including production figures and prices for crops, livestock, dairy and poultry. Most data cover a one year period; select trends are included. Includes data by commodity/sector, county and district. Contains approximately 62 tables.
Data from state and U.S.D.A. sources.
Description based on 1983 imprint covering 1982 data.

S0810
Kentucky. Department of Economic Development. Division of Planning and Research.
(year) Kentucky Economic Statistics.
Approximately 125 pages.   Annual.   1952-
                                LCCN: SC84-1126
Availability: $4.00 + $1.00 P/H from the issuing source.

Presents a broad range of social and economic data for the state of Kentucky. Provides data on population, housing, birth, death, employment, unemployment, personal income, Consumer Price Index, Gross State Product or other measures of production, and the following industries: construction, finance, minerals, and retail trade. Most data cover a three year period; select trends and projections are included. Includes data by industry/ sector, city, S.M.S.A, county and Area Development District. Provides select comparisons to U.S. data. Contains approximately 50 tables. Title and issuing source vary.
Data from federal and state sources.
Description based on 1984 imprint covering 1980-1982 data.

S0820
Kentucky. Health Services Bureau.
(year) Annual Vital Statistics Report.
Approximately 190 pages.   Annual.   1959-
                                LCCN: SN85-16101
Availability: $25.00 from the Health and Vital Statistics Office.

Provides data on population, birth, death, marriage and divorce for the state of Kentucky. Most data cover a one year period; select long term trends are included. Includes data

by county and Area Development District. Contains approximately 36 tables. Title and issuing source vary.
Data from state sources.
Description based on 1983 imprint covering 1982 data.

S0830
Kentucky. Office of Manpower Services.
Annual Planning Report, (fy).
Approximately 640 pages in eight volumes.   Annual.   1985-
                         LCCN: 79-640184
Availability: Free from Labor Market Research and Analysis Branch.

Multi-volume set provides data on population, education, employment, unemployment and personal income for the state of Kentucky and its Service Delivery Areas. Most data cover an eight year period with actual figures for two years and six year projections; select trends and additional projections are included. Includes data by industry/sector, county and Service Delivery Area. Provides select comparisons to U.S. data. Contains approximately 350 tables.
Data from federal, private and state sources.
Description based on 1985 imprint covering 1983-1990 data.

S0840
Louisiana State University, Baton Rouge. College of Business Administration. Division of Research.
Louisiana Economic Indicators.
Approximately 10 pages.   Monthly.   1917-
ISSN: 0279-6392   LCCN: SC82-1131
Availability: Free from the issuing source.

Provides data on business and economic conditions for the state of Louisiana including employment, unemployment, personal income and the following industries: construction, finance, minerals, retail trade, and tourism. Most data cover a one year period. Includes data by industry/sector and S.M.S.A. Provides select comparisons to U.S. and foreign data. Contains approximately 14 tables. Incorporates monthly data formerly published in *Louisiana Business Review.*
Data from federal and state sources.
Description based on 1983 imprint covering 1983 data.

S0850
Louisiana State University, Baton Rouge. Department of Agricultural Economics and Agribusiness.
Agricultural Statistics and Prices for Louisiana (years).
Approximately 80 pages.   Annual.   1924-
                         LCCN: 83-620661
Availability: Free from the issuing source.

Provides data on the agriculture industry for the state of Louisiana including production figures and prices for crops, livestock, dairy and poultry. Most data cover a six year period. Includes data by commodity/sector and parish. Contains approximately 75 tables.
Data from state and U.S.D.A. sources.
Description based on 1984 imprint covering 1978-1983 data.

126

S0860
Louisiana State University in New Orleans. Division of Business and Economic Research.
Statistical Abstract of Louisiana.
Approximately 410 pages.   Irregular.   1965-
ISSN: 0081-4695   LCCN: 65-65408
Availability: $8.50 from the issuing source.

Presents a broad range of social and economic data for the state of Louisiana. Provides data on population, housing, birth, death, marriage, divorce, education, employment, personal income, Consumer Price Index, cost of living, and the following industries: agriculture, energy, finance, forest products, manufacturing, minerals, select service industries, transportation, and wholesale and retail trade. Most data cover a ten year period; select long term trends are included. Includes data by industry/sector and parish. Provides select comparisons to U.S. data. Contains approximately 310 tables. Issuing source varies.
Data from federal, private and state sources.
Description based on 1981 imprint covering 1970-1979 data.

S0870
Louisiana. Department of Labor.
Annual Planning Report.
Approximately 90 pages.   Annual.   1969-
ISSN: 0147-4987   LCCN: 77-646508
Availability: Free from Management and Finance Office, Research and Statistics Unit.

Provides data on population, employment, unemployment and personal income for the state of Louisiana. Most data cover a three year period; select trends and projections are included. Includes data by industry/sector, parish and Service Delivery Area. Contains approximately 25 tables. Title varies.
Data from federal and state sources.
Description based on 1984 imprint covering 1982-1984 data.
Also publishes updated data in *Louisiana Labor Market Information* (monthly).

S0880
Louisiana. Governor.
Louisiana Trends.
Approximately 70 pages.   Monograph.   1983-
                                LCCN: 83-633407
Availability: Free from the State Planning Office.

Presents a broad range of social and economic data for the state of Louisiana. Provides data on population, birth, death, marriage, divorce, education, employment, unemployment, personal income and the following industries: agriculture, energy, fishing, minerals, select service industries, tourism, and transportation. Most data cover a four year period; select trends are included. Includes data by industry/sector. Contains approximately 75 tables.
Data from federal, private and state sources.
Description based on 1983 imprint covering 1979-1982 data.

S0890
Louisiana. Office of Public Health Statistics.
Vital Statistics of Louisiana.
Approximately 107 pages.   Annual.   1967-
ISSN: 0362-322X   LCCN: 76-642575
Availability: Free from the issuing source.

Provides data on population, birth, death, marriage and divorce for the state of Louisiana.
Most data cover a one year period. Includes data by place, parish and Health Services
Area. Contains approximately 41 tables. Title varies.
Data from state sources.
Description based on 1984 imprint covering 1980 data.

S0900
Maine. Bureau of Employment Security. Division of Economic Analysis and Research.
Annual Planning Information, Maine Statewide, (py).
Approximately 105 pages.   Annual.   1979-
                                  LCCN: 82-644275
Availability: $3.00 from the issuing source.

Provides data on population, education, employment, unemployment and personal
income for the state of Maine. Most data cover a three year period; select long term
trends are included. Includes data by industry/sector and county. Provides select
comparisons to regional data. Contains approximately 34 tables.
Data from federal and state sources.
Description based on 1984 imprint covering 1980-1983 data.
Also publishes updated data in *Maine Labor Market Digest* (monthly).

S0910
Maine. Department of Agriculture, Food and Rural Resources.
Maine Agricultural Statistics, (year).
Approximately 45 pages.   Annual.   1981-
Availability: Free from the issuing source.

Provides data on the agriculture industry for the state of Maine including production
figures and prices for crops, livestock, dairy and poultry. Most data cover a twelve year
period. Includes data by commodity/sector. Provides select comparisons to U.S. data.
Contains approximately 23 tables.
Data from state and U.S.D.A. sources.
Description based on 1982 imprint covering 1971-1982 data.

S0920
Maine. Department of Human Services. Division of Research and Data.
Maine Vital Statistics, (year).
Approximately 100 pages.   Annual.   1892-
ISSN: 0160-7421   LCCN: 78-642135
Availability: $5.00 from Health Planning and Development Bureau.

Provides data on population, birth, death, marriage and divorce for the state of Maine.
Most data cover a one year period; select long term trends are included. Includes data

by county. Contains approximately 22 tables. Title varies.
Data from state sources.
Description based on 1982 imprint covering 1981 data.

S0930
Maine. State Development Office.
Maine: A Statistical Summary.
Approximately 55 pages.   Irregular.   1984-
Availability: Free from the issuing source.

Presents a broad range of social and economic data for the state of Maine. Provides data
on population, education, employment, unemployment, personal income, Gross State
Product or other measures of production, and the following industries: energy, forest
products, manufacturing, retail trade, and transportation. Most data cover a one year
period; select trends are included. Includes data by industry/sector, city and county.
Contains approximately 45 tables. Title and issuing source vary.
Data from federal and state sources.
Description based on 1984 imprint covering 1981 data.

S0940
Maryland. Crop Reporting Service.
Maryland Agricultural Statistics, (year).
Approximately 55 pages.   Annual.   1962-
                                LCCN: 64-64330
Availability: Free from the issuing source.

Provides data on the agriculture industry for the state of Maryland including production
figures and prices for crops, livestock, dairy and poultry. Most data cover a two year
period; select short term trends are included. Includes data by commodity/sector and
county. Contains approximately 65 tables. Issuing source varies.
Data from state and U.S.D.A. sources.
Description based on 1984 imprint covering 1982-1983 data.

S0950
Maryland. Department of Economic and Community Development.
Maryland Statistical Abstract, (years).
Approximately 270 pages.   Biennial.   1970-
ISSN: 0580-9029   LCCN: 80-644045
Availability: $20.00 from the Public Affairs Division.

Presents a broad range of social and economic data for the state of Maryland. Provides data
on population, birth, death, marriage, divorce, education, employment, unemployment,
personal income, cost of living, Gross State Product or other measures of production,
and the following industries: agriculture, construction, energy, finance, fishing, forest
products, manufacturing, minerals, select service industries, tourism, transportation, and
wholesale and retail trade. Most data cover a one year period; select trends are included.
Includes data by industry/sector and county. Provides select comparisons to U.S. data.
Contains approximately 220 tables. Issuing source varies.
Data from federal and state sources.
Description based on 1983 imprint covering 1980 data.

S0960
Maryland. Department of Employment and Training. Research and Analysis Division.
Maryland Labor Market Dimensions.
Approximately 15 pages.   Monthly.   1955-
Availability: Free from the issuing source.

Provides data on population, employment, unemployment and Consumer Price Index
for the state of Maryland. Most data cover a one month period with the most current
figures available; select short term trends are included. Includes data by industry/sector,
S.M.S.A. and county. Contains approximately 10 tables. Issuing source varies.
Data from federal and state sources.
Description based on 1984 imprint covering 1984 data.

S0970
Maryland. State Department of Health and Mental Hygiene. Center for Health Statistics.
Annual Vital Statistics Report, Maryland, (year).
Approximately 85 pages.   Annual.   1965-
Availability: Free from the issuing source.

Provides data on population, birth, death, marriage and divorce for the state of Maryland.
Most data cover a one year period; select long term trends are included. Includes data
by area and county. Provides select comparisons to U.S. data. Contains approximately
60 tables. Issuing source varies.
Data from federal and state sources.
Description based on 1983 imprint covering 1981 data.

S0980
Massachusetts. Department of Commerce and Development.
Monograph of the Commonwealth of Massachusetts.
Approximately 40 pages.   Irregular.   1976-
Availability: Free from the issuing source.

Presents a broad range of social and economic data for the state of Massachusetts.
Provides data on population, housing, education, employment, unemployment, personal
income, and the following industries: agriculture, construction, energy, finance, manufacturing, select service industries, transportation, and wholesale and retail trade. Most
data cover a two year period; select trends are included. Includes data by industry/sector
and S.M.S.A. Provides select comparisons to U.S. data. Contains approximately 45 tables.
Data from federal and state sources.
Description based on 1984 imprint covering 1982-1983 data.

S0990
Massachusetts. Department of Food and Agriculture.
Massachusetts Agricultural Statistics, (year).
Approximately 35 pages.   Annual.   1972-
ISSN: 0092-9794   LCCN: 74-640739
Availability: Free from the issuing source.

Provides data on the agriculture industry for the state of Massachusetts including
production figures and prices for crops, livestock, dairy and poultry. Most data cover a

twelve year period. Includes data by commodity/sector. Provides select comparisons to U.S. and regional data. Contains approximately 60 tables. Title varies. Bound together with the agency's annual report with the cover title *Massachusetts Agriculture, (year)*. Data from state and U.S.D.A. sources.
Description based on 1984 imprint covering 1973-1984 data.

S1000
Massachusetts. Division of Employment Security. Labor Area Research Department.
Annual Planning Information Report, Fiscal Year (fy), Massachusetts.
Approximately 100 pages.   Annual.   1977-
                                LCCN: 83-647533
Availability: Free from the issuing source.

Provides data on population, employment, unemployment and personal income for the state of Massachusetts. Most data cover a two fiscal year period; select trends and projections are included. Includes data by industry/sector and county. Provides select comparisons to U.S. and regional data. Contains approximately 42 tables.
Data from federal and state sources.
Description based on 1984 imprint covering FY1982-FY1983 data.
Also publishes updated data in *Massachusetts Employment Review* (monthly).

S1010
Massachusetts. Registry of Vital Records and Statistics.
Annual Report: Vital Statistics of Massachusetts, (year).
Approximately 140 pages.   Annual.   1841-
ISSN: 0542-8998   LCCN: 82-643484
Availability: Free from the issuing source.

Provides data on population, birth, death, marriage and divorce for the state of Massachusetts. Most data cover a one year period; select trends are included. Data by city/town, county and Health Services Area. Provides select comparisons to U.S. data. Contains approximately 36 tables. Issuing source varies.
Data from state and federal sources.
Description based on 1983 imprint covering 1981 data.

S1020
Memphis State University. Fogelman College of Business and Economics. Bureau of Business and Economic Research.
Mid-South Business Journal.
Approximately 30 pages.   Quarterly.   1963-
ISSN: 0279-8174   LCCN: 81-642658
Availability: Free from the issuing source.

Quarterly journal on business and economic conditions for the Mid-South region includes recurring statistical feature "Statistical Supplement: The Mid-South Economy". Provides data on employment, unemployment, personal income and the following industries: construction, finance, and retail trade for the five Mid-South region states: Alabama, Arkansas, Louisiana, Mississippi and Tennessee. Most data cover a one year period; select short term trends are included. Includes data by industry/sector and state. Provides

select comparisons to U.S. data. Contains approximately 7 tables/charts. Title varies.
Data from federal and state sources.
Description based on 1984 imprint covering 1984 data.

S1030
Michigan. Agricultural Reporting Service.
Michigan Agricultural Statistics, (year).
Approximately 90 pages.   Annual.   1962-
ISSN: 0277-5824   LCCN: 54-23119
Availability: $3.00 from Crop Reporting Board Publications, U.S.D.A.

Provides data on the agriculture industry for the state of Michigan including production
figures and prices from crops, livestock, dairy and poultry. Most data cover a one year
period. Includes data by commodity/sector and county. Provides select comparisons to
U.S. data. Contains approximately 65 tables.
Data from state and U.S.D.A. sources.
Description based on 1984 imprint covering 1983 data.

S1040
Michigan. Department of Management and Budget.
Economic Report of the Governor, (year).
Approximately 160 pages.   Annual.   1967-
ISSN: 0196-5980   LCCN: SC79-3795
Availability: Free from Revenue and Tax Analysis Office.

Provides data on business and economic conditions for the state of Michigan including
population, employment, unemployment, personal income, Consumer Price Index and
the following industries: agriculture, construction, energy, finance, manufacturing,
minerals, retail trade, and tourism. Most data cover a two year period; select trends
are included. Includes data by industry/sector, S.M.S.A. and county. Provides select
comparisons to U.S. data. Contains approximately 35 tables. Title varies.
Data from federal and state sources.
Description based on 1984 imprint covering 1982-1983 data.

S1050
Michigan. Employment Security Commission.
Annual Planning Information Report, (fy).
Approximately 80 pages.   Annual.   1978-
                               LCCN: 84-641479
Availability: Free from Labor Market Analysis Unit.

Provides data on population, education, employment, unemployment and personal
income for the state of Michigan. Most data cover a one fiscal year period; select
projections and short term trends are included. Includes data by industry/sector. Contains
approximately 25 tables. Title and issuing source varies.
Data from state sources.
Description based on 1984 imprint covering FY1982 data.
Also publishes updated data in *Michigan Labor Review* (monthly).

S1060
Michigan. Vital and Health Statistics Office.
Michigan Health Statistics, (year).
Approximately 375 pages.   Annual.   1970-
ISSN: 0539-7413   LCCN: 74-644861
Availability: $11.00 from the issuing source.

Provides data on birth, death, marriage and divorce for the state of Michigan. Most data cover a one year period; select long term trends are included. Includes data by place. Contains approximately 160 tables.
Data from state sources.
Description based on 1982 imprint covering 1981 data.

S1070
Minnesota. Crop and Livestock Reporting Service.
Minnesota Agricultural Statistics, (year).
Approximately 80 pages.   Annual.   1923-
                            LCCN: AD47-2732
Availability: $4.00 from Minnesota State Documents Center.

Provides data on the agriculture industry for the state of Minnesota including production figures and prices for crops, livestock, dairy and poultry. Most data cover a one year period; select trends are included. Includes data by commodity/sector and county. Provides select comparisons to U.S. data. Contains approximately 30 tables. Title varies.
Data from state and U.S.D.A. sources.
Description based on 1984 imprint covering 1983 data.

S1080
Minnesota. Department of Economic Security. Research and Statistics Services Office.
Minnesota Labor Market Information Summary for (year).
Approximately 105 pages.   Annual.   1976-
                            LCCN: SC84-1556
Availability: Free from the issuing source.

Provides data on population, education, employment, unemployment and personal income for the state of Minnesota. Most data cover a three year period with actual figures for two years and one year projections; select short term trends are included. Includes data by industry/sector, city and region. Contains approximately 25 tables.
Data from federal and state sources.
Description based on 1984 imprint covering 1983-1985 data.
Also publishes updated data in *Review of Labor and Economic Conditions* (quarterly with monthly supplements).

S1090
Minnesota. Health Statistics Center.
Minnesota Health Statistics, (year).
Approximately 170 pages.   Annual.   1951-
ISSN: 0094-5641   LCCN: 74-645678
Availability: Free from the issuing source.

Provides data on population, birth, death, marriage and divorce for the state of Minnesota. Most data cover a one year period; select short term trends are included. Includes data by city and county. Contains approximately 33 tables.
Data from state sources.
Description based on 1984 imprint covering 1982 data.

S1100
Minnesota. State Planning Agency. Development Planning Division.
Minnesota Pocket Databook, (years).
Approximately 400 pages.   Biennial.   1973-
ISSN: 0094-3983   LCCN: 74-645305
Availability: $24.95 from Blue Sky Marketing.

Presents a broad range of social and economic data for the state of Minnesota. Provides data on population, housing, birth, death, marriage, divorce, education, employment, unemployment, personal income and the following industries: agriculture, construction, energy, forest products, minerals, select service industries, transportation, tourism, and wholesale and retail trade. Most data cover an eight year period; select long term trends are included. Includes data by industry/sector, city and region. Contains approximately 200 tables.
Data primarily from state sources.
Description based on 1983 imprint covering 1975-1982 data.

S1110
Mississippi State University. College of Business and Industry. Division of Research.
Mississippi Business Review.
Approximately 20 pages.   Monthly.   1939-
ISSN: 0026-6167   LCCN: 54-40725
Availability: $3.50 per year from the issuing source.

Monthly report on business and economic conditions for the state of Mississippi includes recurring statistical features. Provides data on employment, unemployment, personal income and the following industries: agriculture, construction, energy, finance, and retail trade. Most data cover a one month period with the most current figures available. Includes data by industry/sector, S.M.S.A. and county. Provides select comparisons to regional data. Also, includes an annual feature which provides a summary of data by county. Contains approximately 8 tables.
Data from federal, private and state sources.
Description based on 1984 imprint covering 1984 data.

S1120
Mississippi State University. College of Business and Industry. Division of Research.
Mississippi Employment (years).
Approximately 100 pages.   Annual.   1975-
                               LCCN: 76-620070
Availability: $6.75 from the issuing source.

Provides data on employment for the state of Mississippi. Most data cover a six year period. Includes data by S.M.S.A. and county. Provides select comparisons to U.S. data.

Contains approximately 3 tables.
Data from federal and state sources.
Description based on 1983 imprint covering 1976-1981 data.

S1130
Mississippi State University. College of Business and Industry. Division of Research.
Mississippi Personal Income: Selected Years (years).
Approximately 120 pages.   Annual.   1971-
                                LCCN: 72-619728
Availability: $8.85 from the issuing source.

Provides data on population and personal income for the state of Mississippi. Most data
cover a six year period. Includes data by S.M.S.A and county. Contains approximately
7 tables.
Data from federal and state sources.
Description based on 1983 imprint covering 1976-1981 data.

S1140
Mississippi State University. College of Business and Industry. Division of Research.
Mississippi Statistical Abstract, (year).
Approximately 810 pages.   Annual.   1968-
                                LCCN: 75-629881
Availability: $19.95 + $1.50 P/H from the issuing source.

Presents a broad range of social and economic data for the state of Mississippi.
Provides data on population, birth, death, marriage, divorce, education, employment,
unemployment, personal income and the following industries: agriculture, construction,
energy, finance, forest products, manufacturing, minerals, select service industries,
transportation, and wholesale and retail trade. Most data cover a two year period; select
trends are included. Includes data by industry/sector and county. Provides select
comparisons to regional data. Contains approximately 280 tables. Issuing source varies.
Data from federal and state sources.
Description based on 1983 imprint covering 1981-1982 data.

S1150
Mississippi. Crop and Livestock Reporting Service.
Mississippi Agricultural Statistics, (years).
Approximately 60 pages.   Annual.   1953-
Availability: Free from the issuing source.

Provides data on the agriculture industry for the state of Mississippi including production
figures and prices for crops, livestock, dairy and poultry. Most data cover a two year
period. Includes data by commodity/sector, county and district. Contains approximately
90 tables. Title and issuing source varies.
Data from state and U.S.D.A. sources.
Description based on 1984 imprint covering 1982-1983 data.

S1160
Mississippi. Employment Security Commission.
Annual Planning Information, State of Mississippi, (fy).
Approximately 110 pages.   Annual.   1976-
Availability: Free from Research and Statistics Department.

Provides data on population, employment, unemployment and personal income for the
state of Mississippi. Most data cover a one year period; select trends and projections are
included. Includes data by industry/sector. Contains approximately 40 tables.
Data from federal and state sources.
Description based on 1984 imprint covering 1983 data.

S1170
Mississippi. State Department of Health.
Vita Statistics, Mississippi, (year).
Approximately 140 pages.   Annual.   1961-
                                  LCCN: 46-34256
Availability: Free from Public Health Statistics Office.

Provides data on population, birth, death, marriage and divorce for the state of Mississippi.
Most data cover a one year period; select trends are included. Includes data by place
and county. Contains approximately 50 tables. Title and issuing source vary.
Data from federal and state sources.
Description based 1984 imprint covering 1983 data.

S1180
Missouri. Center for Health Statistics.
Missouri Vital Statistics, (year).
Approximately 115 pages.   Annual.   1972-
ISSN: 0098-1974   LCCN: 75-643234
Availability: Free from the issuing source.

Provides data on birth, death, marriage and divorce for the state of Missouri. Most data
cover a one year period; select trends are included. Includes data by city, county and
Regional Planning Commission. Contains approximately 53 tables. Issuing source varies.
Data from state sources.
Description based on 1984 imprint covering 1983 data.

S1190
Missouri. Crop and Livestock Reporting Service.
Missouri Farm Facts, (year).
Approximately 55 pages.   Annual.   1904-
ISSN: 0544-5507   LCCN: 77-648377
Availability: Free from the issuing source.

Provides data on the agriculture industry for the state of Missouri including production
figures and prices for crops, livestock, dairy and poultry. Most data cover a two year
period; select trends are included. Includes data by commodity/sector and county.
Contains approximately 71 tables. Title and issuing source varies.
Data from state and U.S.D.A. sources.
Description based on 1984 imprint covering 1982-1983 data.

S1200
Missouri. Department of Labor and Industrial Relations.
Report of the Missouri Department of Labor and Industrial Relations.
Approximately 40 pages.   Annual.   1927-
Availability: Free from the issuing source.

Provides data on employment, unemployment and personal income for the state of
Missouri. Most data cover a one year period; select trends are included. Includes data
by industry/sector. Contains approximately 45 tables. Title and issuing source vary.
Data from state sources.
Description based on 1984 imprint covering 1982 data.
Also publishes *Missouri Area Labor Trends* (monthly).

S1210
Missouri. Division of Community and Economic Development.
Missouri's New and Expanding Manufacturers.
Approximately 20 pages.   Annual.   1952-
                            LCCN: 81-640324
Availability: Free from the issuing source.
Provides data on business and economic conditions for the state of Missouri including
employment, Gross State Product or other measures of production, and the manufactur-
ing and minerals industries. Most data cover a one year period; select trends are included.
Includes data by industry/sector, S.M.S.A. and county. Contains approximately 20 tables.
Title and issuing source vary.
Data from private and state sources.
Description based on 1984 imprint covering 1983 data.

S1220
Montana. Census and Economic Information Center.
Economic Conditions in Montana: A Report to the Governor.
Approximately 155 pages.   Biennial.   1974-
ISSN: 0733-0391   LCCN: 82-643518
Availability: Single copies free from the issuing source.

Provides data on business and economic conditions for the state of Montana including
employment, personal income, and the following industries: agriculture, construction,
manufacturing, minerals, tourism, and transportation. Most data cover a six year period;
select long term trends and projections are included. Provides select comparisons to U.S.
data. Includes data by industry/sector. Contains approximately 42 tables/charts. This
series is supplemented by *Montana Statistical Abstract, (year).* Title varies.
Data from federal and state sources.
Description based on 1985 imprint covering 1979-1984 data.

S1230
Montana. Census and Economic Information Center.
Montana Profile.
Approximately 55 pages.   Biennial.   1978-
Availability: $4.00 from the issuing source.

Presents a broad range of social and economic data for the state of Montana. Provides data on population, housing, birth, death, marriage, divorce, education, employment, unemployment, personal income and the following industries: agriculture, finance, and wholesale and retail trade. Most data cover a four year period; select projections are included. Includes data by industry/sector. Contains approximately 87 tables.
Data from federal, private and state sources.
Description based on 1983 imprint covering 1979-1982 data.
Also publishes data by county in *Montana County Profiles* (for each of Montana's fifty-six counties).

S1240
Montana. Census and Economic Information Center.
Montana Statistical Abstract, (year).
Approximately 485 pages.   Monograph.   1985-
Availability: Single copies free, additional copies $12.50 from the issuing source.

Presents a broad range of social and economic data for the state of Montana. Provides data on population, housing, birth, death, marriage, divorce, education, employment, unemployment, personal income and the following industries: agriculture, construction, energy, finance, forest products, minerals, select service industries, and transportation. Most data cover a four year period; select trends are included. Includes data by industry/sector, place, county and reservation. Provides select comparisons to regional data. Contains approximately 280 tables. This series is a supplement to *Economic Conditions in Montana, 1984.*
Data from federal, private and state sources.
Description based on 1985 imprint covering 1980-1983 data.

S1250
Montana. Crop and Livestock Reporting Service.
Montana Agricultural Statistics, (year).
Approximately 80 pages.   Biennial.   1946-
                             LCCN: 48-13383
Availability: Free from the issuing source.

Provides data on the agriculture industry for the state of Montana including production figures and prices for crops, livestock, dairy and poultry. Most data cover a two year period; select trends are included. Includes data by commodity/sector and county. Contains approximately 80 tables.
Data from state and U.S.D.A. sources.
Description based on 1984 imprint covering 1982-1983 data.

S1260
Montana. Department of Health and Environmental Sciences. Bureau of Records and Statistics.
Montana Vital Statistics, (year).
Approximately 75 pages.   Annual.   1954-
ISSN: 0077-1198   LCCN: 73-641210
Availability: Free from the issuing source.

Provides data on population, birth, death, marriage and divorce for the state of Montana. Most data cover a one year period; select trends are included. Includes data by county. Contains approximately 31 tables. Title varies.
Data from state sources.
Description based on 1984 imprint covering 1983 data.

S1270
Montana. Department of Labor and Industry. Research and Analysis Bureau.
Annual Planning Information, (year), State of Montana.
Approximately 140 pages. Annual. 1977-
LCCN: 79-642770
Availability: Free from the issuing source

Provides data on employment, unemployment and personal income for the state of Montana. Most data cover a three year period; trends and projections are included. Includes data by industry/sector, county and Service Delivery Area. Provides select comparisons to U.S. data. Contains approximately 25 tables.
Data from federal and state sources.
Description based on 1984 imprint covering 1981-1983 data.
Also publishes updated data in *Montana Employment and Labor Force* (quarterly).

S1280
Nebraska. Bureau of Vital Statistics.
Statistical Report of the Bureau of Vital Statistics, (year).
Approximately 110 pages. Annual. 1905-
ISSN: 0095-618X LCCN: 75-640799
Availability: Free from the issuing source.

Provides data on population, birth, death, marriage and divorce for the state of Nebraska. Most data cover a one year period; select trends are included. Includes data by city and county. Contains approximately 80 tables.
Data from state sources.
Description based on 1983 imprint covering 1982 data.

S1290
Nebraska. Crop and Livestock Reporting Service.
Nebraska Agricultural Statistics: Annual Report, (years).
Approximately 165 pages. Annual. 1913-
LCCN: 50-44970
Availability: $5.00 from the issuing source.

Provides data on the agriculture industry for the state of Nebraska including production figures and prices for crops, livestock, dairy and poultry. Most data cover a two year period; select trends are included. Includes data by commodity/sector and county. Provides select comparisons to U.S. data. Contains approximately 110 tables. Issuing source varies.
Data from state and U.S.D.A. sources.
Description based on 1983 imprint covering 1981-1982 data.

S1300
Nebraska. Department of Economic Development. Division of Research.
Nebraska Statistical Handbook.
Approximately 305 pages.   Biennial.   1970-
ISSN: 0097-9325   LCCN: 73-622040
Availability: $5.00 from the issuing source.

Presents a broad range of social and economic data for the state of Nebraska. Provides data on population, housing, birth, death, marriage, divorce, education, employment, unemployment, personal income, Gross State Product or other measures of production, and the following industries: agriculture, construction, energy, finance, manufacturing, minerals, select service industries, tourism, transportation, and wholesale and retail trade. Most data cover a twenty-two year period; select projections and long term trends are included. Includes data by industry/sector and county. Contains approximately 180 tables.
Data from federal, private and state sources.
Description based on 1982 imprint covering 1960-1981 data.

S1310
Nebraska. Division of Employment.
Nebraska Work Trends.
Approximately 30 pages.   Monthly.   1971-
Availability: Free from Research and Statistics Section.

Provides data on employment, unemployment, Consumer Price Index, Producer Price Index and personal income for the state of Nebraska. Most data cover a one month period with the most current figures available; select trends are included. Includes data by industry/sector, S.M.S.A. and county. Contains approximately 20 tables. Title varies.
Data from federal and state sources.
Description based on 1982 imprint covering 1982 data.

S1320
Nelson A. Rockefeller Institute of Government.
New York State Statistical Yearbook, (years).
Approximately 575 pages.   Annual.   1967-
ISSN: 0077-9334
Availability: $15.00 + $2.00 P/H from the issuing source.

Presents a broad range of social and economic data for the state of New York. Provides data on population, birth, death, marriage, divorce, education, employment, unemployment, personal income and the following industries: agriculture, energy, finance, forest products, manufacturing, minerals, select service industries, transportation, and wholesale and retail trade. Most data cover a two year period; select trends and projections are included. Includes data by industry/sector, county and S.M.S.A. Contains approximately 450 tables. Issuing source varies.
Data from federal and state sources.
Description based on 1983 imprint covering 1981-1982 data.

S1330
Nevada. Crop and Livestock Reporting Service.
(year) Nevada Agricultural Statistics.
Approximately 40 pages.   Annual.   1968-
ISSN: 0196-0636   LCCN: SC79-4112
Availability: Free from the Agricultural Statistician.

Provides data on the agriculture industry for the state of Nevada including production figures and prices for crops, livestock, dairy and poultry. Most data cover a one year period; select trends and projections are included. Includes data by commodity/sector and county. Provides select comparisons to U.S. data. Contains approximately 55 tables. Data from state and U.S.D.A. sources.
Description based on 1983 imprint covering 1982 data.

S1340
Nevada. Employment Security Research Section.
(year) Nevada Annual Planning Statistics for State, Las Vegas S.M.S.A., Reno S.M.S.A. and Balance of State.
Approximately 45 pages.   Annual.   1979-
                    LCCN: 83-644135
Availability: Free from the issuing source.

Provides data on population, employment and unemployment for the state of Nevada. Most data are one fiscal year projections. Includes data by industry/sector and S.M.S.A. Contains approximately 75 tables. Title varies.
Data from federal and state sources.
Description based on 1982 imprint covering FY1983 data.
Also publishes updated data in *Economic Update, Nevada* (quarterly).

S1350
Nevada. Governor's Office of Planning Coordination.
Nevada Statistical Abstract, (year) Edition.
Approximately 220 pages.   Annual.   1977-
                    LCCN: 78-648222
Availability: $10.00 from the issuing source.

Presents a broad range of social and economic data for the state of Nevada. Provides data on population, housing, birth, death, marriage, divorce, education, employment, unemployment, personal income, and the following industries: agriculture, construction, energy, finance, gaming, manufacturing, minerals, select service industries, tourism, transportation, and wholesale and retail trade. Most data cover a ten year period; select long term trends are included. Includes data by industry/sector. Contains approximately 160 tables.
Data from federal, private and state sources.
Description based on 1981 imprint covering 1970-1980 data.

S1360
Nevada. Office of Community Service.
Nevada Statewide Profile.
Approximately 100 pages.   Monograph.   1983-
Availability: Limited distribution from the issuing source.

Presents a broad range of social and economic data for the state of Nevada. Provides
data on population, housing, education, employment, unemployment, personal income
and the following industries: construction, energy, gaming, and transportation. Most
data cover a two year period; select trends are included. Includes data by industry/sector
and county. Contains approximately 46 tables.
Data from state sources.
Description based on 1983 imprint covering 1981-1982 data.
Also publishes *Nevada County Profiles* (for Nevada's sixteen counties).

S1370
Nevada. Section of Vital Statistics.
Nevada Vital Statistics Report, (years).
Approximately 55 pages.   Annual.   1974-
ISSN: 0741-1367   LCCN: 83-646886
Availability: Free from the issuing source.

Provides data on population, birth, death, marriage and divorce for the state of Nevada.
Most data cover a one year period. Includes data by county. Contains approximately 15
tables. Title varies.
Data from state sources.
Description based on 1984 imprint covering 1982 data.

S1380
Nevada. State Gaming Control Board.
Nevada Gaming Abstract, (year).
Approximately 95 pages.   Annual.   1975-
                               LCCN: 78-641572
Availability: $10.00 from Publications Office.

Provides data on the gaming industry for the state of Nevada including revenues,
expenses, payouts and employment. Most data cover a one fiscal year period. Includes
data by game, device and location. Contains approximately 77 tables. Issuing source
varies.
Data from private and state sources.
Description based on 1982 imprint covering FY1982 data.

S1390
New Hampshire. Bureau of Vital Records and Health Statistics.
Vital Statistics Report, (year).
Approximately 40 pages.   Annual.   1972-
ISSN: 0737-1896   LCCN: 83-641721
Availability: Free from Public Health Services Division.

Provides data on population, birth, death, marriage and divorce for the state of New Hampshire. Most data cover a one year period; select trends are included. Includes data by city and county. Contains approximately 32 tables. Title and issuing source vary.
Data from federal and state sources.
Description based on 1983 imprint covering 1982 data.

S1400
New Hampshire. Department of Employment Security. Economic Analysis and Reports Section.
Annual Planning Information, New Hampshire, (fy).
Approximately 135 pages.   Annual.   1977-
                              LCCN: 78-646549
Availability: Free from the issuing source.

Provides data on population, employment, unemployment and personal income for the state of New Hampshire. Most data are one fiscal year projections; select trends and long term projections are included. Includes data by industry/sector, occupation and county. Contains approximately 66 tables. Title and issuing source vary.
Data from federal and state sources.
Description based on 1983 imprint covering FY1984 data.
Also publishes updated data in *Economic Conditions in New Hampshire* (bimonthly).

S1410
New Jersey Associates.
The New Jersey Economic Almanac, (year).
Approximately 375 pages.   Annual.   1983-
ISSN: 0736-4210   LCCN: 83-641307
Availability: $33.00 from the issuing source.

Presents a broad range of social and economic data for the state of New Jersey. Provides data on population, housing, birth, death, education, employment, unemployment, personal income, and the following industries: agriculture, construction, energy, finance, fishing, forest products, gaming, manufacturing, minerals, select service industries, tourism, transportation, and wholesale and retail trade. Most data cover an eleven year period; select projections and long term trends are included. Includes data by industry/sector and county. Provides select comparisons to U.S. data. Contains approximately 210 tables.
Data from federal and state sources.
Description based on 1983 imprint covering 1971-1981 data.
Also publishes demographic and governmental data by city and county in *New Jersey Municipal Data Book* (annual).

S1420
New Jersey. Crop Reporting Service.
New Jersey Agricultural Statistics, (year).
Approximately 70 pages.   Annual.   1945-
                              LCCN: 58-63411
Availability: Free from the issuing source.

Provides data on the agriculture industry for the state of New Jersey including production figures and prices for crops, livestock, dairy and poultry. Most data cover a six year period. Includes data by commodity/sector and county. Provides select comparisons to U.S. data. Contains approximately 63 tables.
Data from state and U.S.D.A. sources.
Description based on 1983 imprint covering 1977-1982 data.

S1430
New Jersey. Department of Labor. Division of Planning and Research.
Annual Labor Market Review, State of New Jersey.
Approximately 45 pages.   Annual.   1982-
                              LCCN: 84-640867
Availability: Free from the issuing source.

Provides data on population, employment, unemployment and personal income for the state of New Jersey. Most data cover a ten year period; select projections and long term trends are included. Includes data by county. Contains approximately 26 tables.
Data from federal and state sources.
Description based on 1983 imprint covering 1973-1982 data.
Also publishes updated data in *New Jersey Economic Indicators* (monthly).

S1440
New Jersey. Health Data Services.
Birth.
ISSN: 0735-3227   LCCN: 82-646117
Mortality.
ISSN: 0732-6947   LCCN: 82-642930
Marriage.
ISSN: 0732-6939   LCCN: 82-642929
Approximately 125 pages in three volumes.   Annual.   1962-
Availability: Free from the issuing source.

Provides data on birth, death, marriage and divorce for the state of New Jersey. Most data cover a one year period; select trends are included. Includes data by city and county. Contains approximately 40 tables. Title varies.
Data from state sources.
Description based on 1982 imprint covering 1980 data.

S1450
New Jersey. Office of the Governor.
Economic Report of the Governor.
Approximately 40 pages.   Annual.   1982-
                              LCCN: 84-643875
Availability: Free from Office of Economic Policy.

Provides data on business and economic conditions for the state of New Jersey including employment, unemployment, personal income and the construction and retail trade industries. Most data cover a three year period with actual figures for two years and one

year projections. Includes data by industry/sector. Provides select comparisons to U.S. data. Contains approximately 25 tables.
Data from federal and state sources.
Description based on 1984 imprint covering 1983-1985 data.

S1460
New Mexico. Crop and Livestock Reporting Service.
New Mexico Agricultural Statistics, (year).
Approximately 70 pages.   Annual.   1962-
                            LCCN: 63-54681
Availability: Free from the issuing source.

Provides data on the agriculture industry for the state of New Mexico including production figures and prices for crops, livestock, dairy and poultry. Most data cover a one year period; select trends are included. Includes data by commodity/sector and county. Contains approximately 88 tables. Issuing source varies.
Data from state and U.S.D.A. sources.
Description based on 1982 imprint covering 1981 data.

S1470
New Mexico. Economic Development Division.
New Mexico Fact Book.
Approximately 120 pages.   Looseleaf.   1982-
                            LCCN: 83-620901
Availability: $40.00 (includes one year's updates) from the issuing source.

Presents a broad range of social and economic data for the state of New Mexico. Provides data on population, housing, education, employment, personal income and the following industries: agriculture, construction, energy, finance, manufacturing, minerals, retail trade, select service industries, tourism, and transportation. Most data cover a thirteen year period; select projections are included. Includes data by industry/sector, city, S.M.S.A. and county. Provides select comparisons to U.S. data. Contains approximately 65 tables.
Data from federal, private and state sources.
Description based on 1982 imprint covering 1970-1982 data.

S1480
New Mexico. Employment Security Department. Research and Statistics Section.
Job Training Partnership Act: Labor Market Information System.
Approximately 50 pages.   Annual.   1984-
                            LCCN: 78-642503
Availability: Free from the issuing source.

Provides data on population, employment, unemployment and personal income for the state of New Mexico. Most data cover a two year period; select trends and projections are included. Includes data by S.M.S.A. Provides select comparisons to U.S. data. Contains approximately 26 tables. Title varies.
Data from federal and state sources.
Description based on 1983 imprint covering 1983 data.
Also publishes updated data in *New Mexico Labor Market Review* (monthly).

S1490
New Mexico. Health and Environment Department.
Selected Health Statistics, New Mexico, (years).
Approximately 115 pages.   Annual.   1975-
ISSN: 0161-5416   LCCN: 80-640288
Availability: Free from Health Services Division.

Provides data on population, birth, death, marriage and divorce for the state of New Mexico. Most data cover a one year period; select trends are included. Includes data by city and county. Provides select comparisons to U.S. data. Contains approximately 110 tables. Issuing source varies.
Data from federal and state sources.
Description based on 1983 imprint covering 1980-1981 data.

S1500
New York. Bureau of Health Statistics.
Vital Statistics of New York State, (year).
Approximately 175 pages.   Annual.   1879-
ISSN: 0097-9449   LCCN: 75-642675
Availability: Free from Office of Biostatistics.

Provides data on population, birth, death, marriage and divorce for the state of New York. Most data cover a one year period; select long term trends are included. Includes data by city, county and region. Contains approximately 36 tables. Title varies.
Data from federal and state sources.
Description based on 1983 imprint covering 1982 data.

S1510
New York. Department of Commerce. Bureau of Business Research.
Business Statistics, New York State, Annual Summary.
Approximately 20 pages.   Annual.   1946-
ISSN: 0197-3193   LCCN: 84-643028
Availability: Free from the issuing source.

Provides data on business and economic conditions for the state of New York including employment, personal income, Consumer Price Index, Gross State Product or other measures of production, and the construction and finance industries. Most data cover a one year period. Contains approximately 20 tables. Title and issuing source vary.
Data from federal, private and state sources.
Description based on 1983 imprint covering 1983 data.
Also publishes updated data in *Business Statistics, New York State, Quarterly Summary.*

S1520
New York. Department of Labor. Division of Research and Statistics.
Annual Planning Information, New York State, (fy).
Approximately 90 pages.   Annual.   1980-
Availability: Free from the issuing source.

Provides data on population, birth, death, employment, unemployment and personal income for the state of New York. Most data are one fiscal year projections; select trends are included. Includes data by industry/sector, occupation, city, S.M.S.A. and county. Contains approximately 40 tables.

Data from federal and state sources.

Description based on 1983 imprint covering FY1984 data.

Also publishes updated data in *Employment Review, New York State* (monthly).

S1530

New York. State Crop Reporting Service.
New York Agricultural Statistics, (year).
Approximately 75 pages.   Annual.   1968-
ISSN: 0276-8798   LCCN: 79-648711
Availability: Free from the issuing source.

Provides data on the agriculture industry for the state of New York including production figures and prices for crops, livestock, dairy and poultry. Most data cover a ten year period. Includes data by commodity/sector and county. Provides select comparisons to U.S. data. Contains approximately 100 tables. Title varies.

Data from state and U.S.D.A. sources.

Description based on 1983 imprint covering 1973-1982 data.

S1540

North Carolina. Crop and Livestock Reporting Service.
North Carolina Agricultural Statistics, (year).
Approximately 70 pages.   Annual.   1939-
ISSN: 0091-3693   LCCN: SN79-8189
Availability: Free from the Agricultural Statistician.

Provides data on the agriculture industry for the state of North Carolina including production figures and prices for crops, livestock, dairy and poultry. Most data cover a two year period; select trends are included. Includes data by commodity/sector and county. Provides select comparisons to U.S. data. Contains approximately 110 tables. Issuing source varies.

Data from private, state and U.S.D.A. sources.

Description based on 1983 imprint covering 1981-1982 data.

S1550

North Carolina. Labor Market Information Division.
North Carolina Labor Force Estimates, (year), by County, Defined Multi-County Labor Areas, State, Multi-County Planning Regions.
Approximately 275 pages.   Annual.   1966-
ISSN: 0147-0531   LCCN: 77-648711
Availability: Free from the issuing source.

Provides data on employment and unemployment for the state of North Carolina. Most data cover a one year period; select trends are included. Includes data by industry/sector, S.M.S.A, county and Planning Region. Contains approximately 5 tables.

Data from state sources.

Description based on 1983 imprint covering 1982 data.

Also publishes updated data in *Monthly State Labor Summary, North Carolina.*

S1560
North Carolina. Office of State Budget and Management. Research and Planning Services.
North Carolina State Government Statistical Abstract, (year).
Approximately 575 pages.   Irregular.   1971-
Availability: $15.00 from the issuing source.

Presents a broad range of social and economic data for the state of North Carolina. Provides data on population, housing, birth, death, marriage, divorce, education, employment, unemployment, personal income and the following industries: agriculture, energy, finance, fishing, manufacturing, minerals, select service industries, tourism, transportation, and wholesale and retail trade. Most data cover a thirteen year period; select long term trends are included. Includes data by industry/sector, city, S.M.S.A. and county. Provides select comparisons to U.S. data. Contains approximately 400 tables. Issuing source varies.
Data from federal and state sources.
Description based on 1984 imprint covering 1970-1982 data.

S1570
North Carolina. Office of State Budget and Management. Research and Planning Services.
Profile-North Carolina Counties.
Approximately 270 pages.   Irregular.   1968-
                                LCCN: 78-645452
Availability: 1981 imprint out-of-print; update forthcoming (in late 1985) from the issuing source.

Provides data on business and economic conditions for the state of North Carolina including population, education, employment, unemployment, personal income and the following industries: agriculture, retail trade, and transportation. Most data cover a four year period; select long term trends included. Includes data by county and Planning Region. Contains approximately 200 tables. Issuing source varies.
Data from federal and state sources.
Description based on 1981 imprint covering 1975-1979 data.

S1580
North Carolina. State Center for Health Statistics.
North Carolina Vital Statistics, (year).
Approximately 330 pages in two volumes.   Annual.   1914-
                                LCCN: 79-644285
Availability: Free from the issuing source.

Provides data on population, birth, death, marriage and divorce for the state of North Carolina. Volume One provides data on population, birth, death, marriage and divorce; volume Two provides data on causes of death. Most data cover a one year period; select trends are included. Includes data by city and region. Contains approximately 175 tables. Title and issuing source vary.
Data from state sources.
Description based on 1983 imprint covering 1982 data.

S1590
North Dakota. Crop and Livestock Reporting Service.
North Dakota Agricultural Statistics, (year).
Approximately 100 pages.   Annual.   1956-
ISSN: 0737-1624   LCCN: 83-641803
Availability: $4.00 from the issuing source.

Provides data on the agriculture industry for the state of North Dakota including production figures and prices for crops, livestock, dairy and poultry. Most data cover a two year period; select trends are included. Includes data by commodity/sector and county. Contains approximately 115 tables. Title and issuing source vary.
Data from state sources.
Description based on 1983 imprint covering 1981-1982 data.

S1600
North Dakota. State Department of Health.
Vital Statistics Report, (year).
Approximately 120 pages.   Annual.   1923-
Availability: Free from the issuing source.

Provides data on birth, death, marriage and divorce for the state of North Dakota. Most data cover a one year period. Includes data by county. Provides select comparisons to U.S. data. Contains approximately 79 tables.
Data from state sources.
Description based on 1983 imprint covering 1982 data.

S1610
North Dakota. Economic Development Commission.
North Dakota Growth Indicators.
Approximately 80 pages.   Irregular.   1961-
ISSN: 0549-8368   LCCN: 77-645376
Availability: Free from the issuing source.

Provides data on business and economic conditions for the state of North Dakota including population, housing, education, employment, unemployment, personal income, Gross State Product or other measures of production and the following industries: agriculture, construction, manufacturing, minerals, and wholesale and retail trade. Most data cover an eleven year period; select projections and long term trends are included. Includes data by industry/sector, city, S.M.S.A. and county. Contains approximately 90 tables. Issuing source varies.
Data from federal and state sources.
Description based on 1982 imprint covering 1970-1980 data.

S1620
North Dakota. Job Service. Research and Statistics Section.
Annual Planning Report, (fy), North Dakota.
Approximately 105 pages.   Annual.   1976-
                                LCCN: 82-644178
Availability: Free from the issuing source.

Provides data on population, employment, unemployment and personal income for the state of North Dakota. Most data cover a two year period; select trends and projections are included. Includes data by industry/sector, occupation and county. Provides select comparisons to U.S. data. Contains approximately 40 tables.
Data from federal sources.
Description based on 1983 imprint covering 1981-1982 data.
Also publishes updated data in *Prairie Employer Review* (quarterly).

S1630
Norwest Bank Minneapolis.
Economic Indicators.
Approximately 5 pages.   Bimonthly.   1980-
Availability: Free from Economic Department.

Bimonthly report on business and economic conditions for the state of Minnesota includes several recurring statistical features. Provides data on employment, unemployment, personal income, Consumer Price Index and the construction, finance and retail trade industries. Most data cover a one month or one quarter period with the most current figures available; select short term trends are included. Includes data by S.M.S.A. Provides select comparisons to U.S. data. Contains approximately 10 tables. Title and issuing source vary.
Data from federal and private sources.
Description based on 1984 imprint covering 1984 data.

S1640
Ohio. Bureau of Employment Services. Labor Market Information Division.
Employment, Hours and Earnings in Ohio.
Approximately 30 pages.   Monthly.   1968-
Availability: Free from Statistics Distribution Unit.

Provides data on employment, unemployment and personal income for the state of Ohio. Most data cover a one month period with the most current figures available. Includes data by industry/sector and S.M.S.A. Contains approximately 11 tables.
Data from federal and state sources.
Description based on 1984 imprint covering 1984 data.
Also publishes an annual data in *Employment, Hours and Earnings in Ohio* (annual).

S1650
Ohio. Crop Reporting Service.
Ohio Agricultural Statistics, (year).
Approximately 55 pages.   Annual.   1928-
                        LCCN: 58-40536
Availability: Limited distribution from the issuing source.

Provides data on the agriculture industry for the state of Ohio including production figures and prices for crops, livestock, dairy and poultry. Most data cover a two year period; select trends are included. Includes data by commodity/sector and county. Provides select comparisons to U.S. data. Contains approximately 95 tables. Title and issuing source varies.

Data from state and U.S.D.A. sources.
Description based on 1983 imprint covering 1981-1982 data.

S1660
Ohio. Data Users Center.
(year) Ohio County Profiles.
Approximately 400 pages.   Annual.   1980-
Availability: $80.00 from the issuing source.

Presents a broad range of social and economic data for the state of Ohio. Provides data on population, housing, employment, unemployment, personal income and the following industries: agriculture, finance, manufacturing, select service industries, transportation, and wholesale and retail trade. Most data cover a fourteen year period; select projections are included. Includes data by industry/sector and county. Contains approximately 400 tables.
Data from federal and state sources.
Description based on 1984 imprint covering 1970-1983 data.

S1670
Ohio. Data Users Center.
Ohio Economic Indicators Quarterly.
Approximately 10 pages.   Quarterly.   1981-
Availability: $7.50 per year from the issuing source.

Provides data on business and economic conditions for the state of Ohio including employment, unemployment, personal income, Consumer Price Index, composite index of leading economic indicators and the following industries: construction, energy, finance, and retail trade. Most data cover a one quarter period with the most current figures available; select trends are included. Includes data by industry/sector and S.M.S.A. Contains approximately 10 tables.
Data from federal sources.
Description based on 1984 imprint covering 1984 data.

S1680
Ohio. Department of Health.
Report of Vital Statistics for Ohio, (year).
Approximately 170 pages.   Annual.   1935-
ISSN: 0147-5614   LCCN: 77-646834
Availability: Free from Data Services Division.

Provides data on population, birth, death, marriage and divorce for the state of Ohio. Most data cover a one year period; select trends are included. Includes data by county. Contains approximately 63 tables.
Data from state sources.
Description based on 1984 imprint covering 1982 data.

S1690
Oklahoma State University. Office of Business and Economic Research.
(year) Oklahoma Economic Outlook.
Approximately 30 pages.   Annual.   1980-
ISSN: 0734-404X   LCCN: 82-645098
Availability: Free from the issuing source.

Provides data on business and economic conditions for the state of Oklahoma including
education, employment, personal income, Gross State Product or other measures of
production, and the energy and finance industries. Most data are one year projections;
select short term trends are included. Includes data by industry/sector. Contains approximately 20 tables.
Data from federal, private and state sources.
Description based on 1985 imprint covering 1985 projections.

S1700
Oklahoma. Crop and Livestock Reporting Service.
Oklahoma Agricultural Statistics, (year).
Approximately 110 pages.   Annual.   1971-
                                  LCCN: 80-643362
Availability: $5.00 from the issuing source.

Provides data on the agriculture industry for the state of Oklahoma including production
figures and prices for crops, livestock, dairy and poultry. Most data cover a one year
period; select trends are included. Includes data by commodity/sector and county.
Provides select comparisons to U.S. data. Contains approximately 80 tables. Title and
issuing source vary.
Data from private and state sources.
Description based on 1983 imprint covering 1982 data.

S1710
Oklahoma. Employment Security Commission. Research and Planning Division.
Handbook of Labor Force Data for Selected Areas of Oklahoma.
Approximately 200 pages in two volumes.   Annual.   1950-
                                  LCCN: A60-9860
Availability: Free from the issuing source.

Provides data on employment, unemployment and personal income for the state of
Oklahoma. Volume One provides data on employment and unemployment; Volume
Two provides data on personal income. Most data covers a thirty-four year period.
Includes data by industry/sector and S.M.S.A. Contains approximately 115 tables. Issuing
source varies.
Data from federal and state sources.
Description based on 1984 imprint covering 1950-1983 data.

S1720
Oklahoma. Public Health Statistics Section.
Oklahoma Health Statistics, (year).
Approximately 250 pages.   Annual.   1972-
ISSN: 0098-5651   LCCN: 75-643676
Availability: Free from Data Management Division.

Provides data on population, birth, death, marriage and divorce for the state of Oklahoma.
Most data cover a one year period; select trends are included. Includes data by county.
Contains approximately 25 tables.
Data from state sources.
Description based on 1982 imprint covering 1981 data.

S1730
Oregon. Crop and Livestock Reporting Service.
Oregon Agricultural Statistics.
Approximately 60 pages.   Annual.   1983-
ISSN: 0748-2647   LCCN: 84-645404
Availability: Free from Oregon Department of Agriculture.

Provides data on the agriculture industry for the state of Oregon including production
figures and prices for crops, livestock, dairy and poultry. Most data cover a one year
period; select trends are included. Includes data by commodity/sector and county.
Provides select comparisons to U.S. data. Contains approximately 75 tables.
Data from private, state and U.S.D.A. sources.
Description based on 1983 imprint covering 1981 data.

S1740
Oregon. Department of Economic Development. Research and Information Division.
Oregon: A Statistical Profile, (year).
Approximately 80 pages.   Biennial.   1976-
                              LCCN: 79-623551
Availability: $5.00 from the issuing source.

Presents a broad range of social and economic data for the state of Oregon. Provides
data on population, employment, unemployment, personal income, Gross State Product
or other measures of production, and the following industries: agriculture, forest
products, and tourism. Most data cover a one year period; select trends are included.
Includes data by industry/sector, S.M.S.A. and county. Contains approximately 30 tables.
Data from federal and state sources.
Description based on 1982 imprint covering 1980 data.

S1750
Oregon. Department of Economic Development. Research and Information Division.
Oregon County Economic Indicators.
Approximately 20 pages.   Annual.   1979-
                              LCCN: 79-64419
Availability: $2.50 from the issuing source.

Provides data on business and economic conditions for the state of Oregon including population, employment, unemployment, personal income and the construction and finance industries. Most data cover an eight year period. Includes data by S.M.S.A. and county. Contains approximately 20 tables. Issuing source varies.
Data from federal sources.
Description based on 1983 imprint covering 1975-1982 data.

S1760
Oregon. Employment Division.
Oregon Labor Trends.
Approximately 10 pages.   Monthly.   1979-
                               LCCN: 82-21132
Availability: Free from Research and Statistics-LMI.

Monthly report on employment conditions for the state of Oregon includes recurring statistical feature. Provides data on employment, unemployment, personal income and Consumer Price Index. Most data cover a one month period with the most current figures available; select short term trends are included. Includes data by industry/sector and S.M.S.A. Contains approximately 8 tables.
Data from federal and state sources.
Description based on 1984 imprint covering 1984 data.

S1770
Oregon. Health Division.
Oregon Public Health Statistics Report for Calendar Year (year).
Approximately 150 pages.   Annual.   1971-
                               LCCN: 73-640513
Availability: Free from Center for Health Statistics.

Provides data on population, birth, death, marriage and divorce for the state of Oregon. Most data cover a one year period; select trends are included. Includes data by county. Contains approximately 68 tables.
Data from state sources.
Description based on 1981 imprint covering 1980 data.

S1780
Pennsylvania State University. College of Business Administration. Center for Research.
Pennsylvania Business Survey.
Approximately 4 pages.   Monthly.   1938-
ISSN: 0031-4382   LCCN: A53-9621
Availability: $5.00 per year from issuing source.

Provides data on business and economic conditions for the state of Pennsylvania including employment, personal income, Consumer Price Index, and Gross State Product or other measures of production. Most data cover a one month period with the most current figures available. Contains approximately 15 tables. Title and issuing source vary.
Data from federal and state sources.
Description based on 1984 imprint covering 1984 data.

S1790
Pennsylvania. Crop Reporting Service.
(year) Crop and Livestock Annual Summary, Pennsylvania.
Approximately 70 pages.   Annual.   1914-
ISSN: 0079-046X   LCCN: A55-9126
Availability: $5.00 from Crop Reporting Board Publications, U.S.D.A.

Provides data on the agriculture industry for the state of Pennsylvania including
production figures and prices for crops, livestock, dairy and poultry. Most data cover a
one year period; select trends are included. Includes data by commodity/sector and
county. Contains approximately 90 tables.
Data from state and U.S.D.A. sources.
Description based on 1983 imprint covering 1982 data.

S1800
Pennsylvania. Department of Commerce. Bureau of Statistics, Planning and Research.
(year) Pennsylvania Statistical Abstract.
Approximately 250 pages.   Annual.   1958-
ISSN: 0476-1103   LCCN: A59-9073
Availability: $11.00 from State Book Store.

Presents a broad range of social and economic data for the state of Pennsylvania. Provides
data on population, housing, birth, death, marriage, divorce, education, employment,
unemployment, personal income, Consumer Price Index, Gross State Product or
other measures of production, cost of living and the following industries: agriculture,
construction, energy, finance, minerals, retail trade, and transportation. Most data cover
a thirteen year period; select trends and projections are included. Includes data by
industry/sector, S.M.S.A. and county. Contains approximately 225 tables.
Data from federal and state sources.
Description based on 1983 imprint covering 1970-1982 data.

S1810
Pennsylvania. Health Data Center.
Pennsylvania Vital Statistics, Annual Report, (year).
Approximately 160 pages.   Annual.   1951-
                             LCCN: 81-645515
Availability: Free from the issuing source.

Provides data on population, birth, death, marriage and divorce for the state of Penn-
sylvania. Most data cover a one year period; select trends are included. Includes data by
S.M.S.A. and county. Contains approximately 70 tables. Title and issuing source vary.
Data from state sources.
Description based on 1984 imprint covering 1982 data.

S1820
Pennsylvania. Office of Employment Security.
Annual Planning Information Report, (fy).
Approximately 110 pages.   Annual.   1977-
                             LCCN: 82-644175
Availability: Free from Research and Statistics Section.

Provides data on population, employment, unemployment and personal income for the state of Pennsylvania. Most data cover a one year period; select trends and projections are included. Includes data by industry/sector, occupation and county. Provides select comparisons to U.S. data. Contains approximately 40 tables. Title varies.
Data from federal and state sources.
Description based on 1983 imprint covering 1982 data.
Also publishes updated data in *Pennsylvania Employment and Earnings* (quarterly with monthly supplements).

S1830
Presideo Press.
California Almanac (years).
Approximately 600 pages.   Annual.   1984-
ISSN: 0748-4402   LCCN: 84-645577
Availability: $12.95 from the issuing source.

Presents a broad range of social and economic data for the state of California. Provides data on population, housing, birth, death, marriage, divorce, education, employment, unemployment, personal income, Consumer Price Index and the following industries: agriculture, construction, energy, finance, fishing, forest products, manufacturing, minerals, select service industries, transportation, and wholesale and retail trade. Most data cover a two year period; select trends and projections are included. Includes data by industry/sector and county. Contains approximately 400 tables.
Data from federal and state sources.
Description based on 1984 imprint covering 1982-1983 data.

S1840
Providence Journal Co.
(year) Providence Journal-Bulletin Almanac.
Approximately 300 pages.   Annual.   1887-
                                   LCCN: 51-24546
Availability: $3.25 from the issuing source.

General interest almanac provides data on social and economic conditions for the state of Rhode Island including population, housing, education, employment, unemployment, personal income, Consumer Price Index, and the finance and manufacturing industries. Most data cover a thirteen year period; select long term trends are included. Includes data by industry/sector and county. Provides select comparisons to U.S. data. Contains approximately 50 tables. Data from federal and state sources.
Description based on 1984 imprint covering 1970-1982 data.

S1850
Rhode Island. Department of Employment Security.
Annual Planning Information for State of Rhode Island and Providence/Warwick/ Pawtucket Labor Area.
Approximately 55 pages.   Annual.   1980-
Availability: Free from Labor Market Information Section.

Provides data on population, employment and unemployment for the state of Rhode Island. Most data cover a two year period; select trends and short term projections are included. Includes data by industry/sector, occupation and Labor Area. Contains approximately 15 tables.
Data from federal and state sources.
Description based on 1983 imprint covering 1981-1982 data.
Also publishes updated data in *Rhode Island Employment Bulletin* (monthly).

S1860
Rhode Island. Division of Vital Statistics.
Vital Statistics, (year), Rhode Island.
Approximately 135 pages.   Annual.   1952-
ISSN: 0091-3073   LCCN: 74-643258
Availability: Free from the issuing source.

Provides data on population, birth, death, marriage and divorce for the state of Rhode Island. Most data cover a one year period. Provides select comparisons to U.S. data. Contains approximately 44 tables.
Data from state sources.
Description based on 1982 imprint covering 1981 data.

S1870
Rhode Island. Economic Research Division.
Rhode Island Basic Economic Statistics, (years).
Approximately 170 pages.   Irregular.   1965-
ISSN: 0361-0632   LCCN: 76-643119
Availability: Free from the issuing source.

Presents a broad range of social and economic data for the state of Rhode Island. Provides data on population, housing, birth, death, education, employment, unemployment, personal income and the following industries: agriculture, construction, energy, finance, manufacturing, minerals, retail trade, select service industries, and transportation. Most data cover a twelve year period; select long term trends are included. Includes data by industry/sector and county. Contains approximately 88 tables. Title varies.
Data from federal and state sources.
Description based on 1982 imprint covering 1970-1981 data.

S1880
South Carolina. Crop and Livestock Reporting Service.
South Carolina Crop Statistics, (years).
Approximately 50 pages.   Annual.   1961-
                          LCCN: 81-640880
Availability: Free from the issuing source.

Provides data on the agriculture industry for the state of South Carolina including production figures and prices for crops. Most data cover a two year period; select trends are included. Includes data by commodity/sector and county. Provides select comparisons to U.S. data. Contains approximately 35 tables.

Data from state and U.S.D.A. sources.
Description based on 1983 imprint covering 1981-1982 data.

S1890
South Carolina. Crop and Livestock Reporting Service.
South Carolina Livestock and Poultry Statistics, Inventory Numbers (years).
Approximately 45 pages.   Annual.   1970-
                              LCCN: 81-640886
Availability: Free from the issuing source.

Provides data on the agriculture industry for the state of South Carolina including
production figures and prices for livestock, dairy and poultry. Most data cover a two
year period; select trends are included. Includes data by commodity/sector and county.
Provides select comparisons to U.S. data. Contains approximately 42 tables. Issuing
source varies.
Data from state and U.S.D.A. sources.
Description based on 1983 imprint covering 1981-1982 data.

S1900
South Carolina. Division of Biostatistics.
South Carolina Vital and Morbidity Statistics (year).
Approximately 280 pages in two volumes.   Annual.   1972-
ISSN: 0094-6338   LCCN: 78-645478
Availability: Limited distribution from Vital Records and Public Health Statistics Office.

Provides data on population, birth, death, marriage and divorce for the state of South
Carolina. Volume One provides data on population, birth, death, marriage and divorce;
Volume Two provides data on death by cause. Most data cover a one year period; select
trends are included. Includes data by county. Contains approximately 75 tables. Title
and issuing source vary.
Data from state sources.
Description based on 1983 imprints; Volume One covers 1981 data; Volume Two covers
1982 data.

S1910
South Carolina. Employment Security Commission. Research and Analysis Section.
Annual Planning Information for (year), South Carolina.
Approximately 155 pages.   Annual.   1980-
                              LCCN: 81-645981
Availability: Free from the issuing source.

Provides data on population, employment, unemployment and personal income for the
state of South Carolina. Most data cover a two year period; select trends and projections
are included. Includes data by S.M.S.A. and county. Contains approximately 80 tables.
Issuing source varies.
Data from federal and state sources.
Description based on 1983 imprint covering 1981-1982 data.
Also publishes updated data in *Employment Trends* (monthly).

S1920

South Carolina. State Budget and Control Board. Division of Research and Statistical Services.
Economic Report, the State of South Carolina, (year).
Approximately 180 pages.   Annual.   1974-
ISSN: 0145-3637   LCCN: 76-649684
Availability: $10.50 from the issuing source.

Provides data on business and economic conditions for the state of South Carolina including employment, personal income and the following industries: agriculture, finance, forest products, manufacturing, tourism, and transportation. Most data cover a two year period; select trends and projections are included. Includes data by industry/sector. Provides select comparisons to U.S. data. Contains approximately 85 tables.
Data from federal, private and state sources.
Description based on 1982 imprint covering 1981-1982 data.

S1930

South Carolina. State Budget and Control Board. Division of Research and Statistical Services.
South Carolina Statistical Abstract, (year).
Approximately 360 pages.   Annual.   1972-
ISSN: 0739-9308   LCCN: 72-611159
Availability: $12.00 from the issuing source.

Presents a broad range of social and economic data for the state of South Carolina. Provides data on population, housing, birth, death, marriage, divorce, education, employment, unemployment, personal income and the following industries: agriculture, construction, energy, finance, fishing, forest products, minerals, select service industries, tourism, and transportation. Most data cover a twenty-three year period; select long term trends are included. Includes data by industry/sector, S.M.S.A. and county. Provides select comparisons to U.S. data. Contains approximately 235 tables.
Data from federal and state sources.
Description based on 1984 imprint covering 1960-1982 data.

S1940

South Dakota. Crop and Livestock Reporting Service.
South Dakota Agriculture, (years).
Approximately 46 pages.   Annual.   1919-
Availability: Free from the issuing source.

Provides data on the agriculture industry for the state of South Dakota including production figures and prices for crops, livestock, dairy and poultry. Most data cover a one year period; select trends are included. Includes data by commodity/sector and county. Provides select comparisons to U.S. data. Contains approximately 70 tables. Issuing source varies.
Data from state and U.S.D.A. sources.
Description based on 1984 imprint covering 1983 data.

S1950
South Dakota. Department of Labor. Research and Statistics.
South Dakota Labor Market Bulletin.
Approximately 10 pages.   Monthly.   1975-
ISSN: 0275-0627   LCCN: SC79-4394
Availability: Free from Administrative Services Office.

Provides data on population, employment and unemployment, personal income and Consumer Price Index for the state of South Dakota. Most data cover a one month period. Includes data by industry/sector, S.M.S.A. and county. Contains approximately 6 tables.
Data from state sources.
Description based on 1984 imprint covering 1984 data.

S1960
South Dakota. State Planning Bureau.
South Dakota Facts.
Approximately 380 pages.   Monograph.   1976.
                                    LCCN: 77-621024
Availability: $9.36 from the issuing source.

Presents a broad range of social and economic data for the state of South Dakota. Provides data on population, housing, birth, death, education, employment, unemployment, personal income, Gross State Product or other measures of production, and the following industries: agriculture, energy, finance, minerals, and select service industries. Most data cover a seven year period; select trends are included. Includes data by industry/sector and county. Provides select comparisons to U.S. data. Contains approximately 190 tables.
Data from federal and state sources.
Description based on 1976 imprint covering 1970-1976 data.

S1970
South Dakota. Vital Records Program.
South Dakota Vital Statistics, (year).
Approximately 50 pages.   Annual.   1963-
ISSN: 0732-0442   LCCN: 82-641834
Availability: Free from the issuing source.

Provides data on population, birth, death, marriage and divorce for the state of South Dakota. Most data cover a one year period; select trends are included. Includes data by county. Contains approximately 35 tables. Title and issuing source vary.
Data from state sources.
Description based on 1983 imprint based on 1982 data.

S1980
Tax Foundation of Hawaii.
Government in Hawaii: A Handbook of Financial Statistics.
Approximately 70 pages.   Annual.   1953-
ISSN: 0072-517X   LCCN: 56-23093
Availability: $2.00 from the issuing source.

Provides data on business and economic conditions for the state of Hawaii including population, housing, education, employment, unemployment, personal income, Consumer Price Index and the following industries: agriculture, construction, finance, and tourism. Most data cover a ten year period. Includes data by industry/sector and county. Provides select comparisons to U.S. data. Contains approximately 11 tables.
Data from federal and state sources.
Description based on 1983 imprint covering 1971-1982 data.

S1990
Tayloe Murphy Institute.
Consumer Price Indicators for Virginia Metropolitan Areas, (year).
Approximately 60 pages.   Annual.   1975-
                                    LCCN: 81-641176
Availability: $5.00 from the issuing source.

Provides data on Consumer Price Index and cost of living for the state of Virginia including Relative Price Index and Relative Standard of Living Index. Most data cover an eight year period. Includes data by S.M.S.A. Contains approximately 30 tables. Title varies.
Data from federal, private and state sources.
Description based on 1983 imprint covering 1975-1982 data.

S2000
Tayloe Murphy Institute.
Distribution of Virginia Adjusted Gross Income by Income Class, (year).
Approximately 30 pages.   Annual.   1972-
ISSN: 0148-6772   LCCN: 77-641301
Availability: Free from the issuing source.

Provides data on personal income for the state of Virginia. Most data cover a one year period. Includes data by S.M.S.A. and county. Contains approximately 6 tables.
Data from federal and state sources.
Description based on 1983 imprint covering 1982 data.

S2010
Tayloe Murphy Institute.
Retail Sales in Virginia, (year).
Approximately 40 pages.   Annual.   1972-
ISSN: 0735-9373   LCCN: 82-646888
Availability: $5.20 from the issuing source.

Provides data on the retail trade industry for the state of Virginia. Most data cover a one year period. Includes data by S.M.S.A. and Planning District. Provides select comparisons to U.S. data. Contains approximately 40 tables. Title varies.
Data from federal, private and state sources.
Description based on 1984 imprint covering 1983 data.

S2020
Tayloe Murphy Institute.
Virginia Annual Gross State Product, (years).
Approximately 10 pages.   Annual.   1958-
Availability: Free from the issuing source.

Provides data on Gross State Product or other measures of production for the state of
Virginia. Most data cover a twenty-five year period. Includes data by industry/sector.
Contains approximately 8 tables. Title varies.
Data from federal sources.
Description based on 1983 imprint covering 1958-1982 data.

S2030
Tennessee. Crop Reporting Service.
Tennessee Agricultural Statistics: (year) Annual Bulletin.
Approximately 110 pages.   Annual.   1963-
ISSN: 0497-2317   LCCN: 82-644938
Availability: Free from the issuing source.

Provides data on the agriculture industry for the state of Tennessee including production
figures and prices for crops, livestock, dairy and poultry. Most data cover a six year
period; select long term trends are included. Includes data by commodity/sector, county
and district. Provides select comparisons to U.S. data. Contains approximately 65 tables.
Title and issuing source vary.
Data from state and U.S.D.A. sources.
Description based on 1984 imprint covering 1978-1983 data.

S2040
Tennessee. Department of Employment Security. Research and Statistics Division.
Annual Planning Information (fy), Tennessee and Balance of State.
Approximately 375 pages.   Annual.   1982-
ISSN: 0749-7830   LCCN: SC84-1577
Availability: Free from the issuing source.

Provides data on population, education, employment, unemployment and personal
income for the state of Tennessee. Most data cover a one year period; select trends and
projections are included. Includes data by industry/sector and Service Delivery Area.
Contains approximately 240 tables. Title and issuing source vary.
Data from federal and state sources.
Description based on 1984 imprint covering 1984 data.
Also publishes updated data in *Labor Market Report* (monthly).

S2050
Tennessee. Department of Health and Environment.
Annual Bulletin of Vital Statistics, (year).
Approximately 80 pages.   Annual.   1917-
ISSN: 0363-3020   LCCN: 34-6645
Availability: Free from the State Center for Health Statistics.

Provides data on population, birth, death, marriage and divorce for the state of Tennessee. Most data cover a one year period; select trends are included. Includes data by city and county. Contains approximately 40 tables.

Data from state sources.

Description based on 1982 imprint covering 1981 data.

S2060
Texas. Crop and Livestock Reporting Service.
Bulletin: (year) Texas County Statistics.
Approximately 275 pages.   Annual.   1968-
                                 LCCN: 72-622638
Availability: Free from the Agricultural Statistician.

Provides data on the agriculture industry for the state of Texas including production figures and prices for crops, livestock, dairy and poultry. Most data cover a two year period. Includes data by commodity/sector, county and district. Contains approximately 250 tables. Title varies.

Data from state and U.S.D.A. sources.

Description based on 1984 imprint covering 1982-1983 data.

Also publishes the following detailed annual statistical titles as part of the Bulletin series: *Fruits and Pecans; Livestock, Dairy and Poultry; Field Crops (including Cotton); Vegetables; Cash Receipts and Prices Received and Paid; Small Grains; Yield and Price and Texas Citrus Tree Inventory.*

S2070
Texas. Department of Health.
Texas Vital Statistics, (year).
Approximately 100 pages.   Annual.   1956-
ISSN: 0495-257X   LCCN: 76-641131
Availability: Free from Vital Statistics Bureau, Statistical Services Division.

Provides data on birth, death, marriage and divorce for the state of Texas. Most data cover a one year period; select trends are included. Includes data by county. Contains approximately 30 tables. Issuing source varies.

Data from state sources.

Description based on 1984 imprint covering 1983 data.

S2080
Texas. Employment Commission.
Texas Annual Planning Information.
Approximately 60 pages.   Annual.   1978-
                                 LCCN: 78-642138
Availability: Free from Economic Research and Analysis Department.

Provides data on population, birth, death, employment, and unemployment for the state of Texas. Most data cover a six year period with actual figures for five years and one year projections; select trends are included. Includes data by industry/sector and Service Delivery Area. Contains approximately 33 tables. Title and issuing source vary.

Data from federal and state sources.

Description based on 1984 imprint covering 1980-1985 data.
Also publishes updated data in *Texas Labor Market Reviews* (monthly).

S2090
Transrep Bibliographies.
Statistical Abstract of Colorado, (years).
Approximately 515 pages.   Monograph.   1977.
                                LCCN: 77-641344
Availability: $15.75 from the issuing source.

Presents a broad range of social and economic data for the state of Colorado. Provides
data on population, housing, birth, death, education, employment, unemployment,
personal income and the following industries: agriculture, construction, finance, energy,
forest products, manufacturing, minerals, select service industries, transportation, and
wholesale and retail trade. Most data cover a seven year period; select long term
trends are included. Includes data by industry/sector, S.M.S.A. and county. Contains
approximately 437 tables.
Data from federal and state sources.
Description based on 1977 imprint covering 1970-1976 data.

S2100
University of Alabama. Center for Business and Economic Research.
Economic Abstract of Alabama, (year).
Approximately 430 pages.   Irregular.   1962-
Availability: $8.00 to libraries and government agencies, $10.00 to others, + $2.00 P/H
from the issuing source.

Presents a broad range of social and economic data for the state of Alabama. Provides
data on population, housing, birth, death, marriage, divorce, education, employment,
unemployment, personal income, Gross State Product or other measures of production,
Consumer Price Index and the following industries: agriculture, construction, energy,
finance, manufacturing, select service industries, transportation, and wholesale and retail
trade. Most data cover a six year period; select projections and long term trends are
included. Includes data by industry/sector and county. Contains approximately 150
tables. Issuing source varies.
Data from federal and state sources.
Description based on 1984 imprint covering 1977-1982 data.

S2110
University of Arizona. Division of Economic and Business Research.
Arizona Economic Indicators.
Approximately 50 pages.   Semiannual.   1984-
                                LCCN: SN84-12010
Availability: $9.00 per year from the issuing source.

Provides data on business and economic conditions for the state of Arizona including
population, employment, unemployment, personal income and the following industries:
agriculture, construction, energy, finance, manufacturing, minerals, retail trade, select
service industries, tourism, and transportation. Most data cover an eight year period.
Includes data by industry/sector, S.M.S.A. and county. Contains approximately 44 tables.

Data from federal, private and state sources.
Description based on 1984 imprint covering 1976-1983 data.
Also publishes updated data in *Arizona's Economy* (monthly).

S2120
University of Arizona. Division of Economic and Business Research.
Statistical Abstract of Arizona.
Approximately 640 pages.   Irregular.   1976-
                                LCCN: SC83-6143
Availability: $9.95 +$1.00 P/H from Northland Press.

Presents a broad range of social and economic data for the state of Arizona. Provides data on population, birth, death, marriage, divorce, education, employment, unemployment, personal income and the following industries: agriculture, construction, energy, finance, manufacturing, minerals, select service industries, tourism, transportation, wholesale and retail trade. Most data cover a six year period; select long term trends are included. Includes data by industry/sector and county. Provides select comparisons to U.S. data. Contains approximately 520 tables. Issuing source varies.
Data from federal and state sources.
Description based on 1979 imprint covering 1973-1978 data.

S2130
University of Arkansas. Bureau of Business and Economic Research.
Arkansas Business and Economic Review.
Approximately 50 pages.   Quarterly.   1933-
ISSN: 0004-1742   LCCN: SF78-510
Availability: Free from the issuing source.

Quarterly journal on business and economic conditions for the state of Arkansas includes recurring statistical feature. Provides data on employment, unemployment, personal income, Consumer Price Index and the following industries: construction, finance, manufacturing, minerals, transportation, and wholesale and retail trade. Most data cover a seventeen year period. Includes data by industry/sector. Contains approximately 18 tables. Title varies.
Data from federal, private and state sources.
Description based on 1983 imprint covering 1967-1983 data.

S2140
University of Arkansas at Little Rock. Industrial Research and Extension Center.
State and County Economic Data for Arkansas.
Approximately 20 pages.   Annual.   1977-
Availability: $4.00 from the issuing source.

Presents a broad range of social and economic data for the state of Arkansas. Provides data on population, education, employment, unemployment, personal income and the following industries: finance, manufacturing, select service industries, and wholesale and retail trade. Most data cover a one year period; select trends are included. Includes data industry/sector and by county. Contains approximately 18 tables.
Data from federal, private and state sources.
Description based on 1983 imprint covering 1982 data.

S2150
University of California, Los Angeles. Business Forecasting Project.
Business Forecast for the Nation and California in (year).
Approximately 100 pages.   Annual.   1960-
Availability: $35.00 from the issuing source.

Provides data on business and economic conditions for the United States and the state of California including Gross National Product or other measures of production, imports and exports, employment, personal income, Consumer Price Index, Producer Price Index, and the construction and energy industries. Most data cover a one year period; select projections are included. Contains approximately 60 tables/charts.
Data from federal, private and state sources.
Description based on 1983 imprint covering 1982 data.

S2160
University of Colorado. Business Research Division.
Colorado Business Review.
Approximately 10 pages.   Monthly.   1928-
ISSN: 0010-1524   LCCN: 59-33322
Availability: Free to state residents, $5.00 per year to others.

Monthly journal on business and economic conditions for the state of Colorado includes recurring statistical feature. Provides data on employment, unemployment, personal income and the following industries: construction, energy, finance, and tourism. Most data cover a one month period with most current figures available. Includes data by industry/sector and city. Contains approximately 2 tables. Title varies.
Data from federal, private and state sources.
Description based on 1983 imprint covering 1983 data.

S2170
University of Delaware. Agricultural Experimental Station. Department of Agricultural Economics.
Delaware Farm Income.
Approximately 15 pages.   Annual.   1972-
Availability: Free from the issuing source.

Provides data on the agriculture industry for the state of Delaware including production figures and prices for crops, livestock, dairy and poultry. Most data cover a one year period; select short term trends are included. Includes data by commodity/sector and county. Contains approximately 15 tables.
Data from state and U.S.D.A. sources.
Description based on 1984 imprint covering 1982 data.

S2180
University of Florida. Bureau of Business and Economic Research.
Business and Economic Dimensions.
Approximately 30 pages.   Quarterly.   1965-
ISSN: 0007-6457   LCCN: A65-7913
Availability: $15.00 per year from the issuing source.

Quarterly journal on business and economic conditions for the state of Florida includes annual statistical feature in first quarter issue. Provides data on population, employment, unemployment, personal income and the following industries: construction, finance, manufacturing, retail trade, and tourism. Most data cover a two year period; projections and long term trends are included. Includes data by industry/sector and county. Contains approximately 10 tables.

Data from federal, private and state sources.

Description based on 1983 imprint covering 1981-1982 data.

S2190

University of Florida. Bureau of Economic and Business Research.
(year) Florida Statistical Abstract.
Approximately 700 pages.   Annual.   1967-
ISSN: 0071-6022   LCCN: A67-7393
Availability: $25.00 for hardback, $17.00 for paperback from University Presses of Florida.

Presents a broad range of social and economic data for the state of Florida. Provides data on population, housing, birth, death, marriage, divorce, education, employment, unemployment, personal income, Consumer Price Index, Producer Price Index and the following industries: agriculture, construction, energy, finance, fishing, forest products, manufacturing, minerals, select service industries, tourism, transportation, and wholesale and retail trade. Most data cover a five year period; select trends and projections are included. Includes data by industry/sector and county. Provides select comparisons to U.S. data. Contains approximately 500 tables.

Data from federal and state sources.

Description based on 1983 imprint covering 1978-1982 data.

S2200

University of Georgia. Graduate School of Business Administration. Division of Research.
Georgia Business and Economic Conditions.
Approximately 15 pages.   Bimonthly.   1929-
ISSN: 0279-3857   LCCN: 82-642477
Availability: $12.00 per year from the issuing source.

Bimonthly journal on business and economic conditions for the state of Georgia includes recurring statistical feature "Georgia Business Statistics". Provides data on employment, personal income, Consumer Price Index, Georgia Leading and Coincident Economic Indicators, and the construction and retail trade industries. Most data cover a one year period. Provides select comparisons to U.S. data. Contains approximately 1 table. Title varies.

Data from federal, private and state sources.

Description based on 1984 imprint covering 1984 data.

S2210
University of Georgia. Graduate School of Business Administration. Division of Research.
(year) Georgia Statistical Abstract.
Approximately 480 pages.   Biennial.   1951-
ISSN: 0085-1043   LCCN: 75-646885
Availability: $17.50 from the issuing source.

Presents a broad range of social and economic data for the state of Georgia. Provides data on population, birth, death, marriage, divorce, education, employment, unemployment, personal income, Gross State Product or other measures of production, Consumer Price Index, Producer Price Index and the following industries: agriculture, construction, energy, finance, fishing, forest products, manufacturing, minerals, select service industries, transportation, and wholesale and retail trade. Most data cover a six year period; select trends are included. Includes data by industry/sector, S.M.S.A, county and region. Provides select comparisons to U.S. data. Contains approximately 240 tables. Issuing source varies.
Data from federal, private and state sources.
Description based on 1982 imprint covering 1975-1980 data.

S2220
University of Illinois. Bureau of Economic and Business Research.
Illinois Business Review.
Approximately 12 pages.   Bimonthly.   1938-
ISSN: 0019-1922   LCCN: A44-1688
Availability: Free from the issuing source.

Bimonthly journal on business and economic conditions for the state of Illinois includes recurring statistical feature. Provides data on employment, personal income, Consumer Price Index and the following industries: agriculture, construction, energy, and retail trade. Most data cover a one month period with the most current figures available. Includes data by industry/sector. Contains approximately 2 tables.
Data from federal and state sources.
Description based on 1983 imprint covering 1983 data.

S2230
University of Kansas. Center for Public Affairs.
Kansas Statistical Abstract, (years).
Approximately 280 pages.   Annual.   1958-
ISSN: 0453-2800   LCCN: 80-647969
Availability: $11.00 + $1.00 P/H from the issuing source.

Presents a broad range of social and economic data for the state of Kansas. Provides data on population, housing, birth, death, marriage, divorce, education, employment, unemployment, personal income, Gross State Product or other measures of production and the following industries: agriculture, construction, finance, manufacturing, minerals, select service industries, tourism, and transportation. Most data cover a three year period. Includes data by industry/sector and county. Contains approximately 130 tables. Issuing source varies.

Data from federal and state sources.
Description based on 1983 imprint covering 1980-1982 data.

S2240
University of Kansas. Institute for Economic and Business Research.
Kansas Business Review.
Approximately 25 pages.   Bimonthly.   1977-
ISSN: 0164-8632   LCCN: 79-642737
Availability: Free from the issuing source.

Bimonthly journal on business and economic conditions for the state of Kansas includes
recurring statistical feature. Provides data on employment, unemployment, personal
income, Consumer Price Index and the following industries: agriculture, finance, and
retail trade. Most data cover a one month period with most current data available.
Includes data by industry/sector, S.M.S.A. and county. Contains approximately 9 tables.
Data from federal, private and state sources.
Description based on 1983 imprint covering 1983 data.

S2250
University of Massachusetts. Center for Business and Economic Research.
Massachusetts Business and Economic Report.
Approximately 6 pages.   Quarterly.   1974-
Availability: Free from the issuing source.

Quarterly journal on business and economic conditions for the state of Massachusetts
includes recurring statistical feature. Provides data on employment, unemployment,
personal income and Business Costs Index. Most data cover a three year period with
actual figures for two years and one year projections. Includes data by industry. Contains
approximately 1 table.
Data from federal, private and state sources.
Description based on 1984 imprint covering 1983-1985 data.

S2260
University of Michigan. Survey Research Center.
Economic Outlook USA.
Approximately 20 pages.   Quarterly.   1974-
ISSN: 0095-3830   LCCN: 74-648918
Availability: $13.00 per year to academic subscribers, $27.00 per year to others from the
issuing source.

Quarterly journal on business and economic conditions for the United States includes
recurring statistical feature "Actual and Projected Economic Indicators". Provides
data on employment, unemployment, Gross National Product or other measures of
production, Consumer Price Index, stock market indexes, Leading Economic Indicators,
and the following industries: construction, finance, and manufacturing. Also provides
SRC's own Measures of Consumer Attitude. Most data cover a four year period with
actual figures for four years and one year projections. Contains approximately 14
tables/charts.
Data from original research, federal and private sources.
Description based on 1984 imprint covering 1982-1985 data.

S2270
University of Missouri-Columbia. College of Business and Public Administration.
Missouri Economic Indicators.
Approximately 25 pages.   Quarterly.   1975-
ISSN: 0195-6159   LCCN: 79-644240
Availability: $10.00 per year from the issuing source.

Provides data on business and economic conditions for the state of Missouri including employment, unemployment, personal income, Consumer Price Index and the construction industry. Most data cover a four year period. Includes data by industry/sector and S.M.S.A. Provides select comparisons to U.S. data. Contains approximately 30 tables/charts.
Data from federal and state sources.
Description based on 1984 imprint covering 1981-1984 data.

S2280
University of Missouri-Columbia. College of Business and Public Administration.
Statistical Abstract for Missouri, (year).
Approximately 200 pages.   Biennial.   1961-
ISSN: 0730-7691   LCCN: 81-644761
Availability: $15.00 from the issuing source.

Presents a broad range of social and economic data for the state of Missouri. Provides data on population, birth, death, marriage, divorce, education, employment, unemployment, personal income, Consumer Price Index, Producer Price Index and the following industries: agriculture, construction, finance, manufacturing, minerals, and transportation. Most data cover a ten year period; select long term trends are included. Includes data by industry/sector. Provides select comparisons to U.S. data. Contains approximately 85 tables.
Data from federal, private and state sources.
Description based on 1983 imprint covering 1972-1981 data.

S2290
University of Nebraska-Lincoln.
Business in Nebraska.
Approximately 6 pages.   Monthly.   1941-
ISSN: 0007-683X   LCCN: SN82-8107
Availability: Free from the Bureau of Business Research.

Monthly report on business and economic conditions for the state of Nebraska includes recurring statistical features "Economic Indicators: Nebraska and United States", "Change from 1967", and "Net Taxable Retail Sales of Nebraska Regions". Provides data on Consumer Price Index, Producer Price Index, Gross State Product or other measures of production, and the following industries: agriculture, construction, manufacturing, and retail trade. Most data cover a one month period with the most current figures available; select trends are included. Includes data by industry/sector and region. Provides select comparisons to U.S. data. Contains approximately 3 tables. Title varies.
Data from federal and state sources.
Description based on 1984 imprint covering 1983-1984 data.

S2300
University of Nevada. Bureau of Business and Economic Research.
Nevada Review of Business and Economics.
Approximately 25 pages.   Quarterly.   1957-
ISSN: 0148-5881   LCCN: 77-643077
Availability: Free from the issuing source.

Quarterly journal on business and economic conditions for the state of Nevada includes recurring statistical features. Provides data on employment, unemployment, personal income and the following industries: construction, and wholesale and retail trade. Most data cover a one quarter period with figures available. Includes data by S.M.S.A. and county. Provides select comparisons to U.S. data. Contains approximately 5 tables.
Data from federal, private and state sources.
Description based on 1984 imprint covering 1984 data.

S2310
University of New Mexico. Bureau of Business and Economic Research.
New Mexico Business Current Economic Report.
Approximately 25 pages.   Monthly.   1948-
                               LCCN: SN82-20967
Availability: $12.00 per year from the issuing source.

Monthly journal on business and economic conditions for the state of New Mexico includes monthly and annual recurring statistical features. Provides data on housing, employment, unemployment, personal income, Consumer Price Index and the following industries: agriculture, construction, energy, finance, manufacturing, minerals, tourism, transportation, and wholesale and retail trade. Annual feature also provides data on population. Most data cover a one year period. Annual feature covers a five year period. Includes data by industry/sector and S.M.S.A. Contains approximately 16 tables. Title varies.
Data from federal, private and state sources.
Description based on 1984 imprint covering 1984 data.

S2320
University of New Mexico. Bureau of Business and Economic Research.
New Mexico Statistical Abstract.
Approximately 130 pages.   Biennial.   1970-
ISSN: 0077-8575   LCCN: 81-644287
Availability: $15.00 + $3.00 P/H from the issuing source.

Presents a broad range of social and economic data for the state of New Mexico. Provides data on population, housing, birth, death, marriage, divorce, education, employment, unemployment, personal income and the following industries: agriculture, construction, finance, manufacturing, minerals, select service industries, tourism, transportation, and wholesale and retail trade. Most data cover a three year period; select long term trends are included. Includes data by industry/sector and county. Contains approximately 131 tables.
Data from federal and state sources.
Description based on 1984 imprint covering 1979-1981 data.

171

S2330
University of North Dakota. Bureau of Business and Economic Research.
Statistical Abstract of North Dakota, (year).
Approximately 660 pages.   Irregular.   1979-
                              LCCN: 84-640216
Availability: $14.00 from the issuing source.

Presents a broad range of social and economic data for the state of North Dakota. Provides data on population, housing, birth, death, marriage, divorce, education, employment, unemployment, personal income, Gross State Product or other measures of production, and the following industries: agriculture, construction, energy, finance, manufacturing, minerals, select service industries, tourism, and transportation. Most data cover a three year period; select trends and projections are included. Includes data by industry/sector and county. Provides select comparisons to U.S. and regional data. Contains approximately 300 tables.
Data from federal and state sources.
Description based on 1983 imprint covering 1980-1982 data.

S2340
University of Oklahoma. Center for Economic and Management Research.
Statistical Abstract of Oklahoma, (year).
Approximately 550 pages.   Biennial.   1956-
ISSN: 0191-0310   LCCN: 79-642515
Availability: $15.00 from the issuing source.

Presents a broad range of social and economic data for the state of Oklahoma. Provides data on population, birth, death, marriage, divorce, education, employment, unemployment, personal income, Consumer Price Index, Producer Price Index and the following industries: agriculture, construction, energy, finance, manufacturing, select service industries, transportation, and wholesale and retail trade. Most data cover a one year period; select trends and projections are included. Includes data by industry/sector and county. Contains approximately 200 tables. Title varies.
Data from federal and state sources.
Description based on 1982 imprint covering 1980 data.

S2350
University of Oklahoma. Center for Economic and Management Research.
Oklahoma Business Bulletin.
Approximately 5 pages.   Monthly.   1928-
ISSN: 0030-1671   LCCN: 40-25254
Availability: $4.00 per year from the issuing source.

Monthly report on business and economic conditions for the state of Oklahoma includes recurring statistical feature. Provides data on Consumer Price Index, Producer Price Index, and the construction and retail trade industries. Includes data by city and S.M.S.A. Contains approximately 4 tables. Issuing source varies.
Data from federal and state sources.
Description based on 1983 imprint covering 1982-1983 data.

S2360
University of South Carolina. Division of Research.
South Carolina Economic Indicators.
Approximately 10 pages.   Monthly.   1966-
ISSN: 0038-304X   LCCN: 73-642715
Availability : Free from the issuing source.

Provides data on business and economic conditions for the state of South Carolina including employment, unemployment, personal income, Composite Indices of Leading and Coincident Economic Indicators, and the construction and retail trade industries. Most data cover a two year period; select trends are included. Contains approximately 15 tables.
Data from private and state sources.
Description based on 1984 imprint covering 1983-1984 data.

S2370
University of South Dakota. Business Research Bureau.
South Dakota Business Review.
Approximately 10 pages.   Quarterly.   1942-
ISSN: 0038-3260   LCCN: 58-24864
Availability: Free from the issuing source.

Quarterly report on business and economic conditions for the state of South Dakota includes recurring statistical feature. Provides data on employment, unemployment, personal income, Consumer Price Index, and the following industries: agriculture, construction, and retail trade. Annual feature provides summary data and projections for the coming year. Most data cover a one year period. Includes data by industry/sector and city. Quarterly feature contains approximately 5 tables.
Data from federal and state sources.
Description based on 1984 imprint covering 1984 data.

S2380
University of Tennessee, Knoxville. Center for Business and Economic Research.
Economic Report to the Governor of the State of Tennessee on the State's Economic Outlook and Revenue Prospects.
Approximately 185 pages in two volumes.   Annual.   1976-
Availability: Free from the Tennessee State Planning Office.

Provides data on business and economic conditions for the state of Tennessee including employment, unemployment, personal income, and Gross State Product or other measures of production. Volume One provides a narrative summary; Volume Two, titled *Economic Forecasts for Tennessee*, provides detailed statistical data. Volume One covers a three year period with actual figures for one year and two year projections; select trends and projections are included. Volume Two covers an eleven year period with actual figures for one year and ten year projections. Includes data by industry/sector. Provides select comparisons to U.S. data. Contains approximately 130 tables. Issuing source varies.
Data from federal and state sources.
Description based on 1984 imprint: Volume One covers 1983-1985 data; Volume Two covers 1982-1992 data.

S2390
University of Tennessee, Knoxville. Center for Business and Economic Research.
Survey of Business.
Approximately 30 pages.   Quarterly.   1965-
ISSN: 0099-0973   LCCN: 75-646621
Availability: Free from the issuing source.

Quarterly journal on business and economic conditions for the state of Tennessee includes recurring statistical feature in the Winter issue. Provides data on forecasted economic conditions including employment, unemployment, personal income, Gross State Product or other measures of production, the energy and transportation industries, and expectations of Tennessee executives. Most data are ten year projections. Includes data by industry/sector. Contains approximately 5 tables. Title varies.
Data from federal and state sources.
Description based on 1983 imprint covering 1982-1991 data.

S2400
University of Tennessee, Knoxville. Center for Business and Economic Research.
Tennessee Statistical Abstract, (years).
Approximately 750 pages.   Triennial.   1969-
ISSN: 0082-2760   LCCN: 68-66499
Availability: $20.95 + $1.75 P/H from the issuing source.

Presents a broad range of social and economic data for the state of Tennessee. Provides data on population, housing, birth death, marriage, divorce, education, employment, unemployment, personal income, Gross State Product or other measures of production, and the following industries: agriculture, construction, energy, finance, forest products, manufacturing, minerals, select service industries, transportation, and wholesale and retail trade. Most data cover a two year period; select trends and projections are included. Includes data by industry/sector and county. Contains approximately 400 tables.
Data from federal and state sources.
Description based on 1983 imprint covering 1980-1981 data.

S2410
University of Texas at Austin. Bureau of Business Research.
Texas Fact Book, (year).
Approximately 250 pages.   Annual.   1978-
ISSN: 0163-4666   LCCN: 78-67923
Availability: $6.00 from the issuing source.

Presents a broad range of social and economic data for the state of Texas. Provides data on population, birth, death, marriage, divorce, employment, unemployment, personal income, Consumer Price Index, Gross State Product or other measures of production, and the following industries: agriculture, construction, energy, finance, manufacturing, minerals, select service industries, transportation, and wholesale and retail trade. Most data cover a two year period; select trends are included. Includes data by industry/sector, S.M.S.A. and State Planning Region. Contains approximately 80 tables.
Data from federal and state sources.
Description based on 1983 imprint covering 1981-1982 data.

S2420
University of Utah. Bureau of Economic and Business Research.
Utah Economic and Business Review.
Approximately 12 pages.   Monthly.   1941-
ISSN: 0042-1405   LCCN: 44-45237
Availability: Free from the issuing source

Monthly journal on business and economic conditions for the state of Utah includes recurring statistical features. Provides data on employment, personal income, Consumer Price Index, Gross State Product or other measures of production, and the following industries: agriculture, construction, energy, finance, manufacturing, and tourism. Annual statistical feature provides data on population. Most data cover a one month period with the most current figures available; select trends are included. Includes data by industry/sector, county and Planning District. Provides select comparisons to U.S. data. Contains approximately 3 tables.
Data from federal, private and state sources.
Description based on 1984 imprint covering 1983-1984 data.

S2430
University of Utah. Bureau of Economic and Business Research.
Utah Statistical Abstract, (year).
Approximately 380 pages.   Triennial.   1947-
ISSN: 0278-3770   LCCN: 81-642023
Availability: $25.00 from the issuing source.

Presents a broad range of social and economic data for the state of Utah. Provides data on population, birth, death, marriage, divorce, education, employment, unemployment, personal income and the following industries: agriculture, construction, energy, finance, manufacturing, minerals, retail trade, select service industries, and transportation. Most data cover a ten year period; select long term trends are included. Includes data by industry/sector, S.M.S.A. and county. Contains approximately 230 tables. Issuing source varies.
Data from federal, private and state sources.
Description based on 1983 imprint covering 1971-1981 data.

S2440
University of Wyoming. Institute for Policy Research.
Wyoming Quarterly Update.
Approximately 50 pages.   Quarterly.   1981-
                              LCCN: SN83-11924
Availability: Free from the issuing source.

Provides data on business and economic conditions for the state of Wyoming including employment, unemployment, personal income, Wyoming Coincident Indicator Index, Wyoming Personal Index, Consumer Price Index, cost of living and the following industries: agriculture, construction, energy, finance, minerals, and tourism. Most data cover a three year period. Includes data by industry/sector and county. Contains approximately 15 tables. Title varies.
Data from federal, private and state sources.
Description based on 1985 imprint covering 1982-1984 data.

S2450
Utah Association. of Counties.
Utah: County Facts Book.
Approximately 425 pages.   Irregular.   1981-
Availability: $10.00 from the issuing source.

Presents a broad range of social and economic data for the state of Utah. Provides data on population, education, employment, unemployment, personal income and the following industries: agriculture, construction, energy, forest products, minerals, select service industries, and wholesale and retail trade. Most data cover a one year period; select trends and projections are included. Includes data by industry/sector and county. Contains approximately 380 tables.
Data from federal, private and state sources.
Description based on 1981 imprint covering 1979 data.

S2460
Utah Foundation.
Statistical Review of Government in Utah, (year) Edition.
Approximately 100 pages.   Annual.   1976-
Availability: $10.00 from the issuing source.

Presents a broad range of social and economic data for the state of Utah. Provides data on population, birth, death, marriage, divorce, education, employment, unemployment, personal income, Consumer Price Index and the following industries: agriculture, minerals, retail trade, and transportation. Most data cover a one year period; select trends are included. Includes data by industry/sector, city and county. Provides select comparisons to U.S. data. Contains approximately 85 tables.
Data from federal and state sources.
Description based on 1984 imprint covering 1983 data.

S2470
Utah. Bureau of Health Statistics.
Utah Vital Statistics: Annual Report, (year).
Approximately 95 pages.   Annual.   1968-
ISSN: 0736-4601   LCCN: 83-640087
Availability: $5.00 from the issuing source.

Provides data on population, birth and death for the state of Utah. Most data cover a one year period; select trends are included. Includes data by city and county. Contains approximately 110 tables. Title varies.
Data from state sources.
Description based on 1983 imprint covering 1981 data.

S2480
Utah. Economic and Industrial Development Department.
Utah Facts.
Approximately 110 pages in eight volumes.   Irregular.   1970-
Availability: $2.00 + $1.00 P/H per volume, $16.00 + $2.00 P/H per set from the issuing source.

Presents a broad range of social and economic data for the state of Utah. Provides data on population, birth, death, education, employment, personal income, cost of living and the following industries: agriculture, construction, energy, finance, minerals, retail trade, select service industries, tourism, and transportation. Most data cover a one year period; select trends are included. Includes data by industry/sector. Contains approximately 85 tables.
Data from federal, private and state sources.
Description based on 1983 imprint covering 1981 data.

S2490
Utah. Job Service. Labor Market Information Services Section.
Annual Report: Volume Three: Labor Market Information.
Approximately 125 pages.   Annual.   1981-
Availability: Free from the issuing source.

Provides data on employment, unemployment and personal income for the state of Utah. Most data cover a one year period; select trends are included. Includes data by industry/sector, county and Planning District. Contains approximately 20 tables. Title and issuing source vary.
Data from federal and state sources.
Description based on 1984 imprint covering 1983 data.
Also publishes updated data in *Utah Labor Market Report* (monthly).

S2500
Utah. State Department of Agriculture.
Utah Agricultural Statistics, (year).
Approximately 100 pages.   Annual.   1971-
ISSN: 0276-0193   LCCN: 72-623245
Availability: Free from the issuing source.

Provides data on the agriculture industry for the state of Utah including production figures and prices for crops, livestock, dairy and poultry. Most data cover a one year period; select trends are included. Includes data by commodity/sector and county. Contains approximately 95 tables. Issuing source varies.
Data from state and U.S.D.A. sources.
Description based on 1983 imprint covering 1982 data.

S2510
Valley National Bank, Phoenix. Economic Research Department.
Arizona Statistical Review.
Approximately 75 pages.   Annual.   1949-
ISSN: 0518-6242   LCCN: 50-27371
Availability: Free from the issuing source.

Presents a broad range of social and economic data for the state of Arizona. Provides data on population, birth, death, education, employment, unemployment, personal income, Business Confidence Index, Consumer Price Index and the following industries: agriculture, construction, finance, manufacturing, minerals, retail trade, select service industries, transportation, and tourism. Most data cover a three year period. Includes

data by industry/sector and county. Contains approximately 225 tables. Title and issuing source vary.
Data from federal, private and state sources.
Description based on 1983 imprint covering 1980-1982 data.

S2520
Vermont. Department of Agriculture.
Agriculture of Vermont, (years).
Approximately 30 pages.   Biennial.   1909-
Availability: Free from the issuing source.

Provides data on the agriculture industry for the state of Vermont including production figures and prices for crops, livestock, dairy and poultry. Most data cover a thirty-one year period. Includes data by commodity/sector. Contains approximately 30 tables. Title varies. Published with the *Biennial Report of the Commissioner of Agriculture of the State of Vermont (years)*.
Data from state and U.S.D.A. sources.
Description based on 1982 imprint covering 1950-1980 data.

S2530
Vermont. Department of Employment and Training. Research and Statistics Section.
Vermont Annual Planning Information (year).
Approximately 35 pages.   Annual.   1978-
                              LCCN: SC84-1574
Availability: Free from the issuing source.

Provides data on population, employment, unemployment and personal income for the state of Vermont. Most data cover a two year period; select trends are included. Includes data by industry/sector and county. Contains approximately 20 tables. Title and issuing source vary.
Data from federal and state sources.
Description based on 1984 imprint covering 1982-1983 data.

S2540
Vermont. Division of Public Health Statistics.
(year) Annual Report of Vital Statistics in Vermont.
Approximately 140 pages.   Annual.   1887-
ISSN: 0147-5843   LCCN: 77-641747
Availability: $2.00 from the issuing source.

Provides data on population, birth, death, marriage and divorce for the state of Vermont. Most data cover a one year period; select trends are included. Includes data by town and county. Contains approximately 80 tables. Title varies.
Data from state sources.
Description based on 1983 imprint covering 1982 data.

S2550
Vermont. Office of the Governor.
STF Three Profiles: Ten Largest Towns, Vermont.
Approximately 120 pages.   Monograph.   1983.
Availability: $6.00 from Policy Research Staff.

Provides data on population, housing, education, employment, unemployment and
personal income. Most data cover a one year period. Includes data by town. Contains
approximately 10 lengthy tables.
Data from U.S. Bureau of the Census *Summary Tape File Three.*
Description based on 1983 imprint covering 1980 data.

S2560
Virginia. Crop Reporting Service.
Virginia Agricultural Statistics.
Approximately 115 pages.   Annual.   1974-
ISSN: 0360-3830   LCCN: 75-647372
Availability: Free from the Agricultural Statistician.

Provides data on the agriculture industry for the state of Virginia including production
figures and prices for crops, livestock, dairy and poultry. Most data cover a one year
period; select trends are included. Includes data by commodity/sector and county.
Contains approximately 85 tables.
Data from state and U.S.D.A. sources.
Description based on 1984 imprint covering 1983 data.

S2570
Virginia. Department of Health.
Statistical Annual Report Containing Report of the Bureau of Vital Statistics and
Bureau of Communicable Diseases, Virginia.
Approximately 170 pages.   Annual.   1949-
                            LCCN: 56-32221
Availability: $5.00 from Vital Records and Health Statistics Division, Health Statistics
Center.

Provides data on population, birth, death, marriage and divorce for the state of Virginia.
Most data cover a one year period; select trends are included. Includes data by county
and Planning District. Contains approximately 60 tables. Title varies.
Data from state sources.
Description based on 1983 imprint covering 1981 data.

S2580
Virginia. Division of Industrial Development.
Virginia Facts and Figures, (year).
Approximately 35 pages.   Irregular.   1970-
                            LCCN: 72-632694
Availability: Free from the issuing source.

Primarily narrative work presents an overview of social and economic data for the state
of Virginia including population, education, employment, unemployment, personal

income and the following industries: energy, finance, manufacturing, minerals, tourism, and transportation. Most data cover a one year period; select trends are included. Includes data by industry/sector. Contains approximately 20 tables. Issuing source varies.
Data from federal and state sources.
Description based on 1984 imprint covering 1983 data.

S2590
Virginia. Employment Commission. Research and Analysis Division.
Virginia Economic Indicators.
Approximately 20 pages.   Quarterly.   1967-
Availability: Free from the issuing source.

Provides data on employment, unemployment, personal income, and the energy, finance, and retail trade industries for the state of Virginia. Most data cover a one year period; select trends are included. Includes data by industry/sector. Contains approximately 7 tables. Issuing source varies.
Data from federal and state sources.
Description based on 1984 imprint covering 1984 data.
Also publishes updated data on employment and personal income in *Employment, Hours, and Earnings in Virginia and its Metropolitan Areas* (monthly).

S2600
Washington Research Council.
The Fact Book.
Approximately 70 pages.   Irregular.   1978-
                                LCCN: SC83-7077
Availability: $6.00 from the issuing source.

Provides data on business and economic conditions for the state of Washington including population, education, employment, unemployment, personal income, Consumer Price Index and cost of living. Most data cover a two year period; select trends are included. Includes data by county. Provides select comparisons to U.S. data. Contains approximately 25 tables. Title and issuing source vary.
Data from federal, private and state sources.
Description (of former title: *The Book of Numbers*) based on 1982 imprint covering 1980-1981 data.

S2610
Washington. Department of Social and Health Services.
Vital Statistics Summary, Washington State, (year).
Approximately 95 pages.   Annual.   1955-
                                LCCN: 72-625420
Availability: Free from Health Statistics Center.

Provides data on population, birth, death, marriage and divorce for the state of Washington. Most data cover a one year period. Includes data by place and county. Contains approximately 50 tables. Title varies.
Data from state sources.
Description based on 1983 imprint covering 1982 data.

S2620
Washington. Employment Security Department. Research and Analysis Branch.
Washington Labor Market.
Approximately 15 pages.   Monthly.   1977-
                                     LCCN: SC82-111
Availability: Free from the issuing source.

Provides data on employment, unemployment, personal income and Consumer Price
Index for the state of Washington. Most data cover a two year period. Includes data by
industry/sector, S.M.S.A. and county. Provides select comparisons to U.S. data. Contains
approximately 6 tables.
Data from federal and state sources.
Description based on 1984 imprint covering 1983-1984 data.

S2630
Washington. Office of Finance Management.
Washington State Data Book.
Approximately 290 pages.   Biennial.   1970-
ISSN: 0733-2432   LCCN: 82-643712
Availability: Limited distribution from Division of Policy Analysis and Forecasting.

Presents a broad range of social and economic data for the state of Washington.
Provides data on population, birth, death, marriage, divorce, education, employment,
unemployment, personal income, Consumer Price Index and the following industries:
agriculture, construction, energy, finance, fishing, forest products, select service industries, and transportation. Most data cover a six year period. Includes data by industry/
sector, city/town and county. Contains approximately 205 tables. Title varies.
Data from federal and state sources.
Description based on 1984 imprint covering 1978-1983 data.

S2640
Washington. State Crop and Livestock Reporting Service.
Washington Agricultural Statistics, (years).
Approximately 85 pages.   Annual.   1956-
ISSN: 0095-4330   LCCN: 74-648858
Availability: Free from the issuing source.

Provides data on the agriculture industry for the state of Washington including production
figures and prices for crops, livestock, dairy and poultry. Most data cover a two year
period; select trends are included. Includes data by commodity/sector and county.
Provides select comparisons to U.S. data. Contains approximately 75 tables.
Data from state and U.S.D.A. sources.
Description based on 1984 imprint covering 1982-1983 data.

S2650
Wayne State University. Bureau of Business Research.
Michigan Economy.
Approximately 10 pages.   Bimonthly.   1959-
ISSN: 0730-272X   LCCN: 84-645306
Availability: Free from the issuing source.

Bimonthly report on business and economic conditions for the state of Michigan includes recurring statistical features "Michigan Economic Indicators" and "Permit Authorized Construction in Selected Counties". Provides data on employment, Consumer Price Index and the following industries: agriculture, construction, energy, and manufacturing. Most data cover a two year period. Includes data by industry/sector and county. Contains approximately 2 tables. Title varies.
Data from private and state sources.
Description based on 1984 imprint covering 1983-1984 data.

S2660
Wayne State University. Bureau of Business Research.
Michigan Statistical Abstract, (years).
Approximately 700 pages.   Annual.   1955-
ISSN: 0076-8308   LCCN: 74-644904
Availability: $15.50 from the issuing source.

Presents a broad range of social and economic data for the state of Michigan. Provides data on population, housing, birth, death, marriage, divorce, education, employment, unemployment, personal income, Consumer Price Index, cost of living, imports and exports, and the following industries: agriculture, construction, energy, finance, fishing, forest products, manufacturing, minerals, select service industries, transportation, and wholesale and retail trade. Most data cover a one year period; select trends and projections are included. Includes data by industry/sector and county. Contains approximately 400 tables. Issuing source varies.
Data from federal and state sources.
Description based on 1983 imprint covering 1981 data.

S2670
West Virginia Chamber of Commerce. Research Department.
West Virginia: An Economic-Statistical Profile, (year).
Approximately 290 pages.   Biennial.   1982-
                                          LCCN: 83-161433
Availability: $10.00 to members, $25.00 to others + P/H from the issuing source.

Presents a broad range of social and economic data for the state of West Virginia. Provides data on population, housing, birth, death, education, employment, unemployment, personal income, Consumer Price Index, Gross State Product or other measures of production, and the following industries: construction, energy, finance, retail trade, select service industries, and transportation. Most data cover four year period; select trends are included. Includes data by industry/sector and county. Provides select comparisons to U.S. data. Contains approximately 150 tables.
Data from federal, private and state sources.
Description based on 1982 imprint covering 1978-1981 data.

S2680
West Virginia. Crop Reporting Service.
West Virginia Agricultural Statistics, (year).
Approximately 90 pages.   Annual.   1980-
                                          LCCN: 82-641074
Availability: $5.00 from the issuing source.

Provides data on the agriculture industry for the state of West Virginia including production figures and prices for crops, livestock, dairy and poultry. Most data cover a one year period; select long term trends are included. Includes data by commodity/sector, county and region. Contains approximately 70 tables.
Data from state and U.S.D.A. sources.
Description based on 1983 imprint covering 1982 data.

S2690
West Virginia. Department of Employment Security. Labor and Economic Research Section.
Annual Planning Information, State of West Virginia, (fy).
Approximately 40 pages.   Annual.   1981-
                             LCCN: 82-644422
Availability: Free from the issuing source.

Provides data on population, employment, unemployment and personal income for the state of West Virginia. Most data cover a five year period with actual figures for four years and one year projections. Includes data by industry/sector, county and Service Delivery Area. Contains approximately 26 tables.
Data from federal and state sources.
Description based on 1984 imprint covering 1981-1985 data.

S2700
West Virginia. Health Statistics Center. Health Planning and Evaluation.
Annual Report: Vital Health Statistics of West Virginia, (year).
Approximately 115 pages.   Annual.   1976-
ISSN: 0272-3972   LCCN: 80-648783
Availability: Free from the issuing source.

Provides data on population, birth, death, marriage and divorce for the state of West Virginia. Most data cover a one year period. Includes data by county and region. Contains approximately 45 tables. Title varies.
Data from state sources.
Description based on 1984 imprint covering 1983 data.

S2710
Wichita State University. Center for Business and Economic Research.
Business and Economic Report.
Approximately 25 pages.   Quarterly.   1948-
Availability: $10.00 per year from the issuing source.

Quarterly journal on business and economic condition for the state of Kansas includes recurring statistical feature "Kansas Economic Indicators". Provides data on employment, unemployment, personal income and the following industries: construction, energy, finance, manufacturing, retail trade, and transportation. Most data cover a two year period. Includes data by industry/sector and city. Contains approximately 12 tables. Title and issuing source vary. Alternates with *Kansas Economic Indicators* (monthly) which provides updated data for the above described recurring statistical feature.
Data from federal and state sources.
Description based on 1984 imprint covering 1983-1984 data.

S2720
Wisconsin. Agricultural Reporting Service.
Wisconsin Agricultural Statistics, (year).
Approximately 95 pages.   Annual.   1950-
ISSN: 0512-1329   LCCN: 66-63464
Availability: $3.00 from the issuing source.

Provides data on the agriculture industry for the state of Wisconsin including production figures and prices for crops, livestock, dairy and poultry. Most data cover a two year period; select trends are included. Includes data by commodity/sector and county. Provides select comparisons to U.S. data. Contains approximately 110 tables. Title and issuing source vary.
Data from state and U.S.D.A. sources.
Description based on 1984 imprint covering 1982-1983 data.

S2730
Wisconsin. Demographics Services Center.
Wisconsin Statistical Abstract.
Approximately 350 pages.   Irregular.   1969-
                             LCCN: 79-626144
Availability: $9.50 from Documents Sales and Distribution.

Presents a broad range of social and economic data for the state of Wisconsin. Provides data on population, housing, birth, death, education, employment, unemployment, personal income, Consumer Price Index and the following industries: agriculture, construction, finance, manufacturing, select service industries, tourism, and wholesale and retail trade. Most data cover an eleven year period; select trends are included. Includes data by industry/sector, city and county. Provides select comparisons to U.S. data. Contains approximately 230 tables. Issuing source varies.
Data from federal, private and state sources.
Description based on 1979 imprint covering 1967-1977 data.

S2740
Wisconsin. Department of Development.
Wisconsin Economic Profile.
Approximately 5 pages.   Irregular.   1978-
Availability: Free from the issuing source.

Provides data on business and economic conditions for the state of Wisconsin including population, housing, employment, personal income and the following industries: agriculture, construction, forest products, manufacturing, minerals, retail trade, and select service industries. Most data cover a two year period; select trends are included. Includes data by industry/sector and city. Provides select comparisons to U.S. data. Contains approximately 15 tables.
Data from federal and state sources.
Description based on 1984 imprint covering 1980-1981 data.

S2750

Wisconsin. Division of Health.
Public Health Statistics, (year).
Approximately 45 pages.   Annual.   1948-
ISSN: 0190-5708   LCCN: 79-640448
Availability: Free from Center for Health Statistics.

Provides data on birth, death, marriage and divorce for the state of Wisconsin. Most data cover a one year period. Includes data by county and Minor Civil Division. Contains approximately 15 tables. Title and issuing source vary.
Data from state sources.
Description based on 1984 imprint covering 1983 data.
Also publishes population estimates and all vital event tables which are based upon estimates in *Public Health Statistics, (year): Part II.*

S2760

Wisconsin. Job Service Division.
Economic Planning Information for the State of Wisconsin, (year).
Approximately 40 pages.   Annual.   1979-
Availability: Free from Labor Market Information.

Provides data on population, employment, unemployment and personal income for the state of Wisconsin. Most data cover a one year period; select projections and short term trends are included. Includes data by county. Provides select comparisons to U.S. data. Contains approximately 28 tables. Title varies.
Data from federal and state sources.
Description based on 1984 imprint covering 1983 data.
Also publishes updated data in *Wisconsin Employment and Economic Indicators* (monthly).

S2770

Wyoming. Crop and Livestock Reporting Service.
Wyoming Agricultural Statistics, (year).
Approximately 90 pages,   Annual.   1973-
ISSN: 0363-9339   LCCN: 76-646923
Availability: Free from the Agricultural Statistician.

Provides data on the agriculture industry for the state of Wyoming including production figures and prices for crops, livestock, dairy and poultry. Most data cover a two year period; select trends are included. Includes data by commodity/sector, county and district. Provides select comparisons to U.S. data. Contains approximately 70 tables. Issuing source varies.
Data from state and U.S.D.A. sources.
Description based on 1984 imprint covering 1982-1983 data.

S2780
Wyoming. Department of Administration and Fiscal Control.
Wyoming Data Handbook, (year).
Approximately 200 pages.   Irregular.   1971-
                                   LCCN: 74-645995
Availability: Free from Research and Statistics Division.

Presents a broad range of social and economic data for the state of Wyoming. Provides data on population, housing, birth, death, marriage, divorce, employment, unemployment, personal income, Gross State Product or other measures of production, Consumer Price Index and the following industries: agriculture, construction, energy, finance, fishing, manufacturing, minerals, select service industries, tourism, transportation, and wholesale and retail trade. Most data cover a twelve year period; select long term trends are included. Includes data by industry/sector and county. Provides select comparisons to U.S. data. Contains approximately 150 tables. Title and issuing source vary.
Data from federal and state sources.
Description based on 1981 imprint covering 1970-1981 data.

S2790
Wyoming. Department of Health and Social Services.
Summary of Wyoming Vital Statistics, (year).
Approximately 55 pages.   Biennial.
                                   LCCN: 59-62576
Availability: Free from the Health and Medical Services Division.

Provides data on population, birth, death, marriage and divorce for the state of Wyoming. Most data cover a one year period; select trends are included. Includes data by place and county. Contains approximately 35 tables.
Data from state sources.
Description based on 1983 imprint covering 1981 data.

S2800
Wyoming. Employment Security Commission. Research and Analysis Section.
(year) Wyoming Annual Planning Report.
Approximately 100 pages.   Annual.   1977-
                                   LCCN: 81-646551
Availability: Free from the issuing source.

Provides data on population, employment, unemployment, personal income and cost of living for the state of Wyoming. Most data cover a one year period; select trends and projections are included. Includes data by industry/sector and county. Provides select comparisons to U.S. data. Contains approximately 25 tables. Title varies.
Data from federal and state sources.
Description based on 1984 imprint covering 1983 data.
Also publishes updated data in *Wyoming Labor Force Trends* (monthly).

APPENDIX A: ADDRESSES: ASSOCIATION PUBLICATIONS

Abingdon Press
201 8th Avenue South
Post Office Box 801
Nashville, TN 37202

Administrative Management Society
2360 Maryland Road
Willow Grove, PA 19090

Air Transport Association of America
1709 New York Avenue Northwest
Washington, DC 20006

Aluminium Association
818 Connecticut Avenue Northwest
Washington, DC 20006

American Association of Engineering
    Societies
Engineering Manpower Commission
345 East 47th Street
New York, NY 10017

American Association of Fund-Raising
    Counsel
500 5th Avenue Suite 1015
New York, NY 10036

American Association of University
    Professors
1 DuPont Circle Suite 500
Washington, DC 20036

American Bankers Association
120 Connecticut Avenue Northwest
Washington, DC 20036

American Bureau of Metal Statistics
420 Lexington Avenue
New York, NY 10170

American Cancer Society
777 3rd Avenue
New York, NY 10017

American Chamber of Commerce
    Researchers Association
c/o Robert Palmer
Indianapolis Chamber of Commerce
320 North Meridian Street
Indianapolis, IN 46204

American Chemical Society
1155 16th Street Northwest
Washington, DC 20036

American Council of Life Insurance
1850 K Street Northwest
Washington, DC 20006

American Financial Services Association
1101 14th Street Northwest
Washington, DC 20005

American Frozen Food Institute
1700 Old Meadow Road
McLean, VA 22209

American Gas Association
1515 Wilson Boulevard
Arlington, VA 22209

American Hospital Publishing
211 East Chicago Avenue
Chicago, IL 60611

American Humane Association
Child Protection Division
9725 Hampden Avenue
Denver, CO 80231

American Iron And Steel Institute
1000 16th Street Northwest
Washington, DC 20036

American Iron Ore Association
1501 Euclid Avenue
514 Buckley Building
Cleveland, OH 44115

American Meat Institute
Post Office Box 3556
Washington, DC 20007

American Medical Association
Post Office Box 821
Monroe, WI 53566

American Newspaper Publishers
   Association
Box 17407
Dulles International Airport
Washington, DC 20041

American Petroleum Institute
2101 L Street Northwest
Washington, DC 20037

American Public Transit Association
1225 Connecticut Avenue Northwest
   Suite 200
Washington, DC 20036

American Textile Manufacturers
   Institute
1101 Connecticut Avenue Northwest
   Suite 300
Washington, DC 20036

American Waterways Operators
1600 Wilson Boulevard Suite 1000
Arlington, VA 22209

Association of American Railroads
1920 L Street Northwest
Washington, DC 20036

Association of Information Systems
   Professionals
1015 North York Road
Willow Grove, PA 19090

Association of Research Libraries
1527 New Hampshire Avenue Northwest
Washington, DC 20036

Atomic Industrial Forum
Publications Office
7101 Wisconsin Avenue
Bethesda, MD 20814

Aviation Week and Space Technology
1221 Avenue of the Americas
New York, NY 10020

Bank Administration Institute
60 Gould Center
2550 Golf Road
Rolling Meadows, IL 60008

Battery Council International
111 East Wacker Drive
Chicago, IL 60601

Book Industry Study Group
160 5th Avenue
New York, NY 10010

Chamber of Commerce of the U.S.
Forecast Section
1615 H Street Northwest
Washington, DC 20062

Chamber of Commerce of the U.S.
Survey Research Center
Economic Policy Division
1615 H Street Northwest
Washington, DC 20062

Clothing Manufacturers Association of
   the U.S.A.
135 West 50th Street
New York, NY 10020

College Placement Council
62 Highland Avenue
Bethlehem, PA 18097

The Conference Board
845 3rd Avenue
New York, NY 10022

Copper Development Association
405 Lexington Avenue
New York, NY 10174

Council of the Great City Schools
1413 K Street Northwest 4th Floor
Washington, DC 20005

Council for Financial Aid to Education
680 5th Avenue
New York, NY 10019

Credit Union National Association
Post Office Box 431
Madison, WI 53701

Distilled Spirits Council of the U.S.
425 13th Street Northwest
Washington, DC 20004

Edison Electrical Institute
1111 19th Street Northwest
Washington, DC 20036

Electronic Industries Association
2001 I Street Northwest
Washington, DC 20006

Fibre Box Association
5725 East River Road
Chicago, IL 60631

Food Marketing Institute
1750 K Street Northwest
Washington, DC 20006

General Aviation Manufacturers
  Association
1020 Connecticut Avenue Northwest
  Suite 517
Washington, DC 20036

Gold Institute
1001 Connecticut Avenue Northwest
Washington, DC 20036

Health Insurance Association of America
1850 K Street Northwest
Washington, DC 20006

Independent Petroleum Association of
  America
1101 16th Street Northwest
Washington, DC 20036

Independent Sector
1825 L Street Northwest
Washington, DC 20036

Institute of Real Estate Management
430 North Michigan Avenue
Chicago, IL 60611

Institute of Scrap Iron and Steel
1627 K Street Northwest
Washington, DC 20006

Insurance Information Institute
110 William Street
New York, NY 10038

International City Management
  Association
1140 Connecticut Avenue Northwest
Washington, DC 20036

Investment Company Institute
1775 K Street Northwest
Washington, DC 20006

Macmillan Publishing Co.
866 3rd Avenue
New York, NY 10022

Menswear Retailers of America
National Clothier Service Division
1727 West Devon
Chicago, Il 60660

Morris, Robert Associates
1616 Philadelphia National Bank
   Building
Philadelphia, PA 19107

Mortgage Bankers Association of
   America
1125 15th Street Northwest
Washington, DC 20005

Motor Vehicle Manufacturers
   Association of the U.S.
300 New Center Building
Detroit, MI 48202

Motorcycle Industry Council
Research and Statistics Department
3151 Airway Avenue
Building P-1
Costa Mesa, CA 92626

National Association for State
   Information Systems
Post Office Box 11910
Iron Works Pike
Lexington, KY 40578

National Association of Broadcasters
1771 North Street Northwest
Washington, DC 20036

National Association of Business
   Economists
28349 Chagrin Boulevard
Cleveland, OH 44122

National Association of Hosiery
   Manufacturers
447 South Sharon Amity Road
Charlotte, NC 28211

National Association of Real Estate
   Investment Trusts
1101 17th Street Northwest Suite 700
Washington, DC 20036

National Association of Realtors
777 14th Street Northwest
Washington, DC 20005

National Association of Securities
   Dealers
1735 K Street Northwest
Washington, DC 20006

National Association of State Budget
   Officers
Hall Of States
444 North Capitol Street
Washington, DC 20001

National Association of State Racing
   Commissioners
Box 4216
Lexington, KY 40504

National Association of Wheat Growers
415 2nd Street Northeast Suite 300
Washington, DC 20002

National Automobile Dealers Association
8400 Westpark Drive
McLean, VA 22102

National Business Aircraft Association
1 Farragut Square South
Washington, DC 20006

National Coal Association
1130 17th Street Northwest
Washington, DC 20036

National Cotton Council of America
Post Office Box 12285
Memphis, TN 38112

National Council of Savings Institutions
200 Park Avenue
New York, NY 10166

National Education Association
The Academic Building
Saw Mill Road
West Haven, CT 06516

National Federation of Independent
   Business
150 West 20th Avenue
San Mateo, CA 94403

National Food Processors Association
1133 20th Street Northwest
Washington, DC 20036

National Funeral Directors Association
of the U.S.
135 West Wells Street
Milwaukee, WI 53203

National LP-Gas Association
1301 West 22nd Street
Oak Brook, IL 60521

National Machine Tool Builders'
Association
7901 Westpark Drive
McLean, VA 22102

National Paperbox and Packaging
Association
231 Kings Highway East
Haddonfield, NJ 08033

National Restaurant Association
311 1st Street Northwest
Washington, DC 20001

National Retail Merchants Association
100 West 31st Street
New York, NY 10001

National Safety Council
Order Department
444 North Michigan Avenue
Chicago, IL 60611

Newspaper Advertising Bureau
485 Lexington Avenue
New York, NY 10017

Newsprint Information Committee
633 3rd Avenue
New York, NY 10017

North American Electric Reliability
Council
Research Park
Terhune Road
Princeton, NJ 08540

Northeast-Midwest Institute
Post Office Box 37209
Washington, DC 20013

Pacific Area Travel Association
228 Grant Avenue
San Francisco, CA 94108

Population Reference Bureau
Post Office Box 35012
Washington, DC 20013

Produce Marketing Association
700 Barksdale Plaza
Newark, DE 19711

Public Securities Association
1 World Trade Center
New York, NY 10048

Radio Advertising Bureau
485 Lexington Avenue
New York, NY 10017

Regional Airline Association
1101 Connecticut Avenue Northwest
Suite 700
Washington, DC 20036

Scientific Manpower Commission
1776 Massachusetts Avenue Northwest
Washington, DC 20036

Securities Industry Association
120 Broadway
New York, NY 10271

Silver Institute
1001 Connecticut Avenue Northwest
Suite 1138
Washington, DC 20036

Society of Industrial Realtors
925 15th Street Northwest
Washington, DC 20005

Southern Regional Education Board
1340 Spring Street Northwest
Atlanta, GA 30309

Tax Foundation
1875 Connecticut Avenue Northwest
Washington, DC 20009

Television Bureau of Advertising
485 Lexington Avenue
New York, NY 10017

U.S. Brewers Association
1750 K Street Northwest
Washington, DC 20006

U.S. Conference of Mayors
1620 I Street Northwest
Washington, DC 20006

U.S. League of Savings Institutions
111 East Wacker Drive
Chicago, IL 60601

U.S. Telephone Association
1801 K Street Northwest Suite 1201
Washington, DC 20006

U.S. Travel Data Center
1899 L Street Northwest Suite 610
Washington, DC 20036

Western Wood Products Association
1500 Yeon Building
Portland, OR 97204

Zinc Institute
292 Madison Avenue
New York, NY 10017

APPENDIX B: ADDRESSES: FEDERAL PUBLICATIONS

Association of College and Research
Libraries
50 East Huron Street
Chicago, IL 60611

Bendix Field Engineering Corporation
Technical Library
Post Office Box 1569
Grand Junction, CO 81502

Board of Governors of the Federal
    Reserve System (U.S.)
Publications Section
Division of Administrative Services
Washington, DC 20551

Federal Deposit Insurance Corporation
Corporate Communications
550 17th Street Northwest
Washington, DC 20429

Federal Reserve Bank of Atlanta
Research Department
Post Office Box 1731
Atlanta, GA 30301

Federal Reserve Bank of Boston
Bank and Public Information Center
600 Atlantic Avenue
Boston, MA 02106

Federal Reserve Bank of Chicago
Publications Division
Post Office Box 834
Chicago, IL 60690

Federal Reserve Bank of Cleveland
Research Department
Post Office Box 6387
Cleveland, OH 44101

Federal Reserve Bank of Kansas City
Research Department
925 Grand Avenue
Kansas City, MO 64198

Federal Reserve Bank of Richmond
Public Services Department
Post Office Box 27622
Richmond, VA 23261

Federal Reserve Bank of St. Louis
Research and Public Information
    Department
Box 442
St. Louis, MO 63166

National Center for Health Statistics
    (U.S.)
Room 1-57 Federal Center Building 2
3700 East-West Highway
Hyattsville, MD 20782

National Science Foundation (U.S.)
Division of Science Resources Studies
1800 G Street Northwest
Washington, DC 20550

National Technical Information Service
U.S. Department of Commerce
5285 Port Royal Road
Springfield, VA 22161

Superintendent of Documents
U.S. Government Printing Office
Washington, DC 20402

U.S. Bureau of Indian Affairs
Phoenix Area Office
Post Office Box 7007
3030 North Central
Phoenix, AZ 85011

U.S. Bureau of Labor Statistics
Information Office
GAO Building
441 G Street Northwest
Washington, DC 20212

U.S. Bureau of Mines
Publications Distribution Section
4800 Forbes Avenue
Pittsburgh, PA 15213

U.S. Coast Guard
Commandant (G-BP)
Washington, DC 20593

U.S. Congressional Budget Office
Office of Intergovernmental Relations
2nd and D Streets Southwest
Washington, DC 20515

U.S. Department of Health and Human
  Services
Health Resources and Services
  Administration
Bureau of Health Professions
Office of Data Analysis and Management
5600 Fishers Lane
Rockville, MD 20852

U.S. Department of Labor
Women's Bureau
Washington, DC 20210

U.S. Department of State
Bureau of International Organizations
Bureau of Public Affairs
Washington, DC 20520

U.S. Department of Transportation
Urban Mass Transportation
  Administration
Information Services
Office of Technical Assistance
400 7th Street Southwest
Washington, DC 20590

U.S. Federal Home Loan Bank Board
Office of Communications
1700 G Street Northwest 2nd Floor
Washington, DC 20552

U.S. Federal Housing Administration
Management Information Systems
  Division Room 9134
U.S. Department of Housing and Urban
  Development
Washington, DC 20410

U.S. Forest Service
Post Office Box 2417
Washington, DC 20013

U.S. Internal Revenue Service
Office of Public Affairs
1111 Constitution Avenue Northwest
Washington, DC 20224

U.S. Interstate Commerce Commission
Office of the Secretary
Publications Room B-221
Washington, DC 20423

U.S. National Credit Union
  Administration
Office of Public Information
1776 G Street Northwest
Washington, DC, 20456

U.S. National Marine Fisheries Service
Public Affairs
Page Two Building
3300 Whitehaven Street Northwest
Washington, DC 20235

U.S. National Park Service
Office of Public Affairs
Washington, DC 20240

U.S. Travel and Tourism Administration
Office of Public Affairs
U.S. Department of Commerce
Washington, DC 20230

APPENDIX C: ADDRESSES: STATE PUBLICATIONS

Alabama Crop and Livestock Reporting
Service
Post Office Box 1071
Montgomery, AL 36192

Alabama Department of Industrial
Relations
Labor Market Analysis Unit
649 Monroe Street
Montgomery, AL 36130

Alabama Office of State Planning and
Federal Programs
State Planning Division
State Capitol
Montgomery, AL 36130

Alabama Vital Statistics Bureau
Special Services Administration
State Office Building Room 207
Montgomery, AL 36130

Alaska Crop and Livestock Reporting
Service
Post Office Box 799
Palmer, AK 99645

Alaska Department of Health and Social
Services
Information Systems Office
Statistical Support Section
Pouch H-01G
Juneau, AK 99811

Alaska Department of Labor
Research and Analysis Section
Post Office Box 1149
Juneau, AK 99802

Alaska Division of Budget and
Management
Pouch AM
Juneau, AK 99811

Arizona Crop and Livestock Reporting
Service
Agricultural Statistician
3001 Federal Building
Phoenix, AZ 85025

Arizona Department of Economic
Security
Labor Market Information
Publications
Post Office Box 6123
Phoenix, AZ 85005

Arizona Department of Health Services
Vital Records and Information Services
Bureau
Research and Analysis Section
1740 West Adams Street
Phoenix, AZ 85007

Arizona State University
Bureau of Business and Economic
Research
Tempe, AZ 85287

Arkansas Crop and Livestock Reporting
Service
Post Office Box 1417
Little Rock, AR 72203

Arkansas Division of Health Statistics
4815 West Markham Street
Little Rock, AR 72201

Arkansas Employment Security Division
Research and Analysis Section
Post Office Box 2981
Little Rock, AR 77203

Ball State University
Bureau of Business Research
College of Business
Muncie, IN 47306

Belo, A.H. Corp.
Communications Center
Dallas, TX 75265

Blue Sky Marketing
Publications Division
2935 Humboldt Avenue North
Minneapolis, MN 55411

California Crop and Livestock Reporting
  Service
Post Office Box 1258
Sacramento, CA 95806

California Department of Finance
Finance Research Section
Post Office Box 151
Sacramento, CA 95801

California Department of Health Services
Center for Health Statistics
Health Demographics Unit
714 P Street
Sacramento, CA 95814

California Employment Data and
  Research Division
Labor Market Information Section
800 Capitol Mall
Sacramento, CA 95814

Colorado Crop and Livestock Reporting
  Service
Post Office Box 17066
Denver, CO 80203

Colorado Department of Health
Health Statistics Section
4210 East 11th Avenue
Denver, CO 80220

Colorado Division of Employment and
  Training
Research and Development Section
251 East 12th Avenue
Denver, CO 80203

Connecticut Department of Agriculture
Marketing Division
State Office Building
Hartford, CT 06106

Connecticut Department of Economic
  Development
210 Washington Street
Hartford, CT 06106

Connecticut Employment Security
  Division
Office of Research and Information
200 Folly Brook Boulevard
Wethersfield, CT 06109

Connecticut Governor
Executive Office
2101 Capitol Avenue
Hartford, CT 06115

Connecticut State Department of Health
  Services
Health Statistics Division
Statistics and Demographics Unit
79 Elm Street
Hartford, CT 06106

County Supervisors Association. of
  California
1100 K Street
Sacramento, CA 95814

Crop Reporting Board Publications
U.S.D.A.
South Building Room 5829
Washington, DC 20250

Delaware Bureau of Disease Control
Division of Public Health
Dover, DE 19901

Delaware Department of Labor
Planning, Research and Evaluation
  Office
Post Office Box 9029
Newark, DE 19711

Delaware Development Office
Post Office Box 1401
Townsend Building 3rd Floor
Dover, DE 19903

District of Columbia
Department of Employment Services
Labor Market Information Division
500 C Street Northwest
Washington, DC 20001

District of Columbia
Department of Human Services
Research and Statistics Division
425 I Street Northwest Room 3107
Washington, DC 20001

District of Columbia
Office of Policy and Program Evaluation
District Building Room 412
1350 Pennsylvania Ave Northwest
Washington, DC 20004

Florida Crop and Livestock Reporting
  Service
1222 Woodward Street
Orlando, FL 32803

Florida Division of Employment Security
Research and Analysis Bureau
Caldwell Building
100 East Madison Street
Tallahassee, FL 32301

Florida Governor
Revenue and Economic Analysis Unit
The Capitol
400 South Monroe Street
Tallahassee, FL 32301

Florida Public Health Statistics Section
Post Office Box 210
Jacksonville, FL 32231

Georgia Crop Reporting Service
Stephens Federal Building Suite 320
355 East Hancock Avenue
Athens, GA 30613

Georgia Division of Public Health
State Health Building
47 Trinity Avenue Southwest
Atlanta, GA 30334

Georgia Labor Information Systems
State Labor Building
254 Washington Street Southwest
Atlanta, GA 30334

Georgia Office of Planning and Budget
State Data Center
Trinity-Washington Building
270 Washington Street Southwest
Atlanta, GA 30334

Georgia State University
Economic Forecasting Project
University Plaza
Atlanta, GA 30303

Hawaii Agricultural Reporting Service
Post Office Box 22159
Honolulu, HI 96801

Hawaii Department of Health
Research and Statistics Office
Post Office Box 3378
Honolulu, HI 96801

Hawaii Department of Labor and
  Industrial Relations
Labor Market and Employment Service
  Research Section
Post Office Box 3680
Honolulu, HI 96811

Hawaii Department of Planning and
  Economic Development
Information Office
Post Office Box 2359
Honolulu, HI 96804

Idaho Crop and Livestock Reporting
  Service
Post Office Box 1699
Boise, ID 83701

Idaho Department of Employment
Research and Analysis Bureau
Box 35
Boise, ID 83735

Idaho Department of Health and Welfare
Vital Statistics
Standards and Local Health Services
  Bureau
450 West State Street
Boise, ID 83720

Idaho Division of Economic and
  Community Affairs
State Census Data Center
Statehouse Room 108
Boise, ID 83720

Idaho Division of Finance Management
Statehouse Room 122
700 West State Street
Boise, ID 83720

Illinois Bureau of Employment Security
Research and Analysis Division
910 South Michigan Avenue
Chicago, IL 60605

Illinois Bureau of the Budget
Planning Office
5245 2nd Street Room 315
Springfield, IL 62705

Illinois Cooperative Crop Reporting
  Service
Post Office Box 429
Springfield, IL 62705

Illinois Department of Commerce and
  Community Affairs
Office of Research
620 East Adams
Springfield, IL 62701

Illinois Department of Public Health
Bureau of Statistics
Health Information and Evaluation
  Division
525 West Jefferson Street
Springfield, IL 62761

Indiana Crop and Livestock Reporting
  Service
Agriculture Administration Building
West Lafayette, IN 47907

Indiana Employment Security Division
Research and Statistics Section
10 North Senate Avenue
Indianapolis, IN 46204

Indiana State Board of Health
Public Health Statistics
1330 West Michigan Street
Indianapolis, IN 46206

Indiana University
Graduate School of Business
Research Division
10th and Fee Lane
Bloomington, IN 47405

Iowa Crop and Livestock Reporting
  Service
Federal Building Room 833
210 Walnut Street
Des Moines, IA 50309

Iowa Department of Job Service
Audit and Analysis Department
1000 East Grand Avenue
Des Moines, IA 50319

Iowa Development Commission
Communications Group
250 Jewett Building
Des Moines, IA 50309

Iowa Development Commission
Research and Development Group
250 Jewett Building
Des Moines, IA 50309

Iowa State Department of Health
Division of Records and Statistics
Statistics Services Unit
Lucas Office Building
Des Moines, IA 50319

Iowa State University
World Food Institute
102 E.O. Building
Ames, IA 50011

Kansas Bureau of Registration & Health
  Statistics
Forbes Field
Topeka, KS 66620

Kansas Department of Human Resources
Division of Staff Services
Research and Analysis Section
401 Topeka Avenue
Topeka, KS 66603

Kansas State Board of Agriculture
109 Southwest 19th Street
Topeka, KS 66612

Kansas State University
Office of University Relations
8 Anderson Hall
Manhattan, KS 66506

Kentucky Council of Economic Advisors
University of Kentucky
College of Business and Economics
451 Commerce Building
Lexington, KY 40506

Kentucky Crop and Livestock Reporting
  Service
Post Office Box 1120
Louisville, KY 40201

Kentucky Department of Economic
  Development
Division of Planning and Research
133 Holmes Street
Frankfort, KY 40601

Kentucky Office of Manpower Services
Labor Market Research and Analysis
  Branch
275 East Main Street 2nd Floor West
Frankfort, KY 40621

Kentucky State Center for Health
  Statistics
Health Services Bureau
Health and Vital Statistics Office
275 East Main Street
Frankfort, KY 40621

Louisiana Department of Labor
Management and Finance Office
Research and Statistics Unit
Post Office Box 44094
Baton Rouge, LA 70804

Louisiana Office of Public Health
  Statistics
Post Office Box 60630
New Orleans, LA 70160

Louisiana State Planning Office
State Capitol Building
Baton Rouge, LA 70804

Louisiana State University, Baton Rouge
College of Business Administration
Division of Research
Baton Rouge, LA 70803

Louisiana State University, Baton Rouge
Department of Agricultural Economics
  and Agribusiness
Baton Rouge, LA 70803

Louisiana State University in New
  Orleans
Division of Business and Economic
  Research
New Orleans, LA 70148

Maine Bureau of Employment Security
Division of Economic Analysis and
Research
20 Union Street
Augusta, ME 04330

Maine Department of Agriculture, Food
and Rural Resources
Statehouse Station 28
Augusta, ME 04333

Maine Department of Commerce and
Industry
State Development Office
Executive Department
193 State Street
Augusta, ME 04330

Maine Department of Human Services
Division of Research and Data
Health Planning and Development
Bureau
Statehouse Station 11
Augusta, ME 04333

Maryland Crop Reporting Service
50 Harry S. Truman Parkway Room 202
Annapolis, MD 21401

Maryland Department of Economic and
Community Development
Public Affairs Division
45 Calvert Street
Annapolis, MD 21401

Maryland Department of Employment
and Training
1100 North Eutaw Street
Baltimore, MD 21201

Maryland State Department of Health
and Mental Hygiene
Center for Health Statistics
201 West Preston Street
Baltimore, MD 21201

Massachusetts Department of Commerce
and Development
Leverett Saltonstall State Office Building
100 Cambridge Street
Boston, MA 02202

Massachusetts Department of Food and
Agriculture
Leverett Saltonstall Building
100 Cambridge Street
Boston, MA 02202

Massachusetts Division of Employment
Security
Labor Area Research Department
Charles F. Hurley Building
Boston, MA 02114

Massachusetts Registry of Vital Records
and Statistics
McCormack Building Room 107
1 Ashburton Place
Boston, MA 02108

Memphis State University
Fogelman College of Business and
Economics
Bureau of Business and Economic
Research
Memphis, TN 38152

Michigan Department of Management
and Budget
Revenue and Tax Analysis Office
Post Office Box 30026
Lansing, MI 48909

Michigan Employment Security
Commission
Labor Market Analysis Unit
7310 Woodward Avenue
Detroit, MI 48202

Michigan Vital Health and Statistics
Office
3500 North Logan Street
Post Office Box 30035
Lansing, MI 48909

Minnesota Department of Economic
Security
Research and Statistics Services Office
390 North Robert Street
St. Paul, MN 55101

Minnesota Health Statistics Center
717 Southeast Delaware Street
Post Office Box 9441
Minneapolis, MN 55440

Minnesota State Documents Center
117 University Avenue
St. Paul, MN 55155

Mississippi Crop and Livestock Reporting
Service
Post Office Box 980
Jackson, MS 39205

Mississippi Employment Security
Commission
Research and Statistics Department
Post Office Box 1699
Jackson, MS 39205

Mississippi State Department of Health
Public Health Statistics Office
Post Office Box 1700
Jackson, MS 39205

Mississippi State University
College of Business and Industry
Division of Research
Post Office Box 5288
Mississippi State, MS 39762

Missouri Center for Health Statistics
Post Office Box 570
Jefferson City, MO 65102

Missouri Crop and Livestock Reporting
Service
Post Office Box L
Columbia, MO 65205

Missouri Department of Labor and
Industrial Relations
Post Office Box 59
Jefferson City, MO 65104

Missouri Division of Community and
Economic Development
Post Office Box 118
Jefferson City, MO 65102

Montana Census and Economic
Information Center
Capitol Station
1424 9th Avenue
Helena, MT 59620

Montana Crop and Livestock Reporting
Service
Post Office Box 4369
Helena, MT 59604

Montana Department of Health and
Environmental Science
Bureau of Records and Statistics
Cogswell Building
Helena, MT 59620

Montana Department of Labor and
Industry
Research and Analysis Section
Post Office Box 1728
Helena, MT 59624

Nebraska Bureau of Vital Statistics
301 Centennial Mall South
Lincoln, NE 68509

Nebraska Crop and Livestock Reporting
Service
Post Office Box 81069
Lincoln, NE 68501

Nebraska Department of Economic
Development
Division of Research
Box 94666
Lincoln, NE 68509

Nebraska Division of Employment
Research and Statistics Section
550 South 16th Street
Post Office Box 94600
State House Station
Lincoln, NE 68509

Nelson A. Rockefeller Institute of
   Government
State University of New York
411 State Street
Albany, NY 12203

Nevada Crop and Livestock Reporting
   Service
Agricultural Statistician
Post Office Box 8888
Reno, NV 89507

Nevada Employment Security Research
   Section
500 East 3rd Street
Carson City, NV 89713

Nevada Governor's Office of Planning
   Coordination
Capitol Complex
Carson City, NV 89710

Nevada Office of Community Service
Capitol Complex
Carson City, NV 89710

Nevada Section of Vital Statistics
505 East King Street Room 102
Carson City, NV 89710

Nevada State Gaming Control Board
Publications Office
1150 East William Street
Carson City, NV 89710

New Hampshire Bureau of Vital Records
   and Health Statistics
Public Health Services Division
Health and Welfare Building
Hazen Drive
Concord, NH 03301

New Hampshire Department of
   Employment Security
Economic Analysis and Reports Section
325 South Main Street
Concord, NH 03301

New Jersey Associates
Box 505
Montclair, NJ 07042

New Jersey Crop Reporting Service
Health and Agriculture Building
Room 204 CN 330
Trenton, NJ 08625

New Jersey Department of Labor
Division of Planning and Research
CN056
Trenton, NJ 08625

New Jersey Health Data Services
Room 501 CN 360
Trenton, NJ 08625

New Jersey Office of Economic Policy
1 West State Street
Trenton, NJ 08625

New Mexico Crop and Livestock
   Reporting Service
Post Office Box 1809
Las Cruces, NM 88004

New Mexico Economic Development
   Division
Bataan Memorial Building
Santa Fe, NM 87503

New Mexico Employment Security
   Department
Research and Statistics Section
Post Office Box 1928
Albuquerque, NM 87103

New Mexico Health and Environment
   Department
Health Services Division
Post Office Box 968
Santa Fe, NM 87504

New York Department of Commerce
Bureau of Business Research
99 Washington Avenue
Albany, NY 12245

New York Department of Labor
Division of Research and Statistics
State Campus Building 12
Albany, NY 12240

New York Office of Biostatistics
Room 321 ESP Tower Building
Albany, NY 12237

New York State Crop Reporting Service
State Campus Building 8
Albany, NY 12235

North Carolina Crop and Livestock
   Reporting Service
Agricultural Statistician
Post Office Box 27767
1 West Edenton Street
Raleigh, NC 27611

North Carolina Labor Market
   Information Division
Post Office Box 25903
Raleigh, NC 27611

North Carolina Office of State Budget
   and Management
Research and Planning Services
116 West Jones Street
Raleigh, NC 27611

North Carolina State Center for Health
   Statistics
Post Office Box 2091
Raleigh, NC 27602

North Dakota Crop and Livestock
   Reporting Service
345 U.S. Post Office Federal Building
Post Office Box 3166
Fargo, ND 58108

North Dakota Economic Development
   Commission
1050 East Interstate Avenue
Bismarck, ND 58505

North Dakota Job Service
Research and Statistics Section
1000 East Divide Avenue
Post Office Box 1537
Bismarck, ND 58501

North Dakota State Department of
   Health
Division of Vital Statistics
State Capitol
Bismarck, ND 58505

Northland Press
Post Office Box N
Flagstaff, AZ 86002

Norwest Bank Minneapolis
Economic Department
7th and Marquette Streets
Minneapolis, MN 55479

Ohio Bureau of Employment Services
Labor Market Information Division
Statistical Distribution Unit
1160 Dublin Road
Columbus, OH 43215

Ohio Crop Reporting Service
Federal Building Room 608
202 North High Street
Columbus, OH 43215

Ohio Data Users Center
Post Office Box 1001
Columbus, OH 43216

Ohio Department of Health
Data Services Division
246 North High Street 7th Floor
Columbus, OH 43215

Oklahoma Crop and Livestock Reporting
Service
Post Office Box 1095
Oklahoma City, OK 73101

Oklahoma Employment Security
Commission
Research and Planning Division
310 Will Rogers Building
Oklahoma City, OK 73105

Oklahoma Public Health Statistics
Division
Data Management Division
1000 Northeast 10th Street
Post Office Box 53551
Oklahoma City, OK 73152

Oklahoma State University
Office of Business and Economic
Research
345 Business Building
Stillwater, OK 74078

Oregon Department of Agriculture
635 Capitol Street Northeast
Salem, OR 97310

Oregon Department of Economic
Development
Research and Information Division
155 Cottage Street Northeast
Salem, OR 97310

Oregon Employment Division
Research and Statistics-LMI
875 Union Street Northeast
Salem, OR 97311

Oregon Health Division
Center for Health Statistics
State Office Building
Post Office Box 116
Portland, OR 97207

Pennsylvania Health Data Center
Post Office Box 90
Harrisburg, PA 17108

Pennsylvania Office of Employment
Security
Research and Statistics Section
7th and Forster Streets
Harrisburg, PA 17121

Pennsylvania State Book Store
Management Services Bureau
Post Office Box 1365
Harrisburg, PA 17125

Pennsylvania State University
College of Business Administration
Center for Research
103 Business Administration Building II
University Park, PA 16802

Presideo Press
31 Pamaron Way
Novato, CA 94947

Providence Journal Co.
75 Fountain Street
Providence, RI 02902

Rhode Island Department of
Employment Security
Labor Market Information Section
24 Mason Street
Providence, RI 02903

Rhode Island Division of Vital Statistics
Cannon Building Room 101
75 Davis Street
Providence, RI 02908

Rhode Island Economic Research
Division
7 Jackson Wallway
Providence, RI 02903

South Carolina Crop and Livestock
Reporting Service
Post Office Box 1911
Columbia, SC 29202

South Carolina Division of Biostatistics
Vital Records and Public Health Statistics
 Office
2600 Bull Street
Columbia, SC 29201

South Carolina Employment Security
 Commission
Research and Analysis Section
Post Office Box 995
Columbia, SC 29202

South Carolina State Budget and Control
 Board
Division of Research and Statistics
 Services
Rembert C. Dennis Building Room 337
1000 Assembly Street
Columbia, SC 29201

South Dakota Crop and Livestock
 Reporting Service
3528 South Western Avenue
Post Office Drawer V
Sioux Falls, SD 57117

South Dakota Department of Labor
Research and Statistics
Administrative Services Office
607 North 4th Street
Post Office Box 1730
Aberdeen, SD 57401

South Dakota State Planning Bureau
Capitol Building
Pierre, SD 57501

South Dakota Vital Records Program
Joe Foss Building
Pierre, SD 57501

Tax Foundation of Hawaii
1067 Alakea Street Suite 400
Honolulu, HI 96813

Tayloe Murphy Institute
University of Virginia
Dynamics Building 4th Floor
2015 Ivy Road
Charlottesville, VA 22903

Tennessee Crop Reporting Service
Ellington Agricultural Center
Post Office Box 41505
Nashville, TN 37204

Tennessee Department of Employment
 Security
Research and Statistics Division
519 Cordell Hull Building
Nashville, TN 37219

Tennessee Department of Health and
 Environment
State Center for Health Statistics
Cordell Hull Building
Nashville, TN 37219

Tennessee State Planning Office
1800 James K. Polk State Office Building
505 Deaderick Street
Nashville, TN 37219

Texas Crop and Livestock Reporting
 Service
Agricultural Statistician
Post Office Box 70
Austin, TX 78767

Texas Department of Health
Vital Statistics Bureau
Statistical Services Division
1100 West 49th Street
Austin, TX 78756

Texas Employment Commission
Economic Research and Analysis
 Department
15th and Congress Avenue
Austin, TX 78778

Transrep Bibliographies
Post Office Box 22678
Denver, CO 80222

University of Alabama
Center for Business and Economic
  Research
Post Office Box AK
University, AL 35486

University of Arizona
Division of Economic and Business
  Research
College of Business and Public
  Administration
Tucson, AZ 85721

University of Arkansas
Bureau of Business and Economic
  Research
College of Business Administration
Fayetteville, AR 72701

University of Arkansas at Little Rock
Industrial Research and Extension
  Center
33rd and University Avenue
Little Rock, AR 72204

University of California, Los Angeles
Business Forecasting Project
Graduate School of Management
Room 4371-C
Los Angeles, CA 90024

University of Colorado
Business Research Division
Graduate School of Business
  Administration
Campus Box 420
Boulder, CO 80309

University of Delaware
Agricultural Experiment Station
Department of Agricultural Economics
Newark, DE 19711

University of Florida
Bureau of Business and Economic
  Research
College of Business Administration
221 Matherly Hall
Gainesville, FL 32611

University of Georgia
Graduate School of Business
  Administration
Division of Research
Athens, GA 30602

University of Illinois
Bureau of Economic and Business
  Research
428 Commerce West
1206 S 6th Street
Champaign, IL 61820

University of Kansas
Center for Public Affairs
607 Blake Street
Lawrence, KS 66045

University of Kansas
Institute for Economic and Business
  Research
319 Raymond Nichols Hall
Lawrence, KS 66045

University of Massachusetts
Center for Business and Economic
  Research
Amherst, MA 01003

University of Michigan
Survey Research Center
Post Office Box 1248
426 Thompson Street
Ann Arbor, MI 48106

University of Missouri-Columbia
College of Business and Public
  Administration
10 Professional Building
Columbia, MO 65211

University of Nebraska-Lincoln
Bureau of Business Research
College of Business Administration
  Room 200
Lincoln, NE 68588

University of Nevada
Bureau of Business and Economic
  Research
College of Business Administration
Reno, NV 89557

University of New Mexico
Bureau of Business and Economic
  Research
Institute of Applied Research Services
Albuquerque, NM 87131

University of North Dakota
Bureau of Business and Economic
  Research
Grand Forks, ND 58202

University of Oklahoma
Center for Economic and Management
  Research
307 West Brooks Street Room 4
Norman, OK 73019

University of South Carolina
Division of Research
College of Business Administration
Columbia, SC 29208

University of South Dakota
Business Research Bureau
School of Business
Vermillion, SD 57069

University of Tennessee, Knoxville
Center for Business and Economic
  Research
College of Business Administration
Glocker Building Suite 100
Knoxville, TN 37996

University of Texas at Austin
Bureau of Business Research
Post Office Box 7459 University Station
Austin, TX 78712

University of Utah
Bureau of Economic and Business
  Research
Graduate School of Business
401 Business Office Building
Salt Lake City, UT 84112

University of Wyoming
Institute for Policy Research
Post Office Box 3925 University Station
Laramie, WY 82071

University Presses of Florida
15 Northwest 15th Street
Gainesville, FL 32603

Utah Association. of Counties
10 West Broadway Suite 311
Salt Lake City, UT 84101

Utah Bureau of Health Statistics
Post Office Box 2500
Salt Lake City, UT 84110

Utah Economic and Industrial
  Development Department
6150 State Office Building
Salt Lake City, UT 84114

Utah Foundation
308 Continental Bank Building
Salt Lake City, UT 84101

Utah Job Service
Labor Market Information Services
  Section
174 Social Hall Avenue
Salt Lake City, UT 84111

Utah State Department of Agriculture
Crop and Livestock Reporting Service
Post Office Box 25007
Salt Lake City, UT 84125

Valley National Bank of Phoenix
Economic Research Department
241 North Central Avenue
Post Office Box 71
Phoenix, AZ 85001

Vermont Department of Agriculture
State Office Building
116 State Street
Montpelier, VT 05602

Vermont Department of Employment
and Training
Research and Statistics Section
Post Office Box 488 Green Mountain
Drive
Montpelier, VT 05602

Vermont Division of Public Health
Statistics
115 Colchester Avenue
Post Office Box 70
Burlington, VT 05401

Vermont Office of the Governor
Policy Research Staff
Pavillion Office Building
109 State Street
Montpelier, VT 05602

Virginia Crop Reporting Service
Agricultural Statistician
Post Office Box 1659
Richmond, VA 23213

Virginia Department of Health
Vital Records and Health Statistics
Division
Health Statistics Center
Post Office Box 1000
Richmond, VA 23208

Virginia Division of Industrial
Development
Office of the Governor
1010 State Office Building
Richmond, VA 23219

Virginia Employment Commission
Research and Analysis Division
Post Office Box 1358
730 East Main Street
Richmond, VA 23211

Washington Department of Social and
Health Services
Health Statistics Center
Health Data Center ET 14
Post Office Box 9709
Olympia, WA 98504

Washington Employment Security
Department
Research and Statistics Branch
Olympia, WA 98504

Washington Office of Finance
Management
Division of Policy Analysis and
Forecasting
Insurance Building MS AQ-44
Olympia, WA 98504

Washington Research Council
906 Columbia Street
Olympia, WA 98501

Washington State Crop and Livestock
Reporting Service
909 1st Avenue Room 3039
Seattle, WA 98174

Wayne State University
Bureau of Business Research
209 Prentis Building
Detroit, MI 48202

West Virginia Chamber of Commerce
Research Department
Post Office Box 2789
Charleston, WV 25305

West Virginia
Crop Reporting Service
Charleston, WV 25305

West Virginia Department of
Employment Security
Labor and Economic Research Section
112 California Avenue
Charleston, WV 25305

West Virginia Health Statistics Center
Health Planning and Evaluation
1800 Washington Street East
Charleston, WV 25305

Wichita State University
Center for Business and Economic
  Research
College of Business Administration
Wichita, KS 67208

Wisconsin Agricultural Reporting
  Service
Post Office Box 9160
Madison, WI 53715

Wisconsin Demographic Services Center
Documents Sales and Distribution
202 Thorton Avenue
Box 7840
Madison, WI 53707

Wisconsin Department of Development
123 West Washington Avenue
Post Office Box 7944
Madison, WI 53707

Wisconsin Division of Health
Health Statistics Bureau
Post Office Box 309
Madison, WI 53701

Wisconsin Job Service Division
Labor Market Information
Post Office Box 7944
Madison, WI 53707

Wyoming Crop and Livestock Reporting
  Service
Agricultural Statistician
Box 1148
Cheyenne, WY 82003

Wyoming Department of Administration
  and Fiscal Control
Research and Statistics Division
Emerson Building Room 302
Cheyenne, WY 82002

Wyoming Department of Health and
  Social Services
Health and Medical Services Division
Hathaway Building
Cheyenne, WY 82002

Wyoming Employment Security
  Commission
Research and Analysis Section
Post Office Box 2760
Casper, WY 82602

APPENDIX D: GLOSSARY OF TERMS

Agriculture Industry	The agriculture industry generally includes the following sectors: crops, livestock, dairy and poultry.
Air Transportation	A sector of the transportation industry.
Banking	A sector of the finance industry.
Birth	Data on birth is generally included in vital statistics.
Chemicals	A sector of the manufacturing industry.
Communications	A sector of the transportation industry.
Credit	A sector of the finance industry.
Credit Unions	A sector of the finance industry.
Crops	A sector of the agriculture industry.
Death	Data on death is generally included in vital statistics.
Department Stores	A sector of the retail trade industry.
Dairy	A sector of the agriculture industry.
Divorce	Data on divorce is generally included in vital statistics.
Economic Conditions	Economic conditions generally includes economic indicators such as Consumer Price Index, cost of living, Producer Price Index, measures of production and/or analyses of specific industries.
Energy	The energy industry generally includes various power generating utilities and mining for fuel minerals. However, in some instances, particularly with state publications, the two industry groups may overlap.

Finance	The finance industry generally includes the following sectors: banking, credit, credit unions, securities and commodities, savings institutions, insurance and real estate.
Funeral Services	A sector of the service industries.
Government	Government finance and operations can include such data as defense or military expenditures, government budget and debt, and tax collection.
Health Care Services	A sector of the service industries.
Highway Transportation	A sector of the transportation industry.
Insurance	A sector of the finance industry.
Livestock	A sector of the agriculture industry.
Manufacturing	The manufacturing industry can include the following sectors: food products, tobacco products, textiles, apparel, forest or wood products, publishing, chemicals, metal products, machinery and transportation equipment.
Marriage	Data on marriage is generally included in vital statistics.
Minerals Industries	The minerals industries are generally considered to be all types of mining except those involving fuel minerals. The energy industry generally encompasses mining for fuel minerals. However, in some instances, particularly with state publications, the two industry groups may overlap.
Personal Income	Personal income measures can include wages, salary and other measures of individual personal income, household income, as well as aggregate measures of personal income.
Poultry	A sector of the agriculture industry.
Railroads	A sector of the transportation industry.
Real Estate	A sector of the finance industry.
Restaurants	A sector of the retail trade industry.
Retail Trade	The retail trade industry generally includes the following sectors: Clothing, general merchandise or department stores, food stores or supermarkets and restaurants.

211

S.M.S.A.	Standard Metropolitan Statistical Area is an area designated by the Bureau of the Census as a large population nucleus and nearby communities which have a high degree of economic and social integration with that nucleus. After the 1980 Census, S.M.S.A. boundaries were re-evaluated and redesignated by the Bureau and the term was shortened to M.S.A. (Metropolitan Statistical Area). Publications annotated as containing data by S.M.S.A. may now reflect this change in designation.
Savings Institutions	A sector of the finance industry.
Securities Industry	A sector of the finance industry.
Service Industries	The service industries generally include the following sectors: hotels, etc., repair services, business services including advertising, amusement or recreation, health care and legal services.
Supermarkets	A sector of the retail trade industry.
Tourism	The tourism industry can include data on travel, tourist accommodations, travel related employment and expenditures, volume of visitors to parks or other tourist attractions.
Transportation	The transportation industry includes the following sectors: railroads, urban mass transportation, motor freight or highway transportation, water transportation, air transportation and communications.
Urban Mass Transportation	A sector of the transportation industry.
Vital Statistics	Vital statistics generally include birth, death, marriage and divorce.
Water Transportation	A sector of the transportation industry.

APPENDIX E: ABBREVIATIONS USED

A.A.C.R.	Anglo-American Cataloguing Rules
A.A.C.R. II	Anglo-American Cataloguing Rules second edition
ABA	American Bankers Association
ADI	Area Dominant Influence
AMS	Administrative Management Society
ARL	Association of Research Libraries
Co.	Company
CPC	College Placement Council
CPI	Consumer Price Index
DMA	Designated Marketing Area
EIA	Electronics Industry Association
ERIC	Educational Resources Information Center
FAA	Federal Aviation Administration
F.A.O.	Food and Agriculture Organization (United Nations)
FHA	(U.S.) Federal Housing Administration
FTE	full-time equivalent
(fy)	fiscal year
FY	Fiscal Year
GSU	Georgia State University
IRA	Individual Retirement Account
I.R.S.	(U.S.) Internal Revenue Service
ISSN	International Standard Serial Number
ITEM NO	U.S. Government Printing Office item number
LCCN	Library of Congress Card Number
LPG	liquefied petroleum gas
mf	microfiche
MVMA	Motor Vehicle Manufacturers Association of the U.S.
NABE	National Association of Business Economists
NADA	National Automobile Dealers Association
NASDAQ	National Association of Securities Dealers
NCES	National Center for Education Statistics
NFIB	National Federation of Independent Business
no	number
nos	numbers
N.T.I.S.	National Technical Information Service
O.E.C.D.	Organisation for Economic Cooperation and Development
O.P.E.C.	Organization of Petroleum Exporting Countries

P/H	postage and handling
pt	part
(py)	program year
R&D	research and development
REIT	Real Estate Investment Trust
RMA	Robert Morris Associates
SASE	self-addressed, stamped envelope
SEC	(U.S.) Securities and Exchange Commission
S.M.S.A.	Standard Metropolitan Statistical Area
SRC'S	Survey Research Center
STF	Summary Tape File
SUDOCS	Superintendent of Documents classification system
SUNYA	State University of New York at Albany
suppl	supplement
TV	television
U.S.	United States
U.S.A.	United States of America
U.S.D.A.	U.S. Department of Agriculture
U.S.S.R.	Union of Soviet Socialist Republics
vol	volume
(year)	calendar year

TITLE INDEX

A

B

C

D

E

F

G

H

I

J

K

L

N

O

S

T

W

Y

SUBJECT INDEX

References in bold indicate publications which are primarily about the relevant subject.

Air transportation
[*See also* Transportation *for publications with data breakdown by sector of the industry*]
United States **A0040, A0700, A1030, A1310, F0050**
By state
[*See also* Air transportation: United States *for publications with data breakdown by state*]
Alabama
[*See also* (subject): United States *or* United States: (subject) *for publications with data breakdown by state*]
Agriculture F0080, **S0010**, S2100
[*See also* Alabama: Forest products]
Birth S0030, S0050, S2100
Construction F0080, S0030, S1020, S2100
Consumer Price Index S2100
Death S0030, S0050, S2100
Divorce S0050, S2100
Economic conditions **F0080**, S0030, **S0040, S1020**, S2100
Education **A1380**, S0030, S2100
Employment F0080, **S0020**, S0030, S0040, S1020, S2100
[*For wage and/or salary data, see* Alabama: Personal income]
Energy S0030, S0040, S2100
Finance F0080, S1020, S2100
Forest products S0030
Gross State Product S0040, S2100
Housing F0080, S0030, S1020, S2100
Manufacturing S2100
Marriage S0050, S2100
Minerals industries S0030
[*For fuel minerals, see also* Alabama: Energy]
Personal income A1380, F0080, S0020, S0030, S0040, S1020, S2100
Population A1380, S0020, S0030, S0040, S0050, S2100
Production S0040, S2100
Retail trade S0030, S0040, S1020, S2100
Service industries S0030, S2100
Statistical abstract **S0030, S2100**
Transportation S0030, S2100
Unemployment F0080, S0020, S0030, S1020, S2100
Vital statistics S0030, **S0050**, S2100
[*See also* Alabama: Population]
Wholesale trade S2100
Alaska
[*See also* (subject): United States *or* United States: (subject) *for publications with data breakdown by state*]
Agriculture **S0070**
[*See also* Alaska: Fishing, Alaska: Forest products]
Birth S0060, S0090

Construction S0090
Consumer Price Index S0080, S0090
Cost of living S0080, S0090
Death S0060, S0090
Divorce S0060
Economic conditions S0080, S0090
Employment **S0080**
[*For wage and/or salary data, see* Alaska: Personal income]
Energy
[*For fuel minerals, see also* Alaska: Minerals industries]
Finance S0090
Fishing S0090
Forest products S0090
Housing S0090
Marriage S0060
Minerals industries S0090
Personal income S0080, S0090
Population S0060, S0080, S0090
Statistical abstract **S0090**
Transportation S0090
Unemployment S0080
Vital statistics **S0060**, S0090
[*See also* Alaska: Population]
Aluminium
[*See also* Minerals industries *for publications with data breakdown by sector of the industry*]
United States **A0050**
American Indians
By state
Arizona **F0420**
Nevada **F0420**
Utah **F0420**
Arizona
[*See also* (subject): United States *or* United States: (subject) *for publications with data breakdown by state*]
Agriculture **S0110**, S2110, S2120, S2510
[*Related heading*: Arizona: Forest products]
American Indians **F0420**
Birth S0130, S2120, S2510
Construction S0100, S2110, S2120, S2510
Consumer Price Index S0100, S2510
Death S0130, S2120, S2510
Divorce S0130, S2120
Economic conditions **S0100, S2110**, S2120, S2510
Education S2120, S2510
Employment **S0120**, S2110, S2120, S2510
Energy S0100, S2110, S2120
[*For fuel minerals, see also* Arizona: Minerals industries]
Finance S2110, S2120, S2510
Forest products **A1480**
Housing S0100, S2110, S2120, S2510
Manufacturing S2110, S2120, S2510

Marriage S0130, S2120
Minerals industries S2110, S2120, S2510
[*For fuel minerals, see also* Arizona: Energy]
Native Americans **F0420**
Personal income S2110, S2120, S2510
Population S0120, S0130, S2110, S2120, S2510
Retail trade S0100, S2110, S2120, S2510
Service industries S2110, S2120, S2510
Statistical abstract **S2120, S2510**
Tourism S2110, S2120, S2510
Transportation S2110, S2120, S2510
Unemployment S0120, S2110, S2120, S2510
Vital statistics **S0130**, S2120, S2510
[*See also* Arizona: Population]
Wholesale trade S2120
Arkansas
[*See also* (subject): United States *or* United States: (subject) *for publications with data breakdown by state*]
Agriculture **S0140**
Birth S0150
Construction S1020, S2130
Consumer Price Index S2130
Death S0150
Divorce S0150
Economic conditions **S1020, S2130**, S2140
Education **A1380**, S2140
Employment **S0160**, S1020, S2130, S2140
[*For wage and/or salary data, see* Arkansas: Personal income]
Energy
[*For fuel minerals, see also* Arkansas: Minerals industries]
Finance S1020, S2130, S2140
Housing S1020, S2130
Manufacturing S2130, S2140
Marriage S0150
Minerals industries S2130
Personal income A1380, S0160, S1020, S2130, S2140
Population A1380, S0150, S0160, S2140
Retail trade S1020, S2130, S2140
Service industries S2140
Statistical abstract **S2140**
Transportation S2130
Unemployment S0160, S1020, S2130, S2140
Vital statistics **S0150**
[*See also* Arkansas: Population]
Wholesale trade S2130, S2140
Banking
[*See also* Finance *for publications with data breakdown by sector of the industry*]
United States **A0090, A0100, A0370, A0840, A0860, A1440, F0060, F0140**
By state
[*See also* Banking: United States *for publications with data breakdown by state*]

Colorado **F0140**
Kansas **F0140**
Missouri **F0140**
Nebraska **F0140**
New Mexico **F0140**
Oklahoma **F0140**
Wyoming **F0140**
Batteries (Motor vehicle)
United States **A0380**
[*See also* Batteries (Motor vehicle): World *for publications with data breakdown by country*]
By state
[*See also* Batteries (Motor vehicle): World *for publications with data breakdown by state*]
Birth
World F0710
United States A0170, F0250, F0280, F0290, F0300, F0670, F0680, F0690, F0700
[*See also* Birth: World *for publications with data breakdown by country*]
By state
[*See also* Birth: United States *for publications with data breakdown by state*]
Alabama S0030, S0050, S2100
Alaska S0060, S0090
Arizona S0130, S2120, S2510
Arkansas S0150
California S0200, S0210, S0320, S1830
Colorado S0250, S2090
Connecticut S0310
Delaware S0330
District of Columbia S0370
Florida S0420, S2190
Georgia S0460, S0480, S2210
Hawaii S0500, S0520
Idaho S0560
Illinois S0600, S0630
Indiana S0170, S0670, S0680
Iowa S0740
Kansas S0760, S2230
Kentucky S0810, S0820
Louisiana S0860, S0880, S0890
Maine S0920
Maryland S0950, S0970
Massachusetts S1010
Michigan S1060, S2660
Minnesota S1090, S1100
Mississippi S1140, S1170
Missouri S1180, S2280
Montana S1230, S1240, S1260
Nebraska S1280, S1300
Nevada S1350, S1370
New Hampshire S1390
New Jersey S1410, S1440
New Mexico S1490, S2320
New York S1320, S1500, S1520
North Carolina S1560, S1580
North Dakota S1600, S2330

Birth
  By state [ctd]
    Ohio S1680
    Oklahoma S1720, S2340
    Oregon S1770
    Pennsylvania S1800, S1810
    Rhode Island S1860, S1870
    South Carolina S1900, S1930
    South Dakota S1960, S1970
    Tennessee S2050, S2400
    Texas S2070, S2080, S2410
    Utah S2430, S2460, S2470, S2480
    Vermont S2540
    Virginia S2570
    Washington S2610, S2630
    West Virginia S2670, S2700
    Wisconsin S2730, S2750
    Wyoming S2780, S2790
Boating
  [Related headings: Tourism, Transportation]
  United States **F0750**
Book publishing
  United States **A0390**
Brewing
  [Related heading: Distilled spirits]
  United States **A1410**
Cadmium
  [See also Minerals industries for publications
  with data breakdown by sector of the industry]
  United States **A1490**
California
  [See also (subject): United States or United
  States: (subject) for publications with data
  breakdown by state]
  Agriculture **S0190**, S0200, S0230, S0320,
  S1830
  [Related heading: California: Forest
  products]
  Birth S0200, S0210, S0320, S1830
  Construction S0200, S0230, S0320, S1830,
  S2150
  Consumer Price Index S0200, S0230, S1830,
  S2150
  Death S0200, S0210, S0320, S1830
  Divorce S0200, S0210, S1830
  Economic conditions S0200, **S0230**, S0320,
  S1830, **S2150**
  Education S0200, S0320, S1830
  Employment S0200, **S0220**, S0230, S0320,
  S1830, S2150
  Energy S0200, S0230, S0320, S1830, S2150
  Finance S0200, S0230, S1830
  Fishing S0200, S1830
  Forest products **A1480**, S0200, S0230, S0320,
  S1830
  Gross State Product S2150
  Housing S0200, S0230, S0320, S1830, S2150
  Manufacturing S0200, S1830

  Marriage S0200, S0210, S0320, S1830
  Minerals industries S0200, S0320, S1830
  [For fuel minerals, see also California:
  Energy]
  Personal income S0200, S0220, S0230,
  S1830, S2150
  Population S0200, S0210, S0220, S0230,
  S0320, S1830
  Producer Price Index S2150
  Production S2150
  Retail trade S0200, S1830
  Service industries S0200, S1830
  Statistical abstract **S0200, S0320, S1830**
  Tourism S0230
  [See also California: Transportation]
  Transportation S0200, S0230, S0320, S1830
  Unemployment S0200, S0220, S0230, S0320,
  S1830
  Vital statistics S0200, **S0210**, S0320, S1830
  [See also California: Population]
  Wholesale trade S1830
Cancer
  [See also Disease and Death for publications
  with data breakdown by type of disease or
  cause of death]
  United States **A0120**
  By state
  [See also Cancer: United States for
  publications with data breakdown by state]
Canned food
  [See also Agriculture for publications with data
  breakdown by sector of the industry]
  United States **A1120**
  By state
  [See also Canned food: United States for
  publications with data breakdown by state]
Chemical industries
  World **A0140**
  United States **A0140**
Chemists
  United States A0140
Child abuse
  [See also Crime for publications with data
  breakdown by type]
  United States **A0220**
Churches
  United States **A1080**
Clerical workers
  United States **A0020**
Clothing industry
  United States
    By industry/sector
      Mens/boys **A0420**
Coal
  [See also Minerals industries and Energy for
  publications with data breakdown by sector of
  the industry]
  United States **A1040**

By state
[*See also* Coal: United States *for publications with data breakdown by state*]
Coinage
World **A0710, A1360**
United States **F0720**
[*See also* Coinage: World *for publications with data breakdown by country*]
Colorado
[*See also* (subject): United States *or* United States: (subject) *for publications with data breakdown by state*]
Agriculture **S0240**, S2090
[*Related heading*: Colorado: Forest products]
Birth S0250, S2090
Construction S2090, S2160
Death S0250, S2090
Divorce S0250
Economic conditions S2090, **S2160**
Education S2090
Employment **S0260**, S2090, S2160
Energy S2090, S2160
Finance **F0140**, S2090, S2160
Forest products **A1480**, S2090
Housing S2090, S2160
Manufacturing S2090
Marriage S0250
Minerals industries S2090
[*For fuel minerals, see also* Colorado: Energy]
Personal income S0260, S2090, S2160
Population S0250, S0260, S2090
Retail trade S2090
Service industries S2090
Statistical abstract **S2090**
Tourism S2160
[*See also* Colorado: Transportation]
Transportation S2090
Unemployment S0260, S2090, S2160
Vital statistics **S0250**, S2090
[*See also* Colorado: Population]
Wholesale trade S2090
College graduates
United States **A0430**
Communications
[*See also* Transportation *for publications with data breakdown by sector of the industry*]
United States
By industry/sector
[*See also* Communications: United States *for publications with data breakdown by sector of the industry*]
Radio **A0910, A1300**
Telephone **A1450, F1000**
Television **A0920, A1400**
Computer systems in government
United States
By state **A0900**
Connecticut
[*See also* (subject): United States *or* United

States: (subject) *for publications with data breakdown by state*]
Agriculture **S0270**
[*For related publications, see also* Connecticut: Fishing]
Birth S0310
Construction F0100, S0280
Consumer Price Index F0090, F0100, S0300
Death S0310
Divorce S0310
Economic conditions **F0090, F0100**, S0280, **S0300**
Employment F0090, F0100, S0280, **S0290**, S0300
Energy F0090, F0100, S0300
Finance F0090, F0100, S0280
Fishing F0100
Gross State Product F0100
Housing F0100, S0280
Manufacturing F0090, F0100, S0280, S0300
Marriage S0310
Minerals industries
[*For fuel minerals, see also* Connecticut: Energy]
Personal income F0090, F0100, S0280, S0290, S0300
Population F0100, S0280, S0290, S0300, S0310
Production F0100
Retail trade F0090, F0100, S0280
Service industries F0100
Statistical abstract **S0280**
Transportation F0100, S0280
Unemployment F0090, F0100, S0290, S0300
Vital statistics **S0310**
[*See also* Connecticut: Population]
Wholesale trade F0100
Construction
[*Related heading*: Real estate]
United States A0090, A0860, A0950, A0960, A0970, A1250, A1420, A1430, A1440, F0020, F0080, F0120, F0130, F0160, F0380, F0410, F0430, **F0430**, F0440, F0650, F0670, F0680, F0690, F0700, F0760, F1020, F1150, S0430, S2150, S2260
By state
[*See also* Construction: United States *for publications with data breakdown by state*]
Alabama F0080, S0030, S1020, S2100
Alaska S0090
Arizona S0100, S2110, S2120, S2510
Arkansas S1020, S2130
California S0200, S0230, S0320, S1830, S2150
Colorado S2090, S2160
Connecticut F0100, S0280
District of Columbia F0160, S0380
Florida F0080, S0410, S2180, S2190
Georgia F0080, S0480, S2200, S2210

Construction
  By state [*ctd*]

  Hawaii S0520, S1980
  Idaho S0570, S0580
  Illinois F0120, S2220
  Indiana F0120, S0170, S0640
  Iowa F0120, S0720, S0730
  Kansas S2230, S2710
  Kentucky S0790, S0810
  Louisiana F0080, S0840, S0860, S1020
  Maine F0100
  Maryland F0160, S0950
  Massachusetts F0100, S0980
  Michigan F0120, S1040, S2650, S2660
  Minnesota S1100, S1630
  Mississippi F0080, S1020, S1110, S1140
  Missouri S2270, S2280
  Montana S1220, S1230, S1240
  Nebraska S1300, S2290
  Nevada S1350, S1360, S2300
  New Hampshire F0100
  New Jersey S1410, S1450
  New Mexico S1470, S2310, S2320
  New York S1510
  North Carolina F0160, S1560
  North Dakota S1610, S2330
  Ohio S1660, S1670
  Oklahoma S2340, S2350
  Oregon S1750
  Pennsylvania S1800
  Rhode Island F0100, S1840, S1870
  South Carolina F0160, S1930, S2360
  South Dakota S1960, S2370
  Tennessee F0080, S1020, S2400
  Texas S0180, S2410
  Utah S2420, S2430, S2450, S2480
  Vermont F0100, S2550
  Virginia F0160
  Washington S2630
  West Virginia S2670
  Wisconsin F0120, S2730, S2740
  Wyoming S2440, S2780
Consumer Price Index
  [*Related heading*: Cost of living; *for
  international data, see* Consumer prices]
  United States A0310, A0530, A0620, A1060,
  A1280, A1390, A1420, F0020, F0030,
  F0090, F0110, F0130, F0200, F0340,
  F0370, F0380, F0410, **F0470**, F0500,
  F0520, F0680, F0700, F0760, F0820,
  F1150, S0430, S0440, S0790, S2150, S2260
  [*See also* Consumer prices: World *for
  publications with data breakdown by
  country*]
  By state
  [*See also* Consumer Price Index: United
  States *for publications with data breakdown
  by state*]

Alabama S2100
Alaska S0080, S0090
Arizona S0100, S2510
Arkansas S2130
California S0200, S0230, S1830, S2150
Connecticut F0090, F0100, S0300
District of Columbia S0360
Florida S2190
Georgia S0440, S2200, S2210
Hawaii S0510, S0520, S1980
Illinois F0110, S2220
Indiana F0110
Iowa F0110
Kansas S0750, S2240
Kentucky S0810
Louisiana S0860
Maine F0090, F0100
Maryland S0960
Massachusetts F0090, F0100
Michigan F0110, S1040, S2650, S2660
Minnesota S1630
Missouri S2270, S2280
Nebraska S1310, S2290
New Hampshire F0090, F0100
New Mexico S2310
New York S1510
Ohio S1670
Oklahoma S2340, S2350
Oregon S1760
Pennsylvania S1780, S1800
Rhode Island F0090, F0100, S1840
South Dakota S1950, S2370
Texas S2410
Utah S2420, S2460
Vermont F0090, F0100
Virginia **S1990**
Washington S2600, S2620, S2630
West Virginia S2670
Wisconsin F0110, S2730
Wyoming S2440, S2780
Consumer prices
  [*Related heading*: Cost of living; *for domestic
  data, see* Consumer Price Index]
  World F0180, **F0580**, F1060
Contributions to international organizations
  United States **F0900**
Copper
  [*See also* Minerals industries *for publications
  with data breakdown by sector of the industry*]
  United States **A0570**
Cost of living
  [*Related headings*: Consumer Price Index,
  Consumer prices]
  United States **A0130**, A0690, A1440
  By state
  Alaska S0080, S0090
  Delaware S0350
  Hawaii S0520

Louisiana S0860
Maryland S0950
Michigan S2660
Pennsylvania S1800
Utah S2480
Virginia **S1990**
Washington S2600
Wyoming S2440, S2800
Cotton
[*See also* Agriculture *for publications with data
breakdown by sector of the industry*]
United States **A1050, A1060**
Credit unions
[*See also* Finance *for publications with data
breakdown by sector of the industry*]
United States **A0610, F1090**
By state
[*See also* Credit unions: United States *for
publications with data breakdown by state*]
Crime
United States A0220, **F0450**, F0690, F0700,
F0990
By state
[*See also* Crime: United States *for
publications with data breakdown by state*]
Criminal justice
United States F0450, F0990
Death
World F0710
United States A0120, A0150, A0170, A1200,
F0040, F0280, F0290, F0300, F0670,
F0680, F0690, F0700
[*See also* Death: World *for publications with
data breakdown by country*]
By state
[*See also* Death: United States *for publications
with data breakdown by state*]
Alabama S0030, S0050, S2100
Alaska S0060, S0090
Arizona S0130, S2120, S2510
Arkansas S0150
California S0200, S0210, S0320, S1830
Colorado S0250, S2090
Connecticut S0310
Delaware S0330
District of Columbia S0370
Florida S0420, S2190
Georgia S0460, S0480, S2210
Hawaii S0500, S0520
Idaho S0560
Illinois S0600, S0630
Indiana S0170, S0670, S0680
Iowa S0740
Kansas S0760, S2230
Kentucky S0810, S0820
Louisiana S0860, S0880, S0890
Maine S0920
Maryland S0950, S0970
Massachusetts S1010

Michigan S1060, S2660
Minnesota S1090, S1100
Mississippi S1140, S1170
Missouri S1180, S2280
Montana S1230, S1240, S1260
Nebraska S1280, S1300
Nevada S1350, S1370
New Hampshire S1390
New Jersey S1410, S1440
New Mexico S1490, S2320
New York S1320, S1500, S1520
North Carolina S1560, S1580
North Dakota S1600, S2330
Ohio S1680
Oklahoma S1720, S2340
Oregon S1770
Pennsylvania S1800, S1810
Rhode Island S1860, S1870
South Carolina S1900, S1930
South Dakota S1960, S1970
Tennessee S2050, S2400
Texas S2070, S2080, S2410
Utah S2430, S2460, S2470, S2480
Vermont S2540
Virginia S2570
Washington S2610, S2630
West Virginia S2670, S2700
Wisconsin S2730, S2750
Wyoming S2780, S2790
Defense
World **F0360, F1140**
United States A0030, A1420, **F0350**, F0700
[*See also* Defense: World *for publications with
data breakdown by country*]
Delaware
[*See also* (subject): United States *or* United
States: (subject) *for publications with data
breakdown by state*]
Agriculture **S2170**
Birth S0330
Cost of living S0350
Death S0330
Divorce S0330
Economic conditions S0350
Education S0350
Employment **S0340**, S0350
Energy S0350
Finance S0350
Marriage S0330
Minerals industries
[*For fuel minerals, see also* Delaware: Energy]
Personal income S0350
Population S0340, S0350
[*See also* Delaware: Vital statistics]
Statistical abstract **S0350**
Transportation S0350
Unemployment S0340
Vital statistics **S0330**
[*See also* Delaware: Population]

By state
[*See also* Economic conditions: United States
*for publications with data breakdown by
state*]
Alabama **F0080**, S0030, **S0040**, **S1020**,
  S2100
Alaska S0080, S0090
Arizona **S0100**, **S2110**, S2120, S2510
Arkansas **S1020**, **S2130**, S2140
California S0200, **S0230**, S0320, S1830,
  S2150
Colorado S2090, **S2160**
Connecticut **F0090**, **F0100**, S0280, **S0300**
Delaware S0350
District of Columbia **F0160**, S0360, S0380
Florida **F0080**, **S0410**, **S2180**, S2190
Georgia **F0080**, **S0440**, S0480, **S2200**,
  S2210
Hawaii S0510, S0520, **S1980**
Idaho **S0580**
Illinois **F0110**, **F0120**, S0600, **S0620**, **S2220**
Indiana **F0110**, **F0120**, S0170, **S0640**
Iowa **F0110**, **F0120**, **S0720**, S0730
Kansas **S0750**, S2230, **S2240**, **S2710**
Kentucky **S0790**, S0810
Louisiana **F0080**, **S0840**, S0860, S0880,
  S1020
Maine **F0090**, **F0100**, S0930
Maryland **F0160**, S0950, S0960
Massachusetts **F0090**, **F0100**, S0980, **S2250**
Michigan **F0110**, **F0120**, **S1040**, **S2650**,
  S2660
Minnesota S1100, **S1630**
Mississippi **F0080**, **S1020**, **S1110**, S1140
Missouri **S1210**, **S2270**, S2280
Montana **S1220**, S1230, S1240
Nebraska S1300, S1310, **S2290**
Nevada S1350, S1360, **S2300**
New Hampshire **F0090**, **F0100**
New Jersey S1410, **S1450**
New Mexico S1470, **S2310**, S2320
New York S1320, **S1510**
North Carolina **F0160**, S1560, **S1570**
North Dakota **S1610**, S2330
Ohio S1660, **S1670**
Oklahoma **S1690**, S2340, **S2350**
Oregon S1740, **S1750**, S1760
Pennsylvania **S1780**, S1800
Rhode Island **F0090**, **F0100**, S1840, S1870
South Carolina **F0160**, **S1920**, S1930, **S2360**
South Dakota S1950, S1960, **S2370**
Tennessee **F0080**, **S1020**, **S2380**, **S2390**,
  S2400
Texas S0180, S2410
Utah **S2420**, S2430, S2450, S2460, S2480
Vermont **F0090**, **F0100**
Virginia **F0160**, S1990, S2020, S2580,
  S2590
Washington S2600, S2620, S2630
West Virginia S2670

Wisconsin **F0110**, **F0120**, S2730, **S2740**
Wyoming **S2440**, S2780, S2800
Education
[*Related heading*: Libraries]
World F0730, F0740
United States **A0170**, A0180, **A0580**, **A0590**,
  A0600, A0810, **A1090**, **A1100**, A1250,
  A1320, A1420, **F0220**, **F0230**, **F0250**,
  F0260, F0540, F0650, F0670, F0680,
  F0690, F0700, F0730, F0740
[*See also* Education: World *for publications
  with data breakdown by country*]
By state
[*See also* Education: United States *for
  publications with data breakdown by state*]
Alabama **A1380**, S0030, S2100
Arizona S2120, S2510
Arkansas **A1380**, S2140
California S0200, S0320, S1830
Colorado S2090
Delaware S0350
District of Columbia S0380
Florida **A1380**, S2190
Georgia **A1380**, S0480, S2210
Hawaii S0520, S1980
Illinois S0600
Indiana S0170
Iowa S0730
Kansas S2230
Kentucky **A1380**, S0830
Louisiana **A1380**, S0860, S0880
Maine S0900, S0930
Maryland S0950
Massachusetts S0980
Michigan S1050, S2660
Minnesota S1080, S1100
Mississippi **A1380**, S1140
Missouri **A1380**, S2280
Montana S1230, S1240
Nebraska S1300
Nevada S1350, S1360
New Jersey S1410
New Mexico S1470, S2320
New York S1320
North Carolina **A1380**, S1560, S1570
North Dakota S1610, S2330
Oklahoma S1690, S2340
Pennsylvania S1800
Rhode Island S1840, S1870
South Carolina **A1380**, S1930
South Dakota S1960
Tennessee **A1380**, S2040, S2400
Texas **A1380**, S0180
Utah S2430, S2450, S2460, S2480
Vermont S2550
Virginia **A1380**, S2580
Washington S2600, S2630
West Virginia **A1380**, S2670
Wisconsin S2730

Restaurants
[See also Retail trade for publications with data breakdown by sector of the industry]
United States **A1170**, A1280
Retail trade
United States A0450, A0540, A1110, **A1180**, **A1190**, F0030, F0090, F0130, F0200, F0380, F0410, F0440, F0670, F0690, F0700, F1150, S0430
By industry/sector
[See also Retail trade: United States for publications with data breakdown by sector of the industry]
Department/specialty stores **A1180**, **A1190**
Electronics A0650, A0660
Mens/boys clothing **A0420**, **A0830**
Motor vehicles A0870
Restaurants **A1170**, A1280
Supermarkets **A0680**, **A0690**
By state
[See also Retail trade: United States for publications with data breakdown by state]
Alabama S0030, S0040, S1020, S2100
Arizona S0100, S2110, S2120, S2510
Arkansas S1020, S2130, S2140
California S0200, S1830
Colorado S2090
Connecticut F0090, F0100, S0280
District of Columbia S0360, S0380
Florida S2180, S2190
Georgia S2200, S2210
Hawaii S0520
Illinois S2220
Indiana S0640
Iowa S0720, S0730
Kansas S2240, S2710
Kentucky S0790, S0810
Louisiana S0840, S0860, S1020
Maine F0090, F0100, S0930
Maryland S0950
Massachusetts F0090, F0100, S0980
Michigan S1040, S2660
Minnesota S1100, S1630
Mississippi S1020, S1110, S1140
Montana S1230
Nebraska S1300, S2290
Nevada S1350, S2300
New Hampshire F0090, F0100
New Jersey S1410, S1450
New Mexico S1470, S2310, S2320
New York S1320
North Carolina S1560, S1570
North Dakota S1610
Ohio S1660, S1670
Oklahoma S2340, S2350
Pennsylvania S1800
Rhode Island F0090, F0100, S1870
South Carolina S2360
South Dakota S2370

Tennessee S1020, S2400
Texas S2410
Utah S2430, S2450, S2460, S2480
Vermont F0090, F0100
Virginia **S2010**, S2590
West Virginia S2670
Wisconsin S2730, S2740
Wyoming S2780
Rhode Island
[See also (subject): United States or United States: (subject) for publications with data breakdown by state]
Agriculture S1870
[Related heading: Rhode Island: Forest products]
Birth S1860, S1870
Construction F0100, S1840, S1870
Consumer Price Index F0090, F0100, S1840
Death S1860, S1870
Divorce S1860
Economic conditions **F0090, F0100,** S1840, S1870
Education S1840, S1870
Employment F0090, F0100, S1840, **S1850,** S1870
Energy F0090, F0100, S1870
Finance F0090, F0100, S1840, S1870
Fishing F0100
Gross State Product F0100
Housing F0100, S1840, S1870
Manufacturing F0090, F0100, S1840, S1870
Marriage S1860
Minerals industries S1870
[For fuel minerals, see also Rhode Island: Energy]
Personal income F0090, F0100, S1840, S1870
Population F0100, S1840, S1850, S1860, S1870
Production F0100
Retail trade F0090, F0100, S1870
Service industries F0100, S1870
Statistical abstract **S1840, S1870**
Transportation F0100, S1870
Unemployment F0090, F0100, S1840, S1850, S1870
Vital statistics **S1860,** S1870
[See also Rhode Island: Population]
Wholesale trade F0100
Salaries and/or wages
[Includes personal income data]
World F0740
United States A0170, A0180, A0400, **A0410,** A0470, A0530, A0690, A0970, A1060, A1250, A1440, F0010, F0020, F0030, F0080, F0090, F0120, F0130, F0160, F0200, F0230, **F0340,** F0370, F0380, **F0390,** F0400, F0410, **F0460,** F0480, F0490, F0500, F0510, F0520, **F0530,**

Television
[See also Transportation for publications with
  data breakdown by sector of the industry]
United States **A0920, A1400**
Tennessee
[See also (subject): United States or United
  States: (subject) for publications with data
  breakdown by state]
Agriculture F0080, **S2030,** S2400
Birth S2050, S2400
Construction F0080, S1020, S2400
Death S2050, S2400
Divorce S2050, S2400
Economic conditions **F0080, S1020, S2380,
  S2390,** S2400
Education **A1380,** S2040, S2400
Employment F0080, S1020, **S2040,** S2380,
  S2390, S2400
[For wage and/or salary data, see Tennessee:
  Personal income]
Energy S2390, S2400
Finance F0080, S1020, S2400
Forest products S2400
Gross State Product S2380, S2390, S2400
Housing F0080, S1020, S2400
Manufacturing S2400
Marriage S2050, S2400
Minerals industries S2400
[For fuel minerals, see also Tennessee:
  Energy]
Personal income A1380, F0080, S1020,
  S2040, S2380, S2390, S2400
Population A1380, S2040, S2050, S2400
Production S2380, S2390, S2400
Retail trade S1020, S2400
Service industries S2400
Statistical abstract **S2400**
Transportation S2390, S2400
Unemployment F0080, S1020, S2040, S2380,
  S2390, S2400
Vital statistics **S2050,** S2400
[See also Tennessee: Population]
Wholesale trade S2400
Texas
[See also (subject): United States or United
  States: (subject) for publications with data
  breakdown by state]
Agriculture S0180, **S2060,** S2410
Birth S2070, S2080, S2410
Construction S0180, S2410
Consumer Price Index S2410
Death S2070, S2080, S2410
Divorce S2070, S2410
Economic conditions S0180, S2410
Education **A1380,** S0180
Employment S0180, **S2080,** S2410
[For wage and/or salary data, see Texas:
  Personal income]
Energy S0180, S2410

Finance S0180, S2410
Forest products S0180
Gross State Product S2410
Housing S0180, S2410
Manufacturing S0180, S2410
Marriage S2070, S2410
Minerals industries S0180, S2410
Personal income A1380, S0180, S2410
Population A1380, S0180, S2080, S2410
[See also Texas: Vital statistics]
Production S2410
Retail trade S2410
Service industries S2410
Statistical abstract **S1080, S2410**
Transportation S0180, S2410
Unemployment S0180, S2080, S2410
Vital statistics **S2070,** S2080, S2410
[See also Texas: Population]
Wholesale trade S2410
Textile industry
United States **A0310**
By industry/sector
[See also Textile industry: United States for
  publications with data breakdown by sector
  of the industry]
Cotton **A1050, A1060**
Tourism
[Related heading: Transportation,
  Gaming/gambling]
World **A1260, F1190, F1200**
United States A0450, **A1460, A1470,** F0680
[See also Tourism: World for publications
  with data breakdown by country]
By industry/sector
[See also Tourism: United States for
  publications with data breakdown by sector
  of the industry]
Boating **F0750**
National parks **F1110**
By state
[See also Tourism: United States for
  publications with data breakdown by state]
Arizona S2110, S2120, S2510
California S0230
Colorado S2160
District of Columbia S0380
Florida S0410, S2180, S2190
Georgia S0480
Hawaii S0510, S0520, S1980
Iowa S0730
Kansas S2230
Louisiana S0840, S0880
Maryland S0950
Michigan S1040
Minnesota S1100
Montana S1220
Nebraska S1300
Nevada S1350
New Jersey S1410

271

Motor vehicle **A0880**
Nonferrous metals **A0110**
  [*See also* World: Minerals industries *for*
  publications with data breakdown by sector
  of the industry]
Personal income F0740
Population **A1270,** F0360, **F0710,** F0730,
  F0740, F1140
Production A1270, F0180, F0360, F0730,
  F0740, F1060, F1065, F1140
Silver **A1350, A1360**
  [*See also* World: Minerals industries *for*
  publications with data breakdown by sector
  of the industry]
Statistical abstract **F0730, F0740**
Tourism **A1260, F1190, F1200**
  [*Related heading*: World: Transportation]
Transportation **A1260,** F0730, F0740,
  F1190, F1200
  [*Related heading*: World: Tourism]
Unemployment F0730, F0740, F1060, F1065
Vital statistics F0710
  [*See also* World: Population]
Wholesale prices F0180, F1060
Wyoming
  [*See also* (subject): United States *or* United
  States: (subject) *for publications with data*
  breakdown by state]
Agriculture S2440, **S2770,** S2780
Birth S2780, S2790
Construction S2440, S2780
Consumer Price Index S2440, S2780
Cost of living S2440, S2800
Death S2780, S2790
Divorce S2780, S2790
Economic conditions **S2440,** S2780, S2800
Employment S2440, S2780, **S2800**
Energy S2440, S2780
Finance **F0140,** S2440, S2780
Fishing S2780
Gross State Product S2780
Housing S2440, S2780
Manufacturing S2780
Marriage S2780, S2790
Minerals industries S2440, S2780
Personal income S2440, S2780, S2800
Population S2780, S2790, S2800
Production S2780
Retail trade S2780
Service industries S2780
Statistical abstract **S2780**
Tourism S2440, S2780
Transportation S2780
Unemployment S2440, S2780, S2800
Vital statistics S2780, **S2790**
  [*See also* Wyoming: Population]
Wholesale trade S2780

Zinc
  [*See also* United States: Minerals industries
  for publications with data breakdown by sector
  of the industry]
United States **A1490**